Putting Their Hands on Race

Putting Their Hands on Race

Irish Immigrant and Southern Black Domestic Workers

DANIELLE T. PHILLIPS-CUNNINGHAM

Rutgers University Press

New Brunswick, Camden, and Newark, New Jersey, and London

Library of Congress Cataloging-in-Publication Data

Names: Phillips-Cunningham, Danielle, author.
Title: Putting their hands on race : Irish immigrant and Southern black domestic workers /
    Danielle T. Phillips-Cunningham.
Description: New Brunswick, New Jersey : Rutgers University Press, [2019] | Includes
    bibliographical references and index.
Identifiers: LCCN 2019007524 | ISBN 9781978800465 (pbk.) | ISBN 9781978800472 (hc) |
    ISBN 9781978800489 (epub) | ISBN 9781978800496 (mobi)
Subjects: LCSH: Women household employees—United States—History—19th century. |
    Women household employees—United States—History—20th century. | Irish American
    women—Northeastern States—History. | Women immigrants—Northeastern States—
    History. | African American women—Northeastern States—History. | African American
    women—Southern States—History. | Northeastern States—Race relations—History—
    19th century. | Northeastern States—Race relations—History—20th century.
Classification: LCC HD6072.2.U5 P46 2019 | DDC 331.6/241507309034—dc23
LC record available at https://lccn.loc.gov/2019007524

A British Cataloging-in-Publication record for this book is available from the British Library.

♾ The paper used in this publication meets the requirements of the American National
Standard for Information Sciences—Permanence of Paper for Printed Library Materials,
ANSI Z39.48-1992.

www.rutgersuniversitypress.org

Manufactured in the United States of America

For my father, grandmothers, and great aunts

Contents

Putting Their Hands on Race

Introduction

———————————————◇————————————————

As a Black woman who grew up in the U.S. South, I have come to know the multiple meanings of what my community calls "laying hands." The women who lay hands on a dress or food make it not just better, but a work of art. These women also attempt to solve problems and rescue through the power of hands. They lay hands on bodies, oils, and sacred texts to ward off illnesses, anxieties about bleak circumstances, and foreseeable dangers. These hands heal and sometimes not, but the expression has lingered over time. To lay hands is ritual, a call to arms, and recognition of a problem *and its solution.*

When I came across the stories of southern Black migrant and Irish immigrant women in domestic service in the archive, I imagined them possessing the language, spirit, and impulse to iron out migration uncertainties; protect loved ones and themselves; and find resources in a new place where they did not always have access to what they needed and wanted. I began to think that laying hands for these women of the late nineteenth and early twentieth centuries was to conjure the unknown and the unseen.[1] Women's laboring hands tell stories of struggle and resistance, progress and stagnation, and conformity and imagination in countries with deeply engrained histories of injustice. So, putting their hands on race seemed an appropriate way to describe both Irish immigrant and southern Black women's purposeful and significant ideological and physical work in northeastern cities.[2]

No groups of women in the United States remained servants longer than indigenous, Irish immigrant and Black women.[3] The interracial and interethnic social history that I have written examines how Irish immigrant and southern Black women were racialized and gendered by the manual labors they performed in their homes of employment. I also explore the physical and ideological work both groups of women did to change their circumstances in a highly racialized and exploitative occupation. When they cleaned laundry, swept floors, and cooked meals for white families, they were engaged in what had been categorized as subservient "Black" labor since the beginning of slavery in the United States to better the material circumstances of their families. Their concentration in a subservient occupation confirmed white supremacist beliefs that Irish and serving Black women were racially inferior to native-born whites. The racial stigma of domestic service, however, did not define Irish immigrant and southern Black women. When they organized labor strikes and wrote letters to local newspapers exposing exploitation in domestic service, they were challenging racial discourses that justified the very notion that they were undeserving of livable wages and safe working conditions because they did stigmatized work and were inferior to native-born whites. All of these labors, I argue then, represented women putting hands on race: labor organizing; building settlement homes for migrant and immigrant women; writing letters that exposed exploitative domestic service employers; writing speeches, essays, books, dissertations, and master's theses about race and women's work; and going about the business of everyday work to provide for their families.[4]

Race is an idea that emerged in the United States during the late 1700s to justify enslavement. This early ideology deemed the white race, or people of European descent, superior in mind, body, and spirit, and therefore the rightful rulers of the Black race. According to this ideology, Blacks, due to their unfortunate African ancestry, were in a permanent state of mental and moral inferiority and were not even human.[5] Thus, slavery was the natural order. As Michael Omi and Howard Winant have helped us to understand through their racial formation theory, race is not biological, although nineteenth-century scientist Samuel Morton insisted that there were natural "racial" hierarchies among the world's populations.[6] Race is an idea that is malleable and derives meaning from the context in which it is defined. However, what has remained consistent about race is that it has determined access to vital resources that are promised to American citizens (i.e., safe housing, voting, education, and jobs with livable wages, to name a few). As historical sociologist Evelyn Nakano Glenn explained, "Citizenship has been a principal institutional formation within which race and gender relations, meanings, and identities have been constituted in the United States."[7]

Because of the enormous power of race, people in power and those who are disadvantaged are constantly in a struggle over competing racial projects to establish which groups should have access to these resources.[8] Omi and Winant explained that racial projects do the ideological work of linking representations of race to political, social, and economic structures. People develop racial projects to "reorganize and redistribute resources along particular racial lines."[9]

Racial projects require work, and I use the term "making race" to describe the labor that people performed with their hands to redefine race, or to advance their racial projects. I also see "making race" as a way of bringing into focus the labors working-class and middle-class women did to redefine race.

Some women wrote books, newspaper articles, and pamphlets about the race question; but not all women could. No nineteenth-century and early-twentieth-century women could argue for or against segregation in a court-room. Until 1920, no women could vote in the United States, but domestic workers and women social reformers had their hands, and they used them to assert their own perspectives about race through the home. As with actual household work, making race was messy. It had unequal outcomes that depended upon the women's gender, class, ethnicity, and race. Women also made race in a society that was subject to changes that demanded "constant remarking of the ideological."[10]

This book foregrounds the unexplored connections between southern African American and Irish immigrant domestic workers who put their hands on race, or engaged in race-making. This is also a study of how their move-ments into northern cities molded race, as native-born whites wrote volumi-nous articles and domestic service manuals expressing anger and ambivalence about those migrations. Although they mostly remain separated in academic study, southern African American and Irish immigrant women's labors and migrations were not isolated. As Tanya Hart explained in her health study of poor and working-class African American, British West Indian, and southern Italian immigrant women in New York City, ". . . the effect of separating group migrations by race, while necessary at times and enlightening in monographs, has created a scholarship based upon separate "racialized" and also "gendered" and "classed" group differences.[11] Bronwen Walter, Deirdre Cooper Owens, and Andrew T. Urban have begun putting into conversation the histories of Irish immigrant and African American women.[12] While also integrating these histories, I intend to open new spaces for inquiries about race and how its meanings relied on African American and Irish immigrant women's house-hold labors and migrations.

By doing this, we are able to understand the deeply embedded racial histories that continue to impact women's lives and those of African Americans, white Americans, and immigrants more broadly. The United States has reverted to the latter half of the nineteenth century within the 2016 presidential election cycle. As during the era of African American and Irish immigrant women in this book, the United States is immersed in a resurgence of white rage, misogyny, xenopho-bia, and denial of women's rights and workers' rights. Donald J. Trump and his administration use the same language and evoke the same fears that eerily harken back to Andrew Johnson, the most explicit and violent white supremacist presi-dent in U.S. history.

Similar to what happened during Johnson's presidency, white terrorist groups have emerged in plain sight because they have presidential support to murder and harass African Americans. Local police officers and private white citizens have become a legalized arm of the Ku Klux Klan and other white supremacist groups, murdering hundreds of Black and brown women, men, and children without any legal repercussions. Like his nineteenth-century predecessor, Trump is racist toward all racial minority groups with a particular disdain for African Americans. He laments that the country has forgotten about white working-class men whose jobs have been "given" to undeserving and lazy African Americans and immigrants. He has passed legislation that strengthens the power of white supremacist state governments, primarily in the South, to curtail the voting rights of primarily Africans Americans, the most consistent mass voting block against white supremacist candidates. Trump selected Stephen Miller, a far-right racist, as his senior adviser for immigration policies. Miller put nineteenth century xenophobia and racism on steroids with his cruel and inhumane family separation policy targeting immigrants of color from Latin America. In addition, Trump nominated for attorney general Jefferson Beauregard Sessions III, a former senator of Alabama who has such a long history of hatred for African Americans that Coretta Scott King, civil rights activist and widow of Dr. Martin Luther King Jr., wrote a ten-page letter to Congress in 1986 imploring them to block Sessions' nomination for federal judge. King asserted that Sessions "exhibited so much hostility" to Blacks exercising their right to vote that, if confirmed, he would be given life tenure to do "what local sheriffs accomplished twenty years ago with clubs and cattle prods."[13]

As many African American scholars and activists have argued, this has always been America, yet white Americans have been reluctant to talk about it. There is much that we can learn about the history of these centuries-old issues and women's impact on them from tracing the ways in which Irish immigrant and African American women were racialized and how they confronted, challenged, and, in the case of some Irish immigrant women, reproduced, white supremacy and labor exploitation. Putting women's histories in conversation with each other helps us begin the difficult dialogues about race and women that we have yet to take on as a country. I hope that this book will initiate in white communities largely unexplored questions about whiteness and gender such as: How could over 50 percent of white women, across socioeconomic class, vote for a presidential candidate who bragged about sexually assaulting women and curtailing women's reproductive rights?[14] How could white women, many of whose nineteenth-century ancestors were persecuted for being immigrants and had few options but to work exploitative jobs, vote for a xenophobic and anti-workers'-rights president? Why do some white women, even in progressive academic and activist circles, avoid discussions about race and misogyny with their own family members?

Irish American women historians have captured the special affection that the Irish American community has for their resilient loved ones who braved the long voyage across the Atlantic Ocean, overcame ethnic and religious discrimination, and worked long hours in private homes to chart brighter futures for their families in the United States and Ireland. How can Irish immigrant women be reimagined beyond the matriarchal trope and seen as equally influential as Irish immigrant men on the construction of whiteness in the United States? I also intend to spark dialogue in African American communities about the marginalization of African American women in the telling of our histories. Why are working-class and middle-class African American women excluded from hegemonic narratives about our most significant racial thinkers? The debates between Booker T. Washington and W.E.B. DuBois and the public exchanges between Martin Luther King Jr. and Malcolm X about racism and labor issues in Black communities are touted as the most significant and instructive, racially-defining moments in African American history, and U.S. history more broadly. Given African American women's influential labor and political activism since the nineteenth century, why are we excluded from national analyses about voting, labor, and U.S. citizenship?

Finally, how can we integrate our loving memories of our mothers, aunts, and grandmothers, who cleaned the homes of white families, into our analysis of U.S. politics? We know and remember our loved ones as not simply women who did the work that white women did not want to do. They were our community's mothers and "aunties," breadwinners, fashion trendsetters, culinary experts, event planners, "no-nonsense" church ushers, and spiritual leaders. I intend to extend dialogue about their roles in our communities into discussions about their significance to the country. They actively shaped the nation's history and future through their very migrations, acts of resistance, and the work that they did in private homes.

Women Making Race

Irish immigrant and southern Black women negotiated and developed perspectives about their own migrations and labors, yet comparative studies about Irish immigrant and Black labor histories focus primarily on how men made race.[15] Literature on race and Irish immigration see Irish immigrants as an "undifferentiated mass."[16] The story goes: Catholic Irish immigrants were nonwhite and sometimes referred to as "niggers inside out" when they migrated to America in the mid-nineteenth century because of the potato famine in Ireland. Irish immigrants engaged in acts of violence, established labor unions, and joined the Democratic Party, which supported slavery and racial segregation, to establish themselves as white and thereby deserving of rights afforded to white American citizens. These rights included access to secure jobs that paid livable wages, the right to vote and own property, and access to education. By 1865, Irish immigrants had constructed the white working-class American, an identity with significant political, social, and economic influence. Black men continued to struggle in jobs that paid lower wages than what Irish immigrant men earned and remained second-class Americans until their citizenship privileges were revoked after Reconstruction.

Boundaries of whiteness and blackness were not solely drawn in the courts, factory floors, and halls of labor union buildings where men dominated. Irish immigrant and southern Black domestic workers, who were women, were also engaged in the arduous labor of defining race. The women's work lasted longer. By virtue of their gender and their concentration in domestic work, a racially stigmatized labor niche, Black and Irish immigrant women had to work especially hard at molding race in ways that could benefit them as women, workers, and mothers. They decided to leave their hometowns where opportunities were limited because they were deemed inferior to those of Anglo-Saxon ancestry. With limited political influence, southern Black and Irish immigrant women ventured into new cities where they put their hands on what was most immediate: brooms, pots, pans, picket signs, pencils and pens, and union petitions to better their material circumstances.

As they did not migrate in isolation from each other, Irish immigrant and African American women also did not make race in isolation from other parts of the world. In fact, their perspectives about race, gender, and labor are what we now call transnational. They inserted themselves into the political and social movements of their time overseas to disrupt racial ideologies that deemed them inferior and unworthy of livable wages and safe working conditions. Irish immigrant women labor organizers spoke out against labor exploitation in the United States because they had a deeply rooted sense of themselves as Irish victims of British oppressors and supporters of Ireland's fight for independence. Irish women also brought to the United States the spirit of labor-organizing women in Ireland. While Irish immigrant women organized labor strikes against white Protestant-owned factories and criticized white Protestant employers in newspapers for issuing low wages, their sisters overseas waged strikes against domestic service employers and British-owned factories in Ireland. Some domestic workers connected their struggles in Ireland to racial oppression in the United States. Mary Condon, who worked as a domestic after having migrated to New York City from County Westcommon in 1930, recalled ". . . I equate the Irish and the Blacks in many ways. I think their problems are pretty much the same; colonialism and things like that."[17]

African American women created a discourse of women's equality and labor rights steeped in transnational racial struggles. They delivered speeches in cities across the United States and at conferences in London, Paris, and Berlin about the oppression of the *Afro*-American woman. This keen awareness of racial exploitation of African-descended people around the world was foundational to Anna Julia Cooper's speech "The Negro Problem in America" at the First Pan-African Conference and her doctoral dissertation on slavery in the French colonies, Mary Church Terrell's book *A Colored Woman in a White World,* and Ida B. Wells-Burnett's contributions to the pamphlet *The Reasons Why The Colored American is not in the World's Columbian Exposition: The Afro American's Contribution to Columbian Literature.*[18] They also insisted on the value of Black women's labors to global capitalism. Scholar, civil rights leader, and daughter of a domestic worker, Anna Julia Cooper declared in her critique of the 1893 Chicago World's Fair that whites had yet to acknowledge how much was "given to the world through Negro industry."[19] African American domestic workers themselves framed their demands for better wages and job security with a racial and gendered sense of their relationship to global capitalism. As one striking laundress protesting commercial Chinese laundries told an Atlanta newspaper, "Chinese got no business coming here taking our work from us."[20]

While Irish immigrant and southern Black women's specific goals were distinct and intersected, their outcomes could not have been more different. Irish immigrant women worked at prying open the boundaries of white female respectability to include themselves, while southern Black women challenged the premise of race that denied their humanity. Both women demanded access to resources available to American citizens, some that were not even available to native-born white women at the time. Molding race for Irish immigrant women also required them to reconstruct meanings of "ruralness," and Black women to redefine their "southernness," which whites in the North declared evidence of their inferiority. Southern Black women had the added burden of redefining southernness for northern Blacks who thought that their "backwards" and "country" cousins, aunts, and uncles from the South would destroy the respectable reputation that they had worked so hard to achieve after slavery was abolished in the North.

It was nearly impossible for Black women to dislodge ideologies of race even after emancipation because capitalism and the very definition of whiteness and blackness relied on their reproductive and agricultural labors. The State recaptured control over Black women's labors by establishing exploitative labor systems. Imprisoned Black women in the late-nineteenth and early-twentieth-century South, for example, were contracted out to work as domestic servants in white households. Harnessing Black women's household labors through the criminal legal system and a political economy that relegated Black women to paid domestic service and agricultural labors was integral to the reestablishment of white supremacy and making of the "New South."[21]

Having entered the U.S. labor system as wage laborers who had never been enslaved, Irish immigrant women of the famine era and afterwards had more room to negotiate the terms of race. Reshaping the contours of whiteness was an arduous endeavor, however, for poor Catholic immigrant women who were racialized as nonwhite before immigrating to the United States, and were racialized again as inferior to native-born whites when they reached American homes. Thus, Irish serving women came closest to blackness than any other group of European immigrant women in U.S. history. It would take nearly seventy years for native-born white America to imagine and believe that the Irish immigrant woman who worked hard in low-wage jobs to provide a better future for her children could become a productive, hardworking American citizen. Until then, she was the destitute, brutish, lazy, dirty, uneducated, and immoral woman who suffered the unfortunate circumstance of not being born of white Anglo-Saxon ancestry. She needed to be removed from Britain's care and into the supervision of American mistresses who barely knew what to do with *her* themselves.

As Irish immigrant women became whiter, Black women continued to (and still have to) lay hands on race. Some Irish immigrant women exited domestic service and became teachers and saleswomen in department stores. For the women in my family, "the woman on the other side of the counter" became shorthand for the racially charged interactions in southern department stores where even middle-class, educated Black women could not work as saleswomen—in the 1970s. Southern Black women are still concentrated in service work even in its oldest form. The 50 Cherokee Bend city bus in Alabama, commonly known as "the maid's bus," for example, transported Black women from a downtown Birmingham bus stop on an hour-long route to the Mountain Brook suburb to work in the homes of wealthy white families in the mid-1900s. The "maid's bus" still operates today carrying elderly women who are past retirement age, but have to continue working because they were unable to save up for health care and retirement with the low wages they received from domestic service.[22]

Irish immigrant and southern Black migrant women molded race in a number of ways, including labor organizing, institution-building, letter writing, migrating into cities with fraught racial politics, redefining domestic service to assert their right to better wages, and defining themselves racially in comparison to each other. Before Irish immigrant women began entering domestic service in the North during the famine era, native-born white women were the "help," working temporarily or part-time depending on their personal and family circumstances. When they chose to work, they helped their employers with textile work and farming activities—food and clothing production that were later outsourced to factories during industrialization.[23] Free Blacks were hired in household employment after emancipation in the North during the early 1800s. As Leslie Harris explained, "Whites believed that blacks who had been enslaved and who in freedom held jobs as servants were the most degraded of workers and the farthest removed from the ideal republican citizen."[24] As such, they were viewed differently than their white counterparts in that they were servants, not the "help." When industrialization took off in the United States, a new urban middle class developed that hired domestic servants.[25] Famine-era Irish women emigrated to the United States and quickly outnumbered the free northern-born Black women in the occupation, transforming domestic service from being not only "Black," but also immigrant women's work. Southern African American women who reached northern cities in the late nineteenth century would have to negotiate the racial politics of domestic service that were distinct from the South where African American women dominated domestic service ranks.

Race-making also took place in the settlement homes established by middle-class southern Black women in the North for their working-class sisters, and the missions created by Catholic churches for Erin's daughters. These institutions for women and girls were invested in helping the new arrivals access the resources that were promised American citizens, but denied to them. African American clubwomen redefined the idea that domestic service was a low-status occupation and Black women were second-class citizens when they held national conferences to discuss how to address the exploitation of domestic workers. Sarah Willie Layten, president of the women's auxiliary of the National Baptist Convention, wrote Black serving women into American citizenship when she condemned the harsh living conditions in tenement homes and the racial prejudices that they were subjected to in their places of employment. Layten told her colleagues at a National Association of Colored Women (NACW) meeting in 1908: "The virtue of colored serving girls should be commended."[26] Race-making took place at the tips of pens and pencils that Irish immigrants used to write letters airing their complaints about domestic service employers in local newspapers. Nuns worked at eliminating racial prejudices towards Irish serving women and the racial stigma associated with Catholicism in the United States by writing advice manuals to domestic servants. They instructed Irish immigrant women to uphold the virtues of devout Catholics in their places of employment. Nun of Kenmare told her readers that they should take domestic service seriously because it was a noble occupation. After all, she concluded, ". . . our Lord Jesus lived and worked as the servant of others—and think what an honor it is to be like Him."[27]

Race was also shaped by the hands of southern Black mothers who wrote to educator Nannie Helen Burroughs—a southern migrant herself—asking her to admit their daughters into her National Training School for Women and Girls in Washington, D.C. The hopeful mothers believed that training in domestic science could help their daughters overcome racial barriers that compromised their chances of gainful employment. Working long hours in domestic service, the mothers also believed that the school would ensure the respectability of their daughters in a society that had deemed Black girls inherently immoral and thereby unworthy of legal protection, especially in the South. As a widowed mother of a 16-year-old girl wrote to Burroughs from Chattanooga, Tennessee, "I have to work and leave her alone . . . I would like to send her right away . . . While she is a nice little girl, I would like to keep her that way."[28]

Native-born whites turned to Irish immigrant and southern Black women in domestic service to reassert white supremacy in the midst of the socioeconomic and political transitions of the late nineteenth and early twentieth centuries. The very movements of the descendants of enslaved Blacks and single, Catholic women from a despised country that resisted Anglo-Saxon rule into northern cities prompted discussions of race that drowned the pages of Irish, Black, and white-owned magazines and newspapers. Using drawings and colored inks to portray Irish and Black serving women could be profitable. Cartoonists sold high volumes of magazines when they concocted images of the unruly Irish "Bridget" and when the R. T. Davis Milling Company used bright reds and blacks to build a pancake empire based on the image of Aunt Jemima.

With all of these reassertions and challenges to race that took place during Irish immigrant and southern Black women's migrations, their histories demand that we refrain from simply reducing race to racism and examine how racial inequalities are formed. Identifying an institution, action, or person as racist is undoubtedly necessary in a courtroom or on a congressional floor to hold people and institutional policies legally accountable for racial discrimination and violence. Deconstructing race in U.S. consciousness, however, requires us to examine race beyond an adjective that can be easily dismissed, especially when someone asserts that they are not racist, or what they said or did was not racist to avoid difficult discussions about whiteness. Current-day reassertions of slavery-era claims about the degeneracy of African Americans and the superiority of white men; nineteenth-century xenophobia towards immigrants who are not of WASP ancestry; and nineteenth-century white ethnic working-class anger toward African Americans makes clear that the country has yet to unpack its turbulent racial history that is also the present. A comparative history of Irish immigrant and southern Black women commands us to slow down and trace why such archaic beliefs, practices, and lawmaking decisions remain vibrant nearly two decades into the twenty-first century.

An underlying question of this book is: What happens to our understandings of race when we center the ideas and lives of working-class Black and immigrant women? Racial inequalities in the United States have always depended on the subjugation and participation of women. Domestic workers' histories require us to make women an integral part of the racial history of the United States as workers, scholars, and activists. I argue that bringing African American and Irish immigrant women's racial histories into a comparative framework provokes much-needed conversations about systemic racial and class inequalities among women; working-class white women's roles and participation in upholding and reproducing white supremacy; and the perpetual labor exploitation of working-class Black, immigrant, and white women.

Hands in Context: Race, Domestic Service, and Irish Immigrant and Black Women's Migrations

This book is indebted to the rich literature that exists on Irish immigrant and Black women in domestic service.[29] Scholars have uncovered the family lives, political engagements, and resistance strategies of African American women who worked in private homes from slavery until the late twentieth century. The scholarship on Irish immigrant women has investigated the ways in which Irish immigrant women struggled to etch new lives for themselves in the United States after leaving an Ireland haunted by the potato famine from the 1840s until the early twentieth century. While this book draws from this groundbreaking literature, it offers a distinct perspective on Irish immigrant and African American women's histories by placing them in conversation with each other to advance a gendered history of the social construction of race.

The height of Black women's migrations from the South and Irish women's immigration from Ireland occurred at different times. The bulk of Irish immigration took place in the mid-nineteenth century during the famine years in Ireland, and Black women migrated north in record numbers after World War I. There were overlaps, however, between their arrivals and labor experiences. Irish women continued emigrating to the U.S. North in the late nineteenth century in record numbers to escape the extended aftermath of the famine and the armed conflicts between Irish nationalists and British soldiers. There were enough Irish immigrant women leaving Ireland to seek domestic service employment in the United States to convince the Irish Colonization Society that Charlotte O'Brien, daughter of an Irish nationalist, was right when she insisted that they needed to provide the financial backing for a mission to assist Irish immigrant women who landed at the port of New York.

Father John Riordan opened the doors of the Mission of Our Lady of the Rosary for the Protection of Irish Immigrant Girls in 1884. Arrivals received temporary lodging and help finding domestic service employment. There were also enough southern Black women who pioneered labor migrations to the North during the late nineteenth century to rally the sympathies of Black clubwomen. By 1897, clubwoman and Georgia-native Victoria Earle Matthews started a traveler's aid service for Black women who boarded the Old Dominion Line steamships in Virginia and landed at Pier 26 in New York City. Matthews, along with nine other concerned clubwomen, also established a settlement home as a place for the southern newcomers to stay and get assistance finding domestic service employment and housing in the city.

In a country where race was defined in binary categories of black and white, few women (with the exception of Native American women) worked harder at defining these categories than Black women, who were completely consumed under the socially constructed meanings of blackness, and Irish immigrant women, who were positioned on the outermost edges of whiteness. They entered northern U.S. cities during a period when women's household labors were critical to the settling of racial boundaries, serving triple duty in defining "home," "woman," and who was fully citizen.

Native-born whites used the home as a place and domesticity as an ideology to re-establish boundaries between whites, Blacks, and immigrants during the social, political, and economic shifts of the late nineteenth century. Since slavery, racial classifications had determined that only native-born white men could access the privileges of American citizenship that included educational opportunities, land ownership, affordable and safe housing, voting rights, and jobs that paid livable wages. Emancipation, western expansion, industrialization, the women's suffrage movement, European immigration, and Black migrations disrupted these definitions of race.

In the midst of these political and economic shifts, Irish immigrant and southern Black women entered a region where native-born whites loathed Ireland and were trying to figure out how to reconcile with the U.S. South after the Civil War. Southern Black and Irish immigrant women's employment in northern homes prompted native-born white employers and journalists to redefine race in ways that preserved native-born white supremacy. Certainly, immigrant women across race and ethnicity were scrutinized when they reached the U.S. North. According to native-born whites, German women were "bad" cooks because they prepared food with too much garlic; Italian women could never become "good" domestic workers because they were impulsive, impractical, and, most importantly, the majority were married; Jewish women were grossly unattractive, vulgar, noisy, and immoral; and the Chinese "wore funny clothes, spoke an unknown language, and ate impossible food"; but these complaints did not outweigh comments about Irish and Black serving women.[30] They bore the brunt of the criticisms in the US northeast because they outnumbered other women in domestic service in the region, and they were touted as hailing from some of the most uncivilized corners of the world.

Irish immigrant and southern Black women worked long hours to bring pristine order to northeastern homes, and they also worked at redefining racial ideologies that marked them as outsiders and undeserving of American citizenship. Of course, their goals were different and sometimes in conflict with one another: Irish immigrant women expanded the boundaries of whiteness by inserting themselves into ideologies of whiteness and femininity, and southern Black women disrupted the premise of whiteness, or the idea that only whites, European immigrants, and men could be American citizens. As

Isabel Wilkerson put it, southern African American migrants "did not dream the American Dream, they willed it into being... they declared themselves the Americans that perhaps few others recognized but that they had always been deep within their hearts." [31] Since the early colonial days, European colonists and white American slaveholders had declared Black women beastly, masculine, hypersexual, and uncivilized, and thereby the antithesis to genteel white womanhood, to justify the labor and sexual exploitation of Black women inherent to slavery.[32] After emancipation, domestic service employers in the South and North used these gendered ideologies of race to justify low wages in the occupation and blame Black women when they were raped by white male employers. Hence, unlike Irish immigrant women, Black women had the added burden of asserting their humanity in their struggle for protection in the workplace and better wages and working conditions. Black women challenged employers' perceptions of them and domestic service that were rooted in the history of slavery by declaring that they were American citizens because they were native-born, respectable women who did skilled work.

What Irish immigrant and African American women shared across their distinct trajectories in domestic service and their distinct identities and racial projects was that they reached northeastern homes of employment already racialized as inferior to white Anglo-Saxon Protestants and as the antithesis of virtuous white womanhood. Hence, investigating the laborious ideological work that Irish immigrant and southern African American women did to redefine race, womanhood, and domestic work in U.S. northeastern cities requires starting with their labors in the racialized and gendered political economies from where they migrated.

Irish immigrant and southern African American women did not arrive in northeastern cities as simply workers seeking to create better lives for themselves and their families. They left their hometowns to claim opportunities and resources that had been denied to them in the stratified political economies of Ireland and the U.S. South. Irish and southern Black women had been castigated as racial others and noncitizens, and were relegated to the lowest-paying and most degraded labors for women: domestic service and agricultural work. In nineteenth-century Ireland and the U.S. South, domestic service and agricultural work were servile labor only suitable for racial others, and was certainly unbefitting of ladies. What Irish and Black women did with their hands marked their racial and gender inferiority: tilling soil, cultivating crops, and tending to farm animals on lands owned by whites in power. They also washed dirty linens, cleaned bodies and bodily waste, sanitized floors and toilets, and prepared meals in homes owned by whites.

Northern white American domestic service employers, journalists, and cartoonists adopted similar attitudes towards Irish and Black women in their racial project to reconstitute white supremacy after emancipation. The servant problem, or the perceived "challenge of finding and retaining good servants" was therefore a racial one.[33] White nativists produced fluctuating representations of the Irish and southern newcomers. On one hand, employers lamented that the ignorant and domineering Irish Bridget brought instability to northern homes, and southern Black women were no better. The southerners had been under the rule of uncivilized, rural white southerners and knew nothing about caring for modern homes. On the other hand, employers argued, Irish women could be cheerful and fun-loving, and Black women knew how to cook delicious southern meals, and they were more submissive than all other women in the occupation.

The comparisons between Irish immigrant and Black women in print media illustrated a shift in the country's attention—and racial anxiety—from primarily Irish immigrant and African American men to include their sisters, daughters, nieces, and wives. After emancipation, African American and Irish immigrant women's household labors as domestic workers became a medium through which the country gauged and defined racial hierarchies and undesirables. To demand better wages and living conditions, Irish immigrant and Black women had to challenge racial and gendered discourses that justified their labor exploitation. Such discourses were simultaneously rooted in the political economies of the U.S. South and Ireland and racial anxieties over Irish and Black women's migrations into northeastern cities in a post-slavery society. They also had to redefine domestic work itself as a respectable occupation.

This book takes a thematic and chronological approach to the study of race-making, women's migrations, and domestic service. It begins with examining the "contact" between Irish immigrant and southern Black women before the latter half of the nineteenth century when they were the two largest groups employed in domestic service in northeastern cities. Both groups of women had been relegated to exploitative women's work in labor economies stratified by race, class, and gender that sustained white supremacy in Ireland and the U.S. South. The labors in which they were concentrated simultaneously marked their racial subordinate status to whites of English Protestant ancestry. In the nineteenth century, employment agencies and programs were designed to specifically recruit Irish and southern Black women to provide "cheap" household labor to white northeastern families. The labor schemes induced regional debates about the Irish and southern newcomers that racialized their labors and the women themselves.

Chapter 1, "Putting Racial Formation Theory to Work: A Women-Centered, Transdisciplinary, and Intersectional Approach," lays out the theoretical framework for this book. I explain how I integrate theories of racial formation and intersectionality to construct a comparative and women-centered history of race. I also argue that this integrated framework provides a lens to trace the history of contemporary injustices rooted in race, gender, labor, and immigration.

Chapter 2, "The Lost Files of Irish Immigration History: The Irish Woman Question and Racialized Manual Labors," explores how Irish women came into the United States as racial beings. They were nonwhite in the eyes of British rulers that relegated them to agricultural and household work, the lowest-paid and lowest-status labors in British-controlled Ireland. During the famine era, Irish women emigrated to the United States before slavery was abolished, and they entered a labor niche that was defined as enslaved Black women's work. They also performed this racially stigmatized labor in a white Protestant-controlled nation where women were not full citizens and where native-born whites had adopted British beliefs about the inferiority of the Irish. As such, Irish immigrant women posed serious challenges to whiteness and American citizenship much longer than their fathers, brothers, and uncles. Irish immigrant women also left an indelible print on the occupation in the North. By virtue of their contested and domineering presence in domestic service, Irish women transformed domestic service from being not only "Black" work, but also racially stigmatized immigrant women's work.

Chapter 3, "Southern Mammy and African American 'Immigrant' Women: Reconstituting White Supremacy after Emancipation," examines the relegation of southern Black women to domestic service in the labor economies of the U.S. South and North. The chapter also traces southern Black women who migrated to northern cities after the Civil War in search of better domestic service employment than what was available in the postwar South. They migrated to a region where northern whites remained uncertain about racial equality after emancipation and prided themselves on being superior to southerners—both black and white. The southern newcomers also entered a region where Irish immigration had fueled regional racial debates about whiteness and racial outsiders. As southern and formerly enslaved Black women, I argue, the southern arrivals to the North became integrated into this race, labor, and immigration question such that they were routinely characterized as "refugees" and immigrants.

Chapter 4, "Too Irish, Too Rural, Too Black: aka 'The Servant Problem,'" traces how Irish immigrant and southern Black women's entrance into domestic service in the U.S. North intensified the race question for native-born whites after emancipation. While holding onto hope that native-born white "help" would return to domestic service to solve the servant problem, or the decline of efficient servants, native-born northern whites were concerned about who would care for their homes. Would it be the familiar cantankerous Irish *Bridget* or the "new" southern Black *refugees*? This was not only a practical question, but a racial one. Employers evaluated the "Irishness" of Irish immigrant women and the "southerness" of Black women to solve the domestic service problem.

Chapter 5, "Irish Immigrant Women Whiten Themselves, African American Women Demand the Unseen," places Irish immigrant and African

American women's labor organizing, community work, and individual acts of resistance during the late nineteenth century in conversation to address the domestic service problem. I argue that Irish immigrant domestic workers inserted themselves into the labor reform movement to end "white slavery" and redefined white female respectability to access better jobs and working conditions. The chapter also examines how Black clubwomen and domestic workers worked at severing the deeply rooted ties between race and domestic service and redefining what it meant to be southern, Black, and migrant women to demand better working conditions.

Chapter 6, "Irish Immigrant Women Become Whiter, African American Women Dignify Domestic Service," explores how Irish immigrant women became whiter by the 1920s and exited the ranks of domestic service to enter other occupations. I argue that this period of transition, however, was gradual. Wage-earning Irish immigrant women encountered discrimination in their new places of employment and had to reenter domestic service when their husbands could no longer support the household. Most Irish immigrant women did not completely leave the ranks of domestic service until the 1930s. The chapter also examines how Black clubwomen and domestic workers continued their enormous project of clearing race of ideologies that marked southern Black migrant women outside the boundaries of American citizenship and basic humanity. These working-class and relatively privileged Black women also redefined the meaning of domestic service, an occupation rooted in the history and enduring legacies of slavery. Black women's struggle to be fully recognized as U.S. citizens continues to this day.

The stories of Irish immigrant and southern Black women offer one historical frame by which to examine questions of race and the "home," a subject which seems to fascinate the American public. The proliferation of reality television shows including *Supernanny*, *Devious Maids*, and *The Real Housewives* series signals that the lives of women and their labors in private homes has the ability to garner much attention. National debates about chef Paula Deen requiring the staff in her restaurant to dress like butlers and maids on a plantation; mixed reactions to depictions of Viola Davis and Octavia Spencer in Kathryn Stockett's film *The Help*; and national protests organized by immigrant women of color against labor exploitation in domestic service signal that the nation remains engaged in conversations about race and domestic work. The country is still processing the history of slavery and its impact on race and American citizenship. As historian Edward Baptist explained, "The idea that the commodification and suffering and forced labor of African Americans is what made the United States powerful and rich is not an idea that people necessarily are happy to hear."[34]

There is much that we can learn about Irish immigrant women and Black women's distinct and overlapping struggles in becoming fully recognized as

American citizens. Making race has always been and continues to be deeply embedded in "home" as personal abode and nation. Irish immigrant and southern Black women's histories provide a way to trace enduring tensions between race and women's labor in a country that has struggled to achieve its democratic ideals while holding onto the legacies of slavery that sustain racial, class, and gender inequalities in the home and beyond. The story that I am ultimately reconstructing is about the stubborn and not fully answered questions of race and labor as they pertain to women.

1

Putting Racial Formation Theory to Work

————————————————————————⟨◦⟩—

A Women-Centered,
Transdisciplinary, and
Intersectional Approach

Writer and MSNBC news show correspondent Lawrence O'Donnell is the first Irish American who I have heard speak publicly about the intersections of racism and misogyny in Irish communities in the United States. On October 19, 2017, O'Donnell walked his audience through the history of Irish racism, patriarchy, and disdain for African American women on his show, *Last Word*.[1] O'Donnell embedded this history lesson in his ardent response to General John F. Kelly for making disparaging remarks about African American congresswoman Frederica Wilson.[2] Kelly, the White House Chief of Staff, held a press conference earlier that same day to defend President Donald Trump against Congresswoman Wilson's claim that the president had outright disrespected the family of deceased U.S. army sergeant La David Johnson. Johnson, a twenty-five-year-old African American husband and father of three children, had been killed in the line of duty along with three white American soldiers on a U.S. mission to combat ISIS in Niger.[3]

Wilson, a close friend of the Johnson family who had known Johnson since he was a young boy and participant in her 5000 Role Models of Excellence Program in Florida, was with the family when Trump called to offer his condolences. Wilson and Johnson's wife, Myeisha Johnson, were in disbelief when he could not recall La David's name during the phone call. President Trump also angered them when he said: "He knew what he was signing up for, but I guess it hurt anyway."[4] His comment reeked of his disregard for any life other than his own, especially Black lives.

Trump compounded the family's already considerable state of distress. The U.S. Army failed to notify them of La David's death. They found out about his murder from watching the news, and, to this very day, U.S. military officials have still not been able to answer the family's questions about the events leading to La David's death. As late as November 2017, after his funeral, the military announced that more of Johnson's bodily remains were found in Niger. Congresswoman Wilson appeared on several news shows detailing the president's conversation with the family and how it impacted them. She also demanded answers from the U.S. military regarding the details of La David's death.

Despite the reprehensible treatment of Johnson's family, General Kelly held a press conference to defend the president and the U.S. military by disparaging Congresswoman Wilson. He began criticizing Wilson by accusing her of bragging about securing money for her congressional district at a building dedication ceremony in honor of two slain FBI agents in 2015.[5] Kelly recalled, "A congresswoman stood up in the long tradition of empty barrels making the most noise, stood up there in all of that, and talked about how she was instrumental in getting the funding for that building and how she took care of constituents because she got the money . . . And we were stunned. Stunned that she'd done it, even for someone who is that empty a barrel. We were stunned." Kelly continued, "I thought that was at least sacred. You know when I was a kid growing up a lot of things were sacred in our country. Women were sacred and looked upon with great honor. That's obviously not the case anymore as we see from recent cases."[6]

Kelly's description of Wilson as an "empty barrel" during the press conference was all too familiar to Lawrence O'Donnell. Both men grew up in similar Irish American neighborhoods and went to the same high school in Boston, Massachusetts, yet O'Donnell asserted, "I was stunned that John Kelly would so callously echo the worst part of the culture that he and I grew up in. Stunned."[7] O'Donnell connected Kelly's comments to the long history of Irish-descended men's disdain for African American women and misogyny toward Irish-descended women in the United States. He declared, "You know what wasn't sacred when he was a kid growing up, where he was growing up? Black women, or black people." O'Donnell noted that just like the Irish Americans who threw rocks and cursed at Black children who integrated schools in Boston in the 1960s, Kelly showed outright disdain and hatred toward Wilson because she is a Black woman. As O'Donnell put it, "He talked more about her than he talked about the president or his sons, and he never mentioned her name. He called her an empty barrel. He dehumanized her." O'Donnell recalled that Kelly's comments were rooted in nearly three-centuries-old racist scientific beliefs in the superiority of the white race. As he put it, Kelly delivered a lecture about "his moral superiority over her and Donald Trump's moral superiority over her." His beliefs were colored with the history of racial segregation in the United States and Irish American hatred toward African Americans. According to O'Donnell, he and Kelly grew up in neighborhoods where "calling someone who looked like Frederica Wilson an empty barrel was the kindest thing that would have been said about her."[8]

A native insider, O'Donnell also took on Kelly's remark about the sacredness of women to expose the misogyny in their community. Rooting Irish American anger toward Black women in the history of misogyny in Irish American communities, O'Donnell asserted, "And oh by the way, [Irish] women were not sacred either. They were not honored either. In John Kelly's neighborhood in the Catholic parish that he grew up in, in the Catholic parish that I grew up in, women were getting beaten by their husbands, their drunken husbands, as a normal weekly occurrence. And their parish priests would tell those women you can't get divorced or you'll be excommunicated. You're just gonna have to bear it. And bear it for the children . . . Most women were domestic servants and the women who had jobs outside of the home were not allowed to have most of the jobs in America at that time." O'Donnell drew a parallel between the life histories of Black women and Irish-descended women when he stated that there were "huge barriers for women who wanted to be doctors instead of nurses, and women who wanted to be professors instead of elementary school teachers, which is how Frederica Wilson began her life's work."[9]

O'Donnell's critique of Kelly's remarks illuminates how the racism and sexism endemic to white immigrant hostility is not just a moment in history. It is also the present. The theory that underlies this book is that putting African American and Irish immigrant women's histories into conversation with each other disrupts the silences of race that have loomed, and continue to loom, largely over the United States. As Grace Hale poignantly stated in *Making Whiteness*, "Central to the meaning of whiteness is a broad, collective American silence . . . the denial that whiteness has a history, allows the quiet, the blankness, to stand as the norm." When whiteness is unspoken, it remains the "deepest sense of what it means to be an American," and the racial and gender boundaries of citizenship that have traditionally excluded people of color, immigrants, and women remain unchallenged. [10]

While I do not claim that what we experience in the present can be directly traced to what occurred during the latter half of the nineteenth century and the early twentieth century, many of the tensions among race, gender, labor, and citizenship that Irish immigrant and southern migrant African

American women encountered, resisted, and, in the case of some Irish immigrant women, bolstered, have persisted to this very day. These unresolved struggles are apparent in many sociopolitical events today, including—to name a few—race-based immigration policies, the resurgence of nativist white supremacy as evidenced in the Charlottesville riots, the sexual and labor exploitation of women in the workplace, the continuous concentration of Black and immigrant women in domestic service, and the persistent struggle for labor legislation to protect domestic workers and other low-wage workers. Southern Black and Irish immigrant women's histories provide a lens to trace these deeply institutionalized inequalities and imagine transformative possibilities for the future.

Constructing a comparative women's history requires a methodological approach that centers women in constructions of race. In this chapter, I lay out my methodological framework that puts racial formation theory to work for women by integrating it with intersectionality theory. I argue that the integration of these theories: 1) illuminates the relationality of women's labor struggles and outcomes; and 2) materializes race beyond a figment of the white slave-era imagination into an ideology that confined women to niches of labor, defined the work that they did, and characterized who they were as workers. This integrated framework also permits the fluidity necessary for "moving with the women" to trace and document how their migrations, labors, and acts of resistance impacted race.[11]

Gendered Racial Ideologies in the United States

Women's labors have been integral to the development of racial ideologies since the earliest days of the American Republic. Slaveholders, politicians, and scientists in the United States adopted gendered racial ideologies that European travelers and scientists developed during the Enlightenment period to justify the institution of slavery in the face of a constitutional crisis. White men had fought for independence from Britain on the declaration that all men were created equal and deserved democratic freedom, yet they had established an institution of human bondage that was the foundation of the United States' economy and political and social systems.

Women of African descent were integral to social constructions of race and gender that white Americans developed to defend slavery against these glaring contradictions. They took cues from early gendered discourses of racial difference developed by colonists who traveled to Africa and detailed their first impressions of the women whom they encountered. As historian Jennifer Morgan argued, these travel accounts were instrumental to the construction of racialist discourses imbued with ideas of gender and sexual difference that justified colonialism in Africa and the enslavement of African-descended women.[12] English colonists described African women in their travel diaries as having beastlike, masculine bodies with large breasts that hung so low that they could throw them over their shoulders to breastfeed their babies while working. These descriptions of African women were used to substantiate the colonial project of exploiting African women for productive and reproductive labor.[13]

White male scientific researchers were intrigued by these travel diaries about African women as well as the "new" plants and animals that colonists brought back to Europe after their voyages. Since the primary purpose of the colonial voyages was to establish the transatlantic slave trade and European naturalists became particularly obsessed with creating a human classification system, they divided people into hierarchical racial categories based on observable differences such as skin color, hair, facial features, and bones. They also sought to determine what they considered to be the anatomical differences between women and men, and between women across the races.[14] Naturalists concluded from their erroneous studies deeply influenced by the colonial agenda of enslaving Africans that European males were the most evolved and African negroes were the least evolved of the human species, nearly akin to apes. They also concluded that the inferiority of African women to European women was traceable through the differences in the size of their pelvises. African women were described as having a larger pelvis capable of birthing children with ease and substantiating the presumption that African women were "entirely destitute of the transparent delicacy characteristic of the female European."[15] Charles White, an English physician, concluded from these characteristics that African descended women were "intermediate between the whites and the apes."[16] The fictive descriptions of African women rationalized coercing enslaved women to work through their pregnancies and shortly after giving birth.

By the nineteenth century, these scientific ideas of race and gender had become widely held beliefs in the United States among the white ruling classes. U.S. white male scientists and physicians cited erroneous European studies to assert the claim that Blacks were in a permanent state of moral and intellectual inferiority and they need the moral guidance and rational instruction of whites to survive. Scientists during this early period were white men who made their experimental findings available for public consumption. Scientists spoke openly about race on lecture circuits to right what they thought was wrong and substantiate what they believed was right about society. As Melissa N. Stein noted, "These scientists often saw themselves as reformers, upholding the natural order and curing society of its ills."[17] Only the wealthy could afford to purchase the manuals; however, scientific ideas about race and gender reached a wide audience through local periodicals that printed satirical images and articles that bolstered the myth that there were hierarchies of racial and gender differences.

Scientific researchers categorized people into gendered racial hierar-chies based on phenotypical characteristics such as skin color, hair texture, and the shape and measurement of the skull and facial and bodily features. Philadelphia-born physician and researcher Dr. Samuel Morton based his conclusion that there were innate differences in intelligence and character between whites and Blacks on his collection of human skulls.[18] *Crania Americana* lived well beyond Morton's death in 1840. It was reprinted several times and read by a wide audience ranging from scientists to wealthy slave owners. The idea that there were innate differences between races was also reflected in the cartoons and commentaries published in newspapers and other periodi-cals of the time. Politicians and planters cited *Crania Americana* to defend the institution of slavery against abolitionist arguments nearing the Civil War.[19] As Rana A. Hogarth explained, "The pathological and even normative traits that physicians attributed to black bodies became tools of oppression and power . . . that disqualified them [blacks] from self-government."[20]

The body of literature produced by women's and gender studies schol-ars, historians, and sociologists such as Londa Schiebinger, Deirdre Cooper Owens, and Melissa N. Stein demonstrated that scientific claims about race had become increasingly gendered and sexualized in the nineteenth century.[21] As historian Deborah Gray White asserted, "Although much of race and sex ideology that abounds in America has its roots in history that is older than the nation, it was during the slavery era that the ideas were molded into a peculiarly American mythology."[22] Constructed as the foil to their virtuous, dainty, and moral white mistresses, enslaved Black women were racialized and gendered as immoral, irrational, and licentious with masculine bodies and abnormally large genitalia, breasts, buttocks.[23] The bodily characteristics that marked the perceived inferiority of Black women to white women made the former suitable for the back-breaking work and sexual exploitation of slavery.

Gendered ideologies of race had become widely held and institutional-ized beliefs in the United States by the mid-nineteenth century. Historian Deirdre Cooper Owens makes the argument that American gynecology was birthed from the sexual and labor exploitation of enslaved Black women and poor Irish immigrant women. Dr. James Marion Sims, known as the "Father of Gynecology," experimented on enslaved Black women in the South and poor Irish immigrant women in New York City to find medical cures for white women. Taking cues from eighteenth-century racial scientific studies in England and France, Sims believed that Black women and immigrant women were intellectually and physiologically inferior to native-born white Prot-estant women. As Cooper Owens explained, "Racialized bodies, those that were 'coloured' because they were not white, middle-class, and Protestant became ones that emphasized 'otherness.'"[24] Sims conducted the often fatal and permanently damaging experiments on Irish immigrant and enslaved

Black women under the assumption that they could withstand pain and were thereby perfect specimens for experimentation to find cures for ailing native-born white women.[25]

Medicalized ideas of race and gender reached far beyond the surgical rooms of Sims' Black and Irish immigrant patients. As I examine in Chapter 4, the gendered racial ideology that Black and immigrant women were inferior to white Anglo-Saxon women was illustrated for public consumption in widely circulated periodicals and domestic service manuals impacting how Black and Irish immigrant women were portrayed as domestic servants. These beliefs also impacted how employers thought of the Irish and Black women in their homes.

There has been significant progress since the nineteenth century, such as the abolition of slavery, women and African Americans gaining the right to vote, and the end of legal racial segregation. Race, gender, class, and other categories of difference, however, remain axes of domination determining how social, economic, and political power is distributed, enforced, and institutionalized. Sociologists Michael Omi and Howard Winant developed racial formation theory to explain that race is socially constructed and not a human biological trait.[26] Racial formation theory allows one to trace the development of racial ideologies from slavery until the present and examine how such ideologies have historically and continue to shape institutions and people's lives. Women of color scholars in women's studies, sociology, legal studies, and history developed intersectionality to explain how ideologies of race are simultaneously gendered, classed, and sexualized. While ideologies of gender and race are mutually constitutive, racial formation theory and intersectionality were developed in isolation from each other. My theoretical framework for this book integrates theories of racial formation and intersectionality to construct a comparative racial history of laboring women.

Intersectional Racial Formation Theory

Omi and Winant define race in the United States as a "fundamental organizing principle of social stratification" determining the "definition of rights and privileges, distribution of resources, and the ideologies and practices of subordination and oppression" since slavery.[27] According to Omi and Winant, *racial formation* is race-making, or the "social historical process by which racial identities are created, lived, transformed, and destroyed."[28] *Racialization,* Omi and Winant assert, is the process of assigning people racial identities, or "imparting social and symbolic meaning to perceived phenotypical differences."[29] The travel accounts of European travelers during the Enlightenment period and the conclusions that Samuel Morton and James Marion Sims derived from the experiments are examples of race-making; more specifically, constructing meanings of whiteness and blackness. They produced definitions of blackness and whiteness by racializing African descended women as having abnormal behavioral and phenotypic traits.

Racial formation theory emphasizes that today's racial meanings have their roots in constructions of race that were historically produced and have endured for centuries. A twenty-first-century twist on nineteenth-century depictions of enslaved Black women, African American women today are racialized as having full lips; voluptuous and strong bodies; "nappy" coarse hair, hair weaves, and vulgar personality traits such as being hypersexual, loud, and outspoken. White women are often racialized as having pale skin, thin bodies, and blond hair, and as being frail and weak in body structure, demeanor, and personality. Like contrasting depictions of Black and white women in the nineteenth century, tennis legend Serena Williams, for example, has been compared to white women tennis players throughout her career to racialize her as masculine, cantankerous, unintelligent, and mean. Williams spoke to these characterizations in a 2017 *Vogue* interview. She posed the rhetorical question, "Why the fixation on me playing dudes?" She also observed: "I feel like people think I'm mean," she said. "Really tough and really mean and really street. I believe that the other girls in the locker room will say, 'Serena's really nice.' But Maria Sharapova, who might not talk to anybody, might be perceived by the public as nicer. Why is that? Because I'm black and so I look mean? That's the society we live in."[30] Mark Knight, an Australian artist, illustrated these beliefs in a cartoon that he drew of Williams after she protested a tennis umpire's unfair decision to penalize her during the finals match at the 2018 U.S. Open Tournament, which arguably cost Williams the entire match. Ironically, Williams' opponent, Naomi Osaka, is portrayed as a white woman although she is of Japanese and Haitian descent. Knight's image of Williams and her opponent is similar to nineteenth-century depictions of "uncivilized" African American and Irish immigrant domestic workers and their "civilized" mistresses that appear in subsequent chapters of this book, thereby demonstrating that intersecting nineteenth-century beliefs about race, gender, and women laborers have not diminished from the white imagination.[31]

Omi and Winant's racial formation theory also accounts for people's agency in creating racial meanings in their concept of *racial projects*. They argue that racial meanings change over time because they are created from competing *racial projects*, or political struggles. The Irish, for example, has become a fascinating case study for historians to trace the shift in meanings of whiteness over time. The groundbreaking scholarship of David Roediger, Noel Ignatiev, and Matthew Frye Jacobsen has established that native-born white Protestants racialized the Irish as akin to African Americans to preserve white supremacy amid the demographic shifts and competition for political power sparked by Irish immigration in the mid-nineteenth century. The Irish racial project to become whiter, which included violently and politically distancing themselves from African Americans, eventually shifted meanings of whiteness over time. By the latter half of the nineteenth century, Irish men were unquestionably white.[32]

While racial formation theory demonstrates how race is socially constructed, acquires power, and shifts in meaning over time, it does not explain how race has historically and continues to be gendered. Whiteness studies, such as the literature on Irish immigration, rely heavily on racial formation theory and thereby produce masculinist narratives of race, or racial histories that only center men. Sociologist Evelyn Nakano Glenn argued in her pathbreaking social history of African American, Mexican, and Hawaiian laborers in the United States that there are missed opportunities of engagement between Omi and Winant's theory of racial formation and feminist theories about gender. Glenn asserts that there are significant overlaps between both bodies of thought. Collectively, they demonstrate that race and gender "share three key features: (1) they are relational concepts whose construction involves (2) representation and material relations and (3) in which power is a constitutive element."[33] The concept of relationality, as Glenn argues, is significant because it "suggests that the lives of different groups are interconnected, even without face-to-face relations . . . a white person in America enjoys privileges and a higher standard of living by virtue of the subordination and lower standard of living of people of color, even if that particular white person is not exploiting or taking advantage of a person of color."[34]

Women's labors have always been foundational to the idea that race and gender are mutually constitutive and foundational to interlocking systems of oppression. Since Maria W. Stewart, a free Black woman from Connecticut, delivered speeches during the early 1800s calling attention to the unique exploitation of "Africa's daughters," or enslaved Black women, African American women activists and scholars have insisted that race, class, gender, and other categories of difference underlie hierarchical and interdependent systems of power. As Women's Studies scholar Beverly Guy-Sheftall explained, African American women's "rebellious spirit" was rooted in their distinct gendered experiences from Black men and distinct racial experiences from white women during slavery. According to Guy-Sheftall, "They [African American women] resisted beatings, involuntary breeding, sexual exploitation by white masters, family separation, debilitating work schedules, bad living conditions, and even bringing into the world children who would be slaves."[35]

Barred by white women from leadership positions in women's suffrage organizations and by Black men in churches and abolitionist organizations, African American women created their own organizations proclaiming that the country address the systems of power that shaped the exploitation of Black women. As Mary Church Terrell, founding president of the National

Association of Colored Women, declared in her 1898 speech "The Progress of Colored Women" to the mostly white National American Woman's Suffrage Association: "Not only are colored women with ambition and aspiration handicapped on account of their sex, but they are almost everywhere baffled and mocked because of their race. Not only because they are women, but because they are colored women..."[36]

As feminist scholar Beverly Guy-Sheftall argued in the canonical Black feminist text *Words of Fire,* nineteenth-century African American women's lectures, writings, community organizing, and demonstrations planted the original seeds for what we now know as intersectionality theory.[37] Native American, Xicana, Latinx, Asian American, African American, multiracial, and immigrant women of color scholars and activists built upon this early tradition of feminist thought extending it into the twentieth century.[38] They, like their nineteenth-century predecessors, insist that they do not experience "race and gender as additive, but as simultaneous and linked," thereby making intersectionality vital for social, economic, and political justice for all women.[39] Feminist legal scholar Kimberlé Crenshaw was the first to give a name to this theory that has been in development since the nineteenth century. In her classic article, "Demarginalizing the Intersection of Race and Sex: A Black Feminist Critique of Antidiscrimination Doctrine, Feminist Theory, and Antiracist Politics," Crenshaw called for the legal system, feminist scholars, and activists to adopt the theory of intersectionality. Intersectionality, Crenshaw argued, disrupts the treatment of "race and gender as mutually exclusive categories of experience and analysis." [40] Intersectionality refutes the additive model, or the explanation that women's experiences are first shaped by their gender, secondly their race, and then other socially constructed categories such as class and sexuality. As Crenshaw noted, intersectionality makes visible the discrimination Black women experience that would otherwise remain marginalized in legal policies, feminist theory, and antiracist politics.

Intersectionality also explains how the racialization of women is relational. I find historian Evelyn Higginbotham's intersectional example a useful illustration of the mutual constitution and relationality of race and gender in everyday language. As Higginbotham poignantly revealed, race is metalanguage, or has an "all-encompassing effect on the construction and representation of other social and power relations, namely, gender, class, and sexuality."[41] It "impregnates the simplest meanings we take for granted." It makes hair often associated with white women "good" and hair often associated with Black women "bad."[42] Legal scholar Dorothy Roberts demonstrated that gendered racialist ideologies not only impact how women are viewed socially, but also have guided U.S. policies that directly impact the materiality of Black women's lives. Although most women on public assistance are not Black, welfare reform was predicated on the belief that Black women are lazy, immoral, and birth more children than they can take care of. As such, welfare reform has disproportionately impacted the lives of Black women, and women of color on public assistance programs.[43]

Intersectionality continues to evolve as a theory across academic disciplines and as an organizing tool for activist organizations. As Kimberlé Crenshaw, Leslie McCall, and Sumi Cho assert in their co-authored article, intersectionality is "a gathering place for open-ended investigations of the overlapping and conflicting dynamics of race, gender, class, sexuality, nation, and other inequalities."[44] Massive participation in the Women's Marches on January 21, 2017, that spanned all seven continents reveal the enormous potential and power of intersectionality as a tool for social justice organizing among women across race and ethnicity.[45]

My work employs intersectionality as a bridge to link women's histories across race, and this is important because intersectionality is continuously underused in histories about working-class white women nearly three decades after Crenshaw's groundbreaking article. Historian Dana Frank called for a racial analysis of working-class white women two decades ago when she argued that the history of race and white-working class women had "fallen into a conceptual gap between two historiographical developments" of whiteness studies and the body of literature on white working-class women that had not marked its subjects as white.[46] As Frank suggested, scholars' avoidance of race in white working-class women's histories might stem from their discomfort with acknowledging that white women could be oppressed and oppressors.[47] The time is ripe to take up the task of naming and investigating whiteness in white women's labor histories. Irish immigrant women could not have become whiter without the existence of Black women. Irish immigrant women also could not have exited the ranks of domestic service without a lower class of women, in this case Black women, remaining concentrated in the occupation. My hope is that engaging both intersectionality and racial formation theories in women's histories leads to more comparative historical scholarship and political organizing among women across race on labor issues.

Scholars have begun calling for an explicit engagement of racial formation theory with the theory of intersectionality. Priya Kandaswamy argues that while there has been increasing recognition of analyzing race and gender together, "theoretical frameworks that examine the process by which race and gender are historically produced have not sufficiently engaged each other," although "racial formation is fundamentally a gendered and sexualized process."[48] Placing racial formation theory and intersectionality in conversation with each other not only strengthens racial formation theory, but also pushes forward the underlying project of intersectionality, which has become lost in some scholarship that uses it as a theory simply to include the experiences of women of color. As Kandaswamy explained, intersectionality was a call to "transform (or abandon) frameworks that cannot grapple with racial difference, inclusion frequently preserves those frameworks as they are by simply adding to them."[49] I seek to explore new questions and dimensions about race and women's labors that have yet to be fully examined by bringing together women's histories into an intersectional racial formation framework.

Migrating and Laboring Intersectional Racial Formation

My book "moves" and "labors" intersectional racial formation, a theoretical framework that centers women in constructions of race and foregrounds the relationality of women's lives, to examine how women's labors and migrations impacted race. Hence, rather than a traditional historiography that details the daily lives and work experiences of Irish immigrant and African American women, I offer a women's social history of race.

The labor system in the United States has been organized along the axes of race, class, and gender since slavery. Defenders of the American Revolution fought for independence from Britain on the basis that America was a self-sustaining and democratic republic and they deserved the right to govern themselves. After gaining independence from Britain, the "founding fathers" proclaimed to use Republican ideologies of independence, democracy, and freedom as guiding principles for U.S. social, political, and economic institutions. Their glaring dilemma, however, was that foundational to these so-called democratic institutions was a system of human bondage. In addition, white men performed a range of work activities that could not be easily characterized as free labor. Landowners in the United States continued to import indentured servants, some of whom were Irish, from Britain after the American War of Independence. Their work activities were sometimes indistinguishable from those of enslaved Blacks.[50] It is important to note that servitude of indentured laborers was temporary, unlike the involuntary and lifelong servitude of enslaved Blacks. White men also worked as apprentices, convict laborers, and captives of sailors.[51]

The segmented labor system was the primary determinant of American citizenship. According to Republican ideology, citizens performed free labor and deserved the resources of a democracy because they were self-sufficient, morally responsible, and rational, whereas noncitizens lacked those capabilities and were thereby undeserving of self-governance.[52] The Naturalization Act of 1790 declared that naturalized citizens were "free white persons," meaning men of Anglo Saxon descent who did independent labor.[53] By the early 1800s, the democratic principles of Republican ideology were racialized and gendered to maintain white male rule by establishing sharper distinctions between citizens and noncitizens and independent and dependent labor.

Definitions of U.S. citizenship and labor simultaneously excluded Blacks, Native Americans, immigrants of color, and white women from U.S. citizenship and profitable, independent labor, and reinforced the construction of racial and gender categories.[54] As legal scholar Ian Haney Lopez explained, ". . . laws that discriminated on the basis of race more often than not defined, and thus helped to create, the categories they claimed only to elucidate."[55] In the court of law, white, property-owning men were the quintessential American citizens with rights to vote, own property, file law suits, make contracts, and establish independent businesses, although ironically, the labors of noncitizens (enslaved Blacks, women, immigrants, children, and servants) made the freedom of white men possible. Independent labor such as property ownership and working as independent craftsmen and farmers was defined as white men's labor, and primarily white men occupied those positions because they had access to the capital and slave labor to establish and operate their own businesses.[56]

White women and enslaved Black women and men, Native Americans, and immigrants of color were noncitizens because they performed "unfree" labor.[57] Blacks were the epitome of anti-U.S. citizenship because they performed the most extreme dependent labor as enslaved workers. As David Roediger put it, ". . . the bondage of Blacks served as a touchstone by which dependence and degradation were measured."[58] A small percentage of Black women worked as domestic servants, laundresses, and seamstresses and some Black men worked as pastors of their own churches and independent artisans, yet blackness was so deeply immersed in notions of anti-citizenship that performing wage labor and establishing their own businesses did not grant them the right to vote and exercise other privileges afforded to white men. White women were considered a dependent class too fragile and morally pure to do "dirty" manual labor. Married white women were expected to depend on the earnings of their husbands and the labors of enslaved Blacks for survival. They were also expected to adhere to what were considered their natural instincts of providing moral guidance for their children and instructing Black servants on how to maintain the household. Viewed as dependents on white men, married white women did not have an independent legal identity from their husbands. They also could not earn their own wages, own property, or vote.

After emancipation, the racialized and gendered segmentation of the labor market and definitions of American citizenship changed ever so slightly.[59] White men across all social classes, both immigrant and native-born, were considered most fit for American citizenship, while women, Blacks, Native Americans, and immigrants of color were relegated to the lowest-paying jobs and denied U.S. citizenship. While the prevailing family ideal remained white, heterosexual, and patriarchal, the advancement of capitalist industrialization produced a sharper definition of what was considered men and women's work in relation to the home.

Respectable men's work was racialized as professional, skilled, clean jobs done by white men. This masculinized work was designated as productive wage-labor outside of the home that offered enough earnings for men to comfortably support the household while the reproductive labor of taking care of children and directing women of color servants remained women's work.[60] Domestic servants in this segmented labor market were mostly Black women in the South, Asian immigrant women in the West, and European immigrant women in the North. Andrew Urban's comparative history of Irish immigrant, African American, and Chinese servants is useful for conceptualizing the ways in which particularly domestic service was essential to the U.S. capitalist labor economy and establishing racial distinctions between African American women and immigrant working-classes by the mid-nineteenth century. According to Urban, "Whether a servant was black, white, Chinese, Catholic, Protestant, Irish, English, or German was a characteristic that employers factored into how they evaluated the potential benefits of a transaction and a trait brokers and laborers marketed."[61]

Married native-born white women labored as mothers of their own children and supervisors of servants. Unmarried white women had few options for work, laboring mostly as missionaries and teachers. While these occupations paid the lowest wages in the labor market because they were viewed as "women's work" and thereby "unskilled" and "feminine" labor, the concentration of native-born white women as housewives and teachers seemed to confirm the belief that they were morally and intellectually superior to women of color. The concentration of women of color in agricultural and domestic service confirmed the belief that they were dirty, lazy, and morally and intellectually inept. Of all women's occupations, the most pronounced racial stigma was associated with domestic service because it was dominated by Black women and was thereby considered servile labor. Servantry, field labor, and cleaning jobs were described as "nigger work."[62]

The conundrum for Irish immigrant men before Emancipation was that their work did not fit within the masculinist definition of white labor since they were wage laborers. As Roediger explained, there were "many gradations of unfreedom among whites" that "made it difficult to draw fast lines between any idealized free white worker and a pitied or scorned servile Black worker."[63] Concentrated in occupations defined as servile, Irish immigrant men were frequently referred to as "niggers turned inside out"[64] and portrayed as "low-browed, brutish, and simian" with a "black tint of skin."[65] Similarly, Irish immigrant women were drawn as cantankerous, ill-tempered servants with a darker skin hue than native-born white women and other European immigrant women.[66] A running theme in the scholarship of David Roediger, Noel Ignatiev, and Matthew Frye Jacobson is that racialization was not a passive process for Irish immigrants. They willed themselves into whiteness and

American citizenship by driving Blacks out of their jobs, banning Black membership in labor unions, and physically attacking Blacks.[67]

Scholars such as Hasia Diner, Janet Nolan, Margaret Lynch-Brennan, Marion Casey, Faye Dudden, and Maureen Murphy produced a historiographical counterpart to this male-centered Irish immigrant history.[68] Their richly detailed books detail the family and work lives of Irish immigrant women during the famine era in Ireland and after emigrating to the United States during the nineteenth and early twentieth centuries. This body of literature demarcates Irish women from white native-born Protestant women in the United States through a critical gendered analytical approach to Irish immigrant women's history that documents how the Irish newcomers resisted traditional notions of female respectability. As Hasia Diner put it, "Irish women adhered to a behavioral code that deviated markedly from the celebrated 'cult of true womanhood' that commanded American women to lead lives of sheltered passivity and ennobled domesticity."[69] Race, however, remains undertheorized in the literature on Irish immigrant women, although the newcomers from Ireland were concentrated in servile, Black women's labor and often depicted in local periodicals and domestic service manuals as masculine, cantankerous, and darker than native-born white women in skin complexion and morale. Although more recent scholarship has begun examining the racialization of Irish immigrant women, the resounding silence about race that has casted Irish immigrant women's history for several decades has masculinized Irish immigrant scholarship on race and produced the implicit conclusion that when Irish immigrant men achieved whiteness so did Irish immigrant women.[70]

My intersectional racial formation theoretical framework centers women's labors and migrations to illuminate questions that remain unexamined in this body of scholarship in whiteness studies. Similar to the work that Irish immigrant men did when they first arrived in the United States, domestic service was also defined as servile, Black labor because Black women dominated it. As sociologist Judith Rollins put it, ". . . for wherever Blacks served, domestic service was labeled 'nigger's work.'"[71] Considering that labor racialized and gendered workers, I ask: How were Irish immigrant women characterized by the work that they did? Since labor was also defined by the people in it, did Irish immigrant women's concentration in domestic service influence its racial meanings? Racial formation and intersectionality theories demonstrate that people have agency in defining themselves and deconstructing racial categories. Thus, I ask: How did Irish immigrant women see themselves racially, and what did they do to whiten themselves? These questions will expand our understandings of Irish immigrant women's racial histories and white women's intentional relationship to race.

Similarly, the body of scholarship on African American women's migration and labor history has developed in isolation from immigrant women's labor histories. The groundbreaking scholarship of Elizabeth Clark-Lewis, Bonnie Thornton Dill, Elizabeth Hafkin Pleck, Jacqueline Jones, Judith Rollins, and Gerda Lerner employed an intersectional theoretical lens to document the labor exploitation of southern women migrants in domestic service and how they resisted it by insisting on living outside of their employers' homes, negotiating the terms of their employment, and redefining domestic service as respectable, skilled labor.[72]

What remains unexamined in African American women's history is the impact of their labors and migrations on race, and how their racial status was intricately connected to the immigrant women who were also migrating to U.S. cities for domestic service employment at the turn of the century. I use an intersectional racial formation framework that moves with the women of the nineteenth and twentieth centuries in order to provoke crucial questions such as: How did the concentration of Irish immigrant women in domestic service influence the racialization of African American women? In an era of heightened European immigration, how did African American women's identities as migrants impact their racialization? How did African American women theorize race through their own migrations and labors, and in relation to the immigrant women around them?

Examining the relationality of Irish immigrant and African American women's labor and migration histories brings us closer to unveiling the silences of race that not only haunt women's historical scholarship, but also everyday experiences lived in the present. What happens when we detail the racial formation process of how Irish immigrant women became whiter, rather than just stating the outcome? Tracing Irish immigrant women's engagement with whiteness through their racial projects should initiate much-needed dialogue about white women's voting patterns and disrupt the resounding silence around white women's contributions to white supremacy historically and today. Detailing intersectional racial formation in Irish immigrant women's history also sheds light on the persistent struggles of working-class white women, many of whom reside in Appalachia and are descendants of the famine-era Irish, and their maintenance of white supremacy under the guise of concerns about jobs.

Putting African American women's theories and labor and migration histories into conversation with the histories of immigrant women expands the utility of intersectionality into present-day immigration and labor politics. Women's Studies scholar Brittany Cooper captured the incomplete potential and promises of nineteenth-century women's theories when she aptly noted, "... we have not yet engaged with the content of what Black women intellectuals actually *said,* even as we celebrate all that they *did,* seems to escape notice . . . obscuring other kinds of critical scholarly utility they have for our conversations in history, politics, literary studies, and feminist theory."[73] My intention in revisiting African American women's labor and migration histories is to initiate dialogue about the persistent labor struggles of African American women. Black feminist scholarship on how class inequalities shape the lives of working-class African American women has tapered off since the 1980s. While African American women have greater access than their predecessors to jobs outside of domestic service, working-class African American women remain concentrated in service and cleaning jobs such as working as servers in restaurants and school cafeterias, and cleaning restrooms in schools, airports, and offices. In these occupations they often receive low wages and inadequate health benefits. The concentration of African American women in service occupations, and health disparities that disproportionately impact Black women because of their working and living conditions, demand that dialogue about the stubborn question of race and labor for women is urgent.

I argue that Black women's political activism and writings about the struggles of domestic workers are critical for understanding the struggles of immigrants of color today. African American comedian Katt Williams captured the interconnectedness of the fates of African Americans and immigrants of color when he told his audience: "Immigrants, we are your friends because after they come for you, they are coming for us [African Americans] next."[74] General Kelly seemed to confirm Williams's observation in February 2018. Kelly revealed four months after his press conference about Frederica Wilson that his disdain for Black women is not far removed from racist beliefs about immigrants of color. Kelly blamed Latin American immigrant children for administrative refusal to extend the DACA (Deferred Action for Childhood Arrivals) application deadline. According to Kelly, they did not deserve the protection of DACA because they were too lazy to have applied for it in advance.[75]

Racialized as lazy since slavery, Black women and their theories about the exploitation of women migrants, who were arguably among the most disenfranchised and marginalized workers in the nineteenth and early twentieth century U.S. economy, bear important historical insights into the underlying tensions between race and citizenship that subject immigrants of color to injustices. Examining the connections between the struggles of Black women and immigrants can deepen cross-racial political alliances and advance our national understandings about the intersections of whiteness, citizenship, and labor exploitation.

A Note on Hands and Intersectional Racial Formation

Hands connect the intellectual project and heart of this book. What African American and Irish immigrant women had in common across their differences in race, ethnicity, and occupational outcomes were their hands. Their hands carried tales of race and labor exploitation specific to women. African American and Irish immigrant women touched the materiality of race because they did racially stigmatizing labor. They labored in a country where the ruling white class had adopted British beliefs about domestic service and established that manual labor was unbefitting of respectable white women.

Any labor done with hands tainted women racially in the United States and Britain. British employers often referred to the racial "otherness" of working-class women because they did manual labor.[76] As Anne McClintock explained, "Hands expressed one's class by expressing one's relation to labor. Dainty hands were hands that were unstained by work ... smooth white hands revealed that one could afford to buy the labor of others."[77] So important were the hands and labor to social status that British middle-class women employers who often had to do housework themselves "went to incongruous lengths to disguise their work and erase its evidence from their hands."[78] According to historian Deborah Valenze, the "double stigma of gender and class" for female servants in England was a "foreignness approaching racial difference."[79] In the United States, hands were also the site of intersecting racial and class privileges of white women employers that made the exploitation of servants possible. Housewives avoided traces of doing household work because "to be pure and genteel required not soiling her hands. She had to have a servant to do the heaviest labor."[80]

Foregrounding the work of women's hands deepens understanding of race beyond skin hue. Irish immigrant women, for example, had the same skin complexion as their employers, but that did not dissuade cartoonists and employers from drawing them as dark, animalistic, and masculine. Hands also bring working-class women into focus, especially when their hands, or the site of their labors, were erased in racialized gender stereotypes. Disparaging depictions of African American and Irish immigrant servants as idle and pilfering diminished the work that they did. Scholars have rescued the significance of their household labors from the obscurity of these negative epithets, but seldom are domestic workers recognized for their intellectual work. Hands foreground the discursive labor of working-class women that is often forgotten.

The complex history of race for women in the United States lies in what Irish immigrant and African American women decided to do with their hands to change their life's circumstances. They took hold of the imagined ideology of race that colored their identities, labors, and materiality of their lives by attempting to either disrupt or expand white supremacy through their writings, speeches, petitions, and when they put down brooms, mops, and pans in resistance to the inhumane demands of their employers.

I hope that this book provides a historical perspective that will lead to further interrogation of the complexities of race for women that remain deeply entrenched in the social fabric and political economy of the United States. I also intend to initiate discussions about not only the fluidity of race, but also its permanence. When it is not interrogated as such, white consciousness will continue to forget race after the most shocking displays of racism fade. The lessons that can be gleaned from Irish immigrant and African American women's histories make the words of James Baldwin especially salient today. As he once said about the race problem: "Not everything that is faced can be changed; but nothing can be changed until it is faced."[81] Chapter 2, the next chapter of this book, begins the work that Baldwin alluded to by centering race in Irish immigrant women's labor and migration histories in Ireland and the United States.

2

The Lost Files of Irish Immigration History

◄O►

The Irish Woman Question and Racialized Manual Labors

Irish women were castigated as racial others in a British-controlled and gendered ethnic labor system that confined them to agricultural work and domestic service. Their racial and gender inferiority was marked by the only work they were deemed capable of performing in the nineteenth-century British political economy—manual labor, which was deemed unbefitting of respectable white middle-class and elite British Protestant "ladies." Similar to the racial division of household labor between white women and enslaved Black women in the British colonies, it was expected that white British ladies would not get their hands dirty with the physical tasks of farming and housework. Their hands were for supervising servants, providing moral instruction for children, satisfying the desires and demands of husbands, and engaging in leisurely activities. Pointing to objects for servants to clean to their satisfaction, turning pages while reading Biblical stories to their children, tending to their husband's sexual desires and housekeeping demands, and embroidering linens were respectable tasks that defined virtuous white womanhood. The dirty and demanding work of tilling soil, planting crops, plucking and cleaning fowls for dinner, and cleaning dishes, linens, chamber pots, and bodies was designated for women who were the antithesis of white British ladyhood.

British colonial rule over Ireland left poor Catholic Irish women with few options for survival but to do the racially stigmatized and "manly" work of agricultural labor on tenant farms and domestic service in the big houses of Anglo-Irish families in Ireland. At times, Irish women had to work as domestic servants in England, the center of British colonial power. British colonialism weakened Ireland's economy, curtailing employment opportunities for Irish women. Faced with limited employment options, some Irish women migrated to England to work in middle-class homes. While working on tenant farms and in private homes in Ireland and England, Irish laboring women were routinely characterized as uncivilized, dirty, domineering, and a race apart from the British.

The vast majority of Irish women who left Ireland during the famine era immigrated to the United States. They quickly dominated the ranks of domestic service in northeastern cities, displacing free Black women in the occupation and replacing native-born white women who left domestic service to work in the newly-built factories of the U.S. industrial era. Although Irish women no longer labored under a British colonial labor system, they worked in a country where the native-born whites in power had adopted British attitudes towards the Irish and associated domestic service with the institution of slavery.

In this chapter, I argue that the racialization of Irish women and their labors remains largely unexamined in the literature on British colonialism in Ireland and Irish immigration history in the United States. Gendering Irish labor histories on both sides of the Atlantic illuminates how the construction of Irish women as racially inferior and their subjugation to stigmatized labors was integral to white supremacy in Britain and the United States. It also foregrounds the impact Irish immigrant women's movements into U.S. northeastern cities had on race and domestic service in the United States.

Using the British colony of Ireland as a starting point, I trace how famine-era Irish women arrived in the United States and entered a racially stigmatized niche of labor associated with Black women. While domestic service remained tainted by slavery, it also became closely associated with Irish newcomers in northeastern cities. I argue that Irish women's immigration to the United States and their dominance in domestic service in the mid-nineteenth century incited regional debates about race, household labors, and Irish women's immigration. Irish women's movements across the Atlantic thereby transformed the characterization of domestic service in northeastern U.S. cities into racially stigmatized immigrant women's work.

Race and Irish Women's Labors in the British Colonial Context

The British had declared the Irish a racial other since the twelfth century to justify England's early attempts to assert political, religious, and economic dominance over Ireland in the medieval period. During Elizabeth I's reign from the mid-sixteenth century until the early seventeenth century, England made several attempts to colonize Ireland while also establishing colonies in North America and the Caribbean. The development of England's commercial enterprise involved the construction of racial and gender ideologies to explain why the acquisition of land and exploitation of labor from Ireland and the indigenous populations in the colonies was morally justified and necessary.[1] As Jennifer Duffy put it, "The British [. . .] imagined themselves as not only a distinct race, but a white race, which required a culturally or socially defined 'other.'"[2] Constructing an "other" was integral to British colonialism and divisions of labor. The English portrayed the Irish as lazy and licentious like the Africans who toiled on plantations in English colonies in the Caribbean and North America. While these eighteenth-century characterizations were intended to describe both Irish men and women, the stereotypical depictions relied heavily on representation of Irish men.

After England consolidated its colonial power over Ireland through the Act of Union in 1800, representations of Irish women and their actual labors became more integral to the British colonial enterprise. The Act joined the governments and economies of England, Wales, Scotland, Ireland, and the British provinces of Upper Canada and Lower Canada into a British Parliament based in London.[3] When Britain took control of Ireland, it stunted Ireland's industrial growth and created a pathway of economic dependency in which Irish laborers were subjected to the British Parliament and its economic enterprise.[4] Ireland had the fewest representatives in the governing body and thereby limited political power to alter the economy. Only the Anglo-Irish and Catholic Irish that converted to the Church of Ireland could hold public office, attend the University of Dublin, and pursue careers in law, medicine, or the military.

The Act was thus successful in institutionalizing racial, ethnic, religious, and class hierarchies that positioned the English and the Anglo-Irish Protestants as the ruling classes over the Catholic Irish. The Anglo-Irish, a mixture of English, Irish, and Welsh ancestry, who intermarried with the British ruling classes became the native ruling class of Ireland until the twentieth century. Although the Anglo-Irish replaced the Gaelic Irish and Old English aristocracies, they sided with England and protected its political and economic interests in Ireland. Hence, England exerted control over Ireland's social, economic, and political institutions through the Anglo-Irish. The rise of the Anglo-Irish earned them the nickname "New English" and the British parliament used this ruling class as its strong arm against Irish Catholics until the end of the Irish War of Independence in 1921.[5]

British representations of the feminized Celtic race reified the subordination of the Irish to the British colonial power and the racialized, gendered, and stratified labor system in Ireland. After the Act of Union was passed, England restricted the types of resources that Ireland could import and export in an effort to curtail Ireland's power in the commercial Atlantic trade. Ireland's thriving textile and cotton industries plunged into chaos within four years due to intense competition with England. The British Parliament coerced Ireland into becoming an agrarian-based economy and food supplier for England. They confiscated land from Irish Roman Catholics who refused to convert to the Church of Ireland, which severely compromised their political and economic power against the Anglo-Irish gentry. The Anglo-Irish became the owners of the confiscated lands on which Catholic Irish families lived and converted the property into tenant farms. The tenant farming system that the Anglo-Irish imposed on Catholic Irish tenants with the backing of the British Parliament kept the Irish in a subordinate economic and political position. British representations of the Celtic Irish reflected the British patriarchal belief that this political and social hierarchy was the natural order. As L. P. Curtis Jr. explained, "Feminine signified uncontrollable emotions and thereby meant the Celtic race was incapable of self-government."[6]

Unemployed Irish women who had worked in the textile and cotton industries before the Act of Union had few options but to earn a living selling potatoes, corn, eggs, alcohol, dairy products, and livestock that they raised on tenant farms for English and Irish markets. Irish women produced these goods alongside the men in their families while living on small tenant farms owned by Anglo-Irish landlords. As with the late-nineteenth century sharecropping system in the U.S. South, tenant farming reified white male supremacy through the labor exploitation of those deemed racial others. As with white male landowners in the U.S. South, Anglo-Irish landlords kept families in poverty by demanding high rent payments and crop yields that were nearly impossible to meet. Landlords extracted as much rent and labor as possible from tenants to support their lavish lifestyles while living in large estates in the Irish countryside. Consequently, the revenue from food cultivation never reached the tenant farming communities, resulting in impoverished living conditions for Irish women and their families.

The racism that undergirded the human suffering that resulted from the tenant farming system resonated with abolitionist and former slave Frederick Douglass when he visited Ireland in 1845. He most eloquently described the similarity between the labor exploitation and racial oppression of the Irish and enslaved Blacks in his book *My Bondage and My Freedom*. While describing the expressions of suffering and frustrations that enslaved Blacks poured into their work songs, Douglass declared, "I have never heard any songs like those anywhere since I left slavery, except when in Ireland. There I heard the same *wailing notes,* and was much affected by them."[7]

Racialized and gendered representations of Irish home life were used to justify British colonialism and the labor exploitation of Irish women that sustained it. British periodicals associated Irish women with dirt and pro-duced disparaging characterizations of Irish homes to illustrate the belief that Irish women were antithetical to respectable white femininity. These represen-tations placed the blame on Irish women for their poor living conditions as tenant farmers. English tourists who traveled throughout rural communities in Ireland also commented frequently on Irish cabins, or rural dwellings. In their letters to friends and family describing Irish rural life, they detailed piles of dung outside cabin doors, the "absence of ventilation and light inside the dwellings," dirt-based cabin floors, the "filthy pile of straw on which the entire family slept," "the fetid smell of people and pigs living together in cramped quarters, and the half-naked and barefoot children."[8]

These stereotypical observations of Irish homes and children directly impli-cated Irish women, who by Victorian standards were responsible for maintain-ing clean and orderly homes. Evaluated by British ideologies of domesticity, Irish women were portrayed as inept housekeepers, unlike middle-class and elite English women, who took pride in and knew how to maintain clean homes. The notion that Irish women lacked the ability to even discern the difference between dirt and cleanliness in the home was strong evidence that they were not only beneath middle-class English women, but the antithesis to white Anglo-Saxon femininity. Disparaging descriptions of rural Irish home life naturalized the exploitative tenant farming system and masked the poverty and disease that it caused for Irish women and their families.

English observers declared that the disorderly rural cabins and the concen-tration of the Irish in degrading work signaled why Ireland needed to be under the colonial rule of England. Historian David Lloyd concluded in his analysis of the exploitation of Irish and enslaved Black male labor: "It is, clearly, dif-ficult to separate the racialization of labor from the racialization of political emancipation and citizenship." British depictions of the "not yet ready for independence" Irish echoed British portrayals of the "never to be ready for emancipation" enslaved Blacks in the West Indies.[9] Both representations jus-tified Britain's refusal to relinquish power over Ireland and the West Indies in the face of organized resistance to British rule among the Irish in Ireland and enslaved Blacks on Caribbean plantations.[10] As historian L. P Curtis Jr. put it, "The most crucial question of all those that went to make up the Irish Question was whether or not the 'native Irish' could be trusted with responsi-bility for attending to the myriad problems of Irish government . . ."[11] The Eng-lish evaluated Irish women's housekeeping to conjure evidence that the Irish could not manage their own abodes much less the local issues in their home of Ireland.

Irish women laboring as domestic servants in the homes of the Anglo-Irish gentry was endemic to the racial hierarchies of British colonialism in Ireland. After the Act of Union in 1800, the Irish Protestant gentry left their homes in the cities and rebuilt estates along Ireland's countryside that the Catholic gentry had left behind after the British Parliament ousted them from power. Irish women sought domestic service employment in Anglo-Irish big houses to escape the poverty of tenant farming and provide more steady income for their families. [12] The vast majority of the house servant staff in the big houses were Irish women, except for Irish men who primarily labored as butlers and footmen. Serving in the big houses was distinct from the domestic service jobs that Irish women sought in Dublin and other major cities in Ireland. Irish women in cities primarily worked for Irish Catholic employers where the division of household labors was based on gender and class hierarchies. Anglo-Irish gentry employers in the big houses, on the other hand, adopted British customs of household service grounded in racial, religious, and gender divisions of household labor to manage servants.

The organization of domestic service in Anglo-Irish families reinforced beliefs that the white Anglo-Saxon race was superior to the Catholic Irish. Anglo-Irish employers hired a cadre of Catholic Irish servants to do the "dirty" manual labors of caring for their homes, like their British counterparts who lived in manors in England and relied on the labors of working-class English and Irish servants casted as racial others. Racial, ethnic, and religious differences determined the hierarchy and rank of servants within an estate. Similar to the English, Anglo-Irish families employed servants for specific housekeeping roles. Within one household there was a scullery maid, kitchen maid, cook, laundry maids, butler, housekeeper, footmen, parlor maid, lady's maid, governess, and head gardener. Historian Mona Hearn noted, "The normal difference between upper and lower servants based only on status was exacerbated in Irish country houses by differences in religion and nationality, because upper staff tended to be Protestant and British, while many of the lower staff were Catholic and Irish."[13]

In addition, I argue that British racial ideologies about the inherent differences between Catholics and Protestants also influenced the hierarchy of servants. As historian J. J. Lee argued, although there were no observable physical differences between Catholics and Protestants, "Irish Catholics conformed in Protestant minds to the classic stereotype of the native ... They were lazy, dirty, improvident, irresolute, feckless made menacing only by their numbers and by their doltish allegiance to a sinister and subversive religion."[14] Such descriptions were used to demonstrate that Irish Catholics were an inferior race and it is likely that this pervasive belief influenced the hiring decisions of Anglo-Irish employers. Estate owners typically sought British and Protestant servants for the most respected positions of steward, butler, housekeeper, and cook. Catholic Irish servants were hired for the lower status manual labor positions of kitchen, scullery, laundry, and dairy maids, which required them to come into closer contact with "dirty" substances.[15] The racialization of Irish servants is also reflected in Irish elite's descriptions of the country homes that employed Irish servants. When Frances Cobbe, Irish social reformer, animal rights activist, and member of the London National Society for Women's Suffrage, visited a "big house" that was under the care of Irish servants, she expressed her discontent with how the home was managed. Cobbe recalled that the country house was in disarray and resembled "that condition of disorder and slatternliness" which she had "heard described as characteristic of Irish houses," among the rural Irish poor.[16]

The actual interactions between Anglo-Irish families and servants were dictated by domestic customs and the architecture of estates in England that reinforced social, ethnic, and class distance between servants, mistress, and master. Mistresses, for example, could order meals without coming into physical contact with servants. Servants walked through tunnels to avoid disruption of the master and mistress's view of the landscape from the home and coming into direct contact with them.[17] The gentry rarely set foot in the kitchen and the servants stayed mostly in the kitchen and the servants' quarters except when performing specific tasks around the manor. Irish servants were central to the everyday operations of the big houses, and they received room, board, and a set wage for their labors, albeit their earnings were rarely enough for them to retire in old age. Irish servants also rarely earned enough money to send back to their families to help them move out of their thatch-roofed homes. The male head of big houses was the administrator of the estate benefitting the most from the labors of servants, and the mistress managed the servants and directed the moral upbringing of their children.[18]

While the big houses offered employment and lodging to Irish women who wanted to escape poverty in rural communities and overcrowded cities, servants were severely underpaid for the arduous work required. Their wages were low, the hours were long, and the manual work was dangerous. It took extreme physical effort to maintain the Victorian ovens in the kitchen, hand scrub the floors of massive houses, make meals from scratch, clean laundry by hand and iron with heavy cast irons, draw the curtains and light the fires, clean tall windows at high altitudes, empty the chamber pots, and fulfill the personal requests of the Sir, Madam, and their guests. Cooking was an especially arduous task because houses did not have gas and electricity. Irish women cooked over open-hearth fires, which required constant bending to maneuver heavy pots on the floor-level flame.[19]

Irish women also migrated to England to work as domestic servants. In the English Victorian era, women who did manual labor for wages had a looser connection with whiteness than middle-class and elite British women. According to the cult of domesticity, women who worked for wages outside of their own homes were not only non-feminine, but also a race apart from respectable Anglo-Saxon women. As Anne McClintock explained, working-class women in England, including domestic workers, female minors, and prostitutes, were "stationed on the threshold between the white and black races," and were sometimes referred to as "white negroes."[20] The construction of the inept Irish servant certainly supported British colonialism in Ireland. A Catholic immigrant and "foreign" female migrant labor workforce considered incompetent at maintaining order, cleanliness, and Christian morals in their own rural homes in Ireland, Irish domestic servants in England were touted as an imminent threat to the purity and moral order of white Anglo-Saxon homes in England. Descriptions of the rude and illogical Irish servant also provided evidence that the Irish were in fact a subordinate race to the English and needed to be colonized.[21] As such, Irish women were "implicated in both [the colonial and domestic] spaces, "reinforcing their association with degeneracy."[22] While English domestic service manuals and magazines featured incessant complaints from mistresses about the domineering and clumsy Irish servant, their persistent employment of Irish immigrant women signaled that these depictions were in fact stereotypes.

The negative evaluation of Irish women's housekeeping standards were also informed by the stigma associated with English working-class women in domestic service. As Deborah Valenze explained in her study of the Industrial Revolution and domestic service in England: "For in the eyes of many masters and mistresses, class operated in ways parallel to racial categories; lower-class people were closer to nature and less pure and clean than the more civilized middle-classes. Female servants suffered from the double stigma of gender and class, and the effect was a foreignness approaching racial difference."[23] The colonial status of Ireland sharpened the stigma of domestic service associated with Irish immigrant women such that it was in fact racialized. As immigrants in overcrowded cities, Irish women were also used as a scapegoat to avoid discussions about the lack of infrastructure in England to accommodate the Irish migrant labor force. As geographer Bronwen Walter explained, "Irish settlement was seen as a cause of decay and ill-health, rather than a symptom of the failure of the economic system to provide adequate housing for the labour force."[24] To acknowledge the lack of resources in urban cities would compromise England's superior stance towards Ireland based on artificial representations of orderly Anglo-Saxon homelife. English commenters concluded from eyewitness accounts of the living conditions in Ireland's rural communities that poverty and disease plagued England's cities because Irish migrant laborers brought with them their culture of unsanitary housekeeping and personal hygiene.[25]

The English also constructed racialized representations of Irish women as uncivilized and incapable of maintaining well-ordered homes to blame them for the famine. British exploitation of Irish workers and the land was the actual cause of the famine. Anglo-Irish landlords' demands for excessive crop yields coupled with their minimal oversight of agricultural production on tenant farms compromised the fertility of the soil by facilitating the growth of a fungus that destroyed over eighty percent of the potato crop beginning in 1845. The potato famine resulted in widespread starvation, poverty, and unemployment in Ireland.[26] The British Parliament passed successive relief policies to stabilize Ireland's economy, yet these interventions were unsuccessful. British colonialism had stagnated economic growth and the labor force before the famine. Ireland thereby lacked the commercial, physical, and human infrastructure to recover from the famine, especially under relief policies that further re-entrenched Britain's economic and political control over Ireland."[27] England blamed Irish domestic culture for the failure of its policy interventions rather than addressing Britain's colonial dominance over Ireland. [28]

British print media representations of the Catholic Irish as uncivilized, lazy, and thereby "the idle and ungrateful recipient of British tax payers'—and imperial generosity" were deeply racialized and gendered.[29] Unlike Anglo-Saxon households ruled by the stern guidance of the patriarchal husband and father, Irish households were portrayed in the British media as homes under the direction of domineering Irish wives who ruled violently over their weak and drunken husbands. In the English imagination, Irish women were deviant, lacked morals, and were incapable of teaching their children how to become productive British citizens. It was thus concluded that the relief policies did not help Ireland because Irish households were inherently matriarchal and consequently dysfunctional.

Cultural representations of Irish women and their families did not account for the actual factors that caused the economic crisis and the failure of the relief policies. In 1847, the British Parliament passed the Poor Law Extension Act in an effort to modernize Ireland's agricultural economy by encouraging Irish peasants to become industrial and independent workers."[30] Transitioning Ireland's agricultural economy into an industrial market was a difficult endeavor. The Act of Union and the potato famine created a pathway of dependence that the Poor Law Extension Act could not avert. Ireland's economy was severely weakened and remained stagnant from the 1840s until the early twentieth century.

Irish women had lesser chances of surviving the economic devastation of the famine than the men in their families. The famine altered land inheritance traditions of dividing property among siblings after the parents died. Due to limited resources, Irish families adopted less risky land inheritance practices by leaving property to the eldest son. Restrictions on inheritances and dowry expectations made it nearly impossible for most Irish women to marry, and if they could marry it might be based on economic considerations rather than romantic ones. Historian Hasia Diner explained, "They had no realistic chances for marriage or employment. For Irish women to attain either, they had to turn their backs on the land of their birth."[31] Irish women who were non-dowered and did not want to remain unpaid workers on their family farms, join a convent, or work on farms owned by the family of their future husbands immigrated to neighboring countries and overseas.

Britain's solution for impoverished Irish families was to instill a strong work ethic in Irish women by sending them to work as domestic servants in the United States and British colonies abroad. British colonialism and the stratified labor system established by the British in Ireland determined Irish women's immigration routes and their occupational outcomes when they reached their destinations. Since Irish women were considered an excess population draining resources from the British government, British emigration societies were created to transport women from Ireland to work as servants in white Protestant homes in the British colonies and the United States. The immigration options of Irish women who were fortunate enough to receive financial assistance from their families to pay for their steerage remained confined to the British Isles, British territories, and the former British colony of North America. What unified Irish women across their different destinations and means of getting there was that they mostly worked for white Protestant employers, as they did in Ireland and England. Also, whether Irish women immigrated to England, Australia, New Zealand, British provinces in Canada, or the United States, they were primarily concentrated in domestic service. As such, British colonialism and domestic service remained integral to the exploitation of Irish women's labors after they left Ireland.

British government officials and philanthropists created the London Female Emigration Society, the Women's Emigration Society, the British Ladies Emigration Society, and the Girls' Friendly Society that sustained Irish women's emigration to the United States and British colonies from the mid-nineteenth century well into the late nineteenth century.[32] Vere Foster, a philanthropist and member of the Anglo-Irish gentry, also financed the voyages of Irish immigrant women to the United States to work as domestic servants.[33] Some Irish women consented to participating in the labor schemes because they had few options for survival in Ireland, and their families could not afford to pay for their steerage. The British societies paid for steerage and secured jobs for them as domestic servants. Irish women earned less laboring in private homes than what the emigration societies earned from sending them aboard.[34]

Irish girls who sought assistance from agencies were susceptible to labor and sexual exploitation. Corrupt U.S.-based employment agencies encouraged Irish immigrant women to migrate to the United States and Canada with false promises of employment opportunities in domestic service. After reaching their destinations, the newcomers discovered that there were no domestic service placements for them. Many women could not afford the passage back to Ireland and remained in the United States and Canada where they found most immediate employment as domestic servants and sex workers.[35] In the

United States, Irish sex workers were often blamed for diseases and crime in urban cities. They were overrepresented in the prison system and were often subjected to medical experimentation when they sought medical services from local hospitals.[36] Irish women who worked as domestic servants in private Protestant homes were also targeted as the cause of social problems. As Trevor McClaughlin, explained, when primarily orphaned teenage Catholic Irish girls reached Australia, they were "condemned in the colonial press, and by upper and middle-class opinion, as immoral, useless, and untrained domestic servants" and were "ill-suited to the needs of the Australian colonies." [37] Australian employers relied on these disparaging characterizations to justify paying Irish girls low wages, if any at all.

The most attractive option for Irish women and girls was to emigrate to the United States, and it was their first-choice destination from the mid-nineteenth century until the 1930s. [38] Prospective employers in U.S. northern cities were eager to hire Irish women as domestics to remedy what had been touted as the domestic service problem. The strong demand for domestic servants in northern U.S. cities convinced the vast majority of Irish women that they could attain better lives for themselves and their families in the United States. Since the early 1800s, native-born whites in the U.S. North had complained about the disruption in home life caused by the abolition of slavery. Supporters of the Society for the Encouragement of Faithful Domestic Servants lamented that the number of loyal and respectable Black domestic servants had declined since emancipation. After slavery was abolished, white families claimed that the formerly enslaved insisted on moving from household to household to find working arrangements that only suited themselves.[39] In a sense, the complaints reflected the actual decisions Blacks made to establish ownership over their labor after emancipation. While some Black women lived with their employers, others worked as self-employed washerwomen to assert independence from the expectations and requirements of domestic service that they were subjected to under slavery.[40] The Society for the Encouragement of Faithful Domestic Servants, a short-lived organization, was created to instill moral character in household workers to control their mobility and labors. The society offered small monetary prizes and public recognition to servants who remained loyal to their employers and established a hiring service that matched employers and servants in what the society considered mutually satisfactory situations.

Employers' complaints about free Black female and male servants and the preference of Irish newcomers to live with their employers certainly made the first wave of Catholic Irish immigrant women in the 1840s and 1850s a highly sought-after source of domestic service labor. Irish immigrant women were initially willing to "live-in" and thus be at the beck and call of their employers twenty-four hours a day because their lodging options were limited as single women with few friends and relatives in the United States. Living with their employers also made it easier for them to save and send a portion of their earnings to their family back in Ireland. This type of arrangement suited the needs of servants and the desires of employers. Employers could demand work from live-in servants anytime during the day for unspecific lengths of time in the absence of laws that regulated labor in private homes. Irish immigrant women quickly outnumbered the small free Black population in domestic service by the mid-nineteenth century. By 1846, only 156 out of 4,249 female servants living with white families were Black.[41]

When Irish women were seeking domestic work in the United States during the famine era, employers were no longer able to rely on native-born white women, who they had hired as "help" in the past to perform certain domestic tasks for specific lengths of time.[42] The rise of industrialization provided opportunities for white working-class women to work in textile factories. Industrialization also ushered in a new white middle class, and some of those who had previously been employed as "help" were soon able to employ domestic servants themselves.[43] Beginning in the late 1700s, factories emerged along the eastern shore board that produced goods that women used to make at home. By the mid-nineteenth century, domestic labors expected of women, such as cultivating crops for a home's food supply, making soap and candles, and spinning thread to make clothes, were exported to factories. Respectable women's household labors shifted to child-rearing, upholding Christian morals, adhering to the desires of the patriarchal head of the home, and supervising servants.[44]

The sheer number of Irish immigrant women in comparison to Black women, and the freed women's insistence on self-employment coupled with the transition of native-born white women out of domestic service, made it more convenient for employers to hire the Irish newcomers. Although German and Scandinavian women were also employed in domestic service by the mid-nineteenth century, they did not migrate in large enough numbers to overshadow the Irish.[45] In addition, employers preferred Irish women because there was no language barrier.[46] Between six and nine thousand Irish people entered the United States in 1816 and 1817. Most of the emigrants in this wave were Presbyterian. The 1840s, however, marked a significant shift in the Irish immigration patterns. More women immigrated in the 1840s and afterwards than in previous decades, and overall Irish immigration increased.[47] While some immigrant women found employment in mills and factories scattered throughout the United States, most were concentrated in domestic service and remained so for several decades.[48] In 1845, approximately 40,000 Catholic Irish emigrants had settled in the United States, more than half of whom were women who worked primarily in domestic service.[49] In places like New York City and Boston, three out of four serving women were Irish immigrants.[50]

Irish women's dominance in domestic service and their emigration from the British colony of Ireland did not shatter the notions that they were racial outsiders and that domestic service was unbefitting of respectable white women. The occupation remained tainted by the presence of Black women in its ranks. While the percentage of Black women in domestic service in northeastern cities declined, they remained concentrated in places where there were large Irish immigrant communities. One-half or more of all Blacks in New York, Philadelphia, and Boston worked in service occupations that included employment in private homes and second-class hotels. When hired in domestic service, they worked as live-in servants, laundresses, and extra attendants at special events.[51] Irish immigrant women brought their own history to the occupation. They had come to the United States as colonized subjects that the British had cast as racially inferior and relegated to the most menial and stigmatized labors in Ireland for women. While live-in domestic work in the United States was initially a convenient arrangement for Irish women, their concentration in the occupation was endemic to their British colonial past. As in Ireland, they remained relegated to the most stigmatized occupation for women. Already defined as Black work before the arrival of the Irish in the United States, domestic service became more stigmatized in the North after the slovenly, belligerent, and racially inferior Irish "Bridget" dominated it.

Race and the "Irishization" of Domestic Service in the U.S. North

Cast as women who defied the terms of virtuous womanhood and occupied the lowest rung of the white race, the very movement of Irish women into U.S. northern cities intensified and molded debates about race. Politicians, scientists, doctors, slaveholders and abolitionists had been immersed in national debates about the abolition of slavery by the time Irish immigrant women planted their feet on U.S. soil in the mid-nineteenth century. These debates called into question the white supremacist racial hierarchies that politicians had cemented into U.S. laws, social institutions, and governing structures of the country. The WASP (white Anglo-Saxon Protestant) ruling classes that upheld these hierarchies embraced British Anglo-Saxon beliefs about the inferiority of working-class women, Blacks, and the Irish.[52] Irish immigrants in northeastern cities "were among the first wave of impoverished peoples from across the Atlantic to receive the full brunt of this ethnocentric" and racial hostility in the late 1840s and 50s.[53]

Irish immigrant women entered a racialized labor economy and political landscape shaped by slavery when they arrived in the United States. According to historian Andrew T. Urban, Vere Foster was discouraged from pursuing his initial plan to finance Irish women's voyages to the U.S. South. Foster's correspondent in Florida told him that the racial divisions between labor were so stark that slaveholders would not hire white servants "even when the costs of wages were less than what they would pay in leasing a black slave."[54] The majority of Irish women settled into northeastern cities that had engaged in contentious and unsettled debates about race, citizenship, and labor that emanated from the legal battles between proslavery legislators and abolitionists petitioning states to outlaw slavery. While northeastern state governments ultimately decided to abolish slavery, they did not grant immediate emancipation to enslaved Blacks, and after full emancipation laws were passed, state governments remained resistant to granting Blacks full citizenship rights.

The Pennsylvania legislature, for example, passed the first gradual emancipation law in 1780 only for children born after February of the same year.[55] It took three trials of the Quock Walker case, based on legal changes to the re-enslavement of Walker after he fled from his deceased owners' property, for the Supreme Judicial Court in Massachusetts to outlaw slavery completely in 1783.[56] Gradual emancipation in New York, a state where many of the Irish newcomers settled, did not begin until over a decade later after decisions in both Massachusetts and Pennsylvania. As historian Leslie Harris put it, "The system of racial slavery became the foundation of New Yorkers' definitions of race, class, and freedom far into the nineteenth century."[57] Since the 1700s, free and enslaved Blacks were denied full citizenship in the North. They could not vote, nor serve on juries and in public offices, and they were forbidden from marrying whites and serving as witnesses in courts of law.[58] In 1785, Quaker Edmond Prior introduced a petition to the lower house of the New York State Legislature to abolish slavery in New York.[59] This bill spurred contention in the full Assembly because it had the potential of transforming the political economy of New York and challenging the basis of American citizenship. The legislature was initially resistant to granting Blacks citizenship rights. Legislators voted on several laws that eventually granted enslaved Blacks emancipation. After debating the terms of emancipation for fourteen years since Prior presented the petition to the lower house, New York passed a Gradual Emancipation Act that granted partial freedom to enslaved Black children born after July 4, 1799. Children, however, were required to remain indentured servants until young adulthood.[60]

It was not until nearly eighteen years later that New York passed another act that granted another form of partial emancipation. The 1817 Assembly approved a law that mandated that enslaved Blacks born before 1799 be freed beginning in 1827.[61] They had been granted emancipation, but not equality with whites. The history of slavery loomed over their lives defining what types of jobs they could do and where they could live. The majority of Blacks, whether born free or enslaved, in New York City were working-class and concentrated in manual labor employment. Black women mostly worked in domestic service and Black men worked in the artisan and maritime trades and sometimes in household employment. Their freedom was tenuous. They were always in danger of being sold back into slavery and transported to the South through the 1850 Fugitive Slave Law.[62] In addition, northern political economies still relied on slave labor. From the 1820s throughout the mid-nineteenth century, warehouses in New York City received shipments of cotton, tobacco, and sugar exports produced by slave labor on plantations in New Orleans, Louisiana; Mobile, Alabama; Savannah, Georgia; and Charleston, South Carolina.[63]

The not-so-distant past of slavery shaped the experiences of famine-era Irish Catholic women. Race remained foundational to the political and social hierarchies of northeastern cities when Irish women emigrated to the United States in the 1840s and 50s. In the mid-nineteenth century, the white ruling class adopted Social Darwinism, or the belief that race was a natural trait that determined the rightful positioning of nations and people in a human hierarchy.[64] As historian John Kelly explained, "It was a special misfortune of the famine Irish to arrive in America just as the 'scientific' study of race was becoming popular. The racial 'scientists' who studied the immigrants came back shaking their heads in dismay. The Irish had the wrong head shape, the wrong facial contours, the wrong pattern of skull bumps."[65] The Irish were classified as Caucasian because they were European, yet they were placed in a subordinate European subgroup that was beneath the Anglo-Saxons.[66]

As abolitionist arguments gained strength across the U.S. North and Europe, proslavery supporters in the U.S. South relied on Philadelphia physician Samuel George Morton's erroneous scientific findings that Blacks were naturally inferior to whites to justify slavery. Morton's experiments became the basis of scientific racism that spread far and wide through his publications that circulated across the United States and Europe throughout the 1840s.[67] Slavery proponents believed that race was an inherent trait and the natural rules of evolution made evident that people of African descent were innately the weakest race in mind, spirit, and intellect and the morally and intellectually superior Anglo-Saxon white race was the most evolved. Native-born white Americans adopted Anglo-Saxon attitudes towards the Irish and integrated the Irish newcomers into these racist scientific findings developed to justify slavery. Morton cited erroneous measurements of Irish skulls and facial contours as evidence that the Irish occupied the lowest subgroup among Caucasians and were almost akin to the African "Negro."[68]

The concentration of free Blacks and Irish in the Lower Manhattan section of Five Points reaffirmed scientists' beliefs that both races were similar. The Five Points was the first free Black settlement in New York City and became an interracial neighborhood of poor Irish and free Blacks by the Civil War. White nativists established a mission in the Five Points to "civilize" the "immoral" Irish and Black residents who they declared were a "major threat to

New York's racial and social order" because they often engaged in interracial sex. The reformers also accused working-class Blacks and Irish of engaging in violence at the saloons, dance halls, theaters, and gambling houses where both races interacted.[69]

While missionaries concentrated their efforts on the entire Irish immigrant and Black populations, physicians focused on what they believed were the biological similarities between Irish and enslaved Black women. These white male physicians concluded that Irish immigrant women and enslaved Black women had a lot in common: they were hypersexual and resistant to pain and thereby sturdy enough to withstand medical experimentation. Historian Deirdre Cooper Owens explained, "Medical case records and journal articles evidence that many of the negative beliefs about Black women's bodies were mapped onto Irish women's bodies too . . ."[70] Physicians concluded that enslaved Black women and Irish immigrant women were perfect specimens on which to practice gynecological surgeries that could potentially cure ailing native-born white women. As racially inferior women, Irish immigrants and enslaved Black women were regarded as masculine sexual deviants immune to childbirth pain who could therefore withstand the agonizing discomfort of surgical experiments.

While physicians practiced experimental surgeries on enslaved Black women in the antebellum South, impoverished Irish immigrant women were test subjects for gynecological surgeries in charity hospitals, lunatic asylums, and almshouses in mid-nineteenth century New York, Boston, Chicago, and Philadelphia. Among the most common experimental procedures that white male doctors performed on Irish and enslaved Black women's bodies were hysterectomies. Contrary to physicians' beliefs that Irish and enslaved Black women's bodies could withstand medical experimentation because they were masculine, subhuman, and thereby stronger than white women, some patients did not survive the dangerous procedures. Determined to find cures for native-born white women, some physicians did not cease medical experimentation after Irish patients died. Irish immigrant and Black women's corpses were used as cadavers in classrooms in New York City medical schools. The women who survived underwent several surgical trials and suffered long-term health complications due to permanent damage to their reproductive organs.[71]

Similar to British depictions of Irish women incapable of managing their own homes, Irish immigrant women were targeted by Protestant social reformers for destroying the moral fabric of northern cities. Charles Loring Brace founded the Children's Aid Society in New York in 1853 to rescue poor and immigrant children from the slums of New York City. While the Society provided resources for all children from poor families, Brace was especially concerned about Irish children and what he considered the inability of Irish immigrant women to socialize them into productive American citizens. He sent Irish children on trains to farms out West to escape the streets of New York City and what he believed were immoral, overcrowded households lacking a strong patriarchal father and headed by uncivilized Irish immigrant women who birthed more children than they could care for. Brace believed that providing these Irish children with formal education and teaching them the value of hard work would save them from what he perceived to be immoral upbringings.[72] He felt so strongly about the danger that Irish immigrant mothers posed to the urban city that he documented detailed stories attesting to how his organization had aided Irish children, and thereby the larger New York City area.

In 1877, Brace recounted a story of how the Cottage Place Industrial School rescued a four-year old Irish girl named Maggie from her mother who had not cared for her properly and had to be sent to a white woman in the "country" who nursed her back to health.[73] Brace reported, ". . . arrangements were made by which Maggie was sent to the country in June, where she remained for over four months, when she returned to her home, in looks an altered child. It was strange that Maggie, only four years old, should be willing to leave mother, brother, and sister, and go among strangers. But she appreciated the change, and a happier child could not be found than Maggie, roaming over the fields and enjoying country life."[74]

Representations of inept Irish immigrant mothers certainly confirmed the belief that they were not respectable white women. As with representations of the Irish migrant labor force in England, portrayals of Irish women as social contagions averted attention from the lack of infrastructure in northern cities to accommodate expanding immigrant populations. Social reformers' preoccupation with Irish women's fertility was also simultaneously religious and political. Native-born white Americans feared that "not only would [Irish] incessant childbearing ensure an Irish political takeover of American cities but Catholicism would become the reigning faith of the hitherto Protestant nation."[75]

Irish immigrant women's concentration in domestic service, a niche of Black women's labor, also reified the notion that they were masculine and racially inferior to the WASP ruling class. The shift in domestic service to an Irish-dominated occupation did not diminish the racial stigma associated with it. Despite Irish immigrant women's displacement of Black women in domestic service in the North, the newcomers from Ireland entered a labor niche that had been defined as servile, Black, and non-feminine since slavery. The very term "servant" held significant racial meanings in a country that had long celebrated the Republican ideologies of independence and free labor as certifiable virtues of whiteness and Americanness. The indentured servitude system for white men disappeared in the early nineteenth century and "the category of unfree labor thus became racialized as nonwhite at the same time that free labor was racialized as white."[76] The prevailing Republican ideologies that informed the racial and gender divisions of labor in the United States deemed domestic service dependent and "degraded" labor only suitable for enslaved African Americans in the South and free African Americans in the North.[77] Native born whites in the North and South believed that domestic servants needed the guidance of masters of the home and, like wives and children, they were not ready for full Republican citizenship.[78]

The racial stigma of domestic service was so deeply rooted that all workers in the occupation had to define themselves in relation to African Americans and slavery. As Judith Rollins explained, the close association of enslaved Blacks with domestic service "had the effect of both reinforcing racial prejudice and degrading the occupation even further for any group involved."[79] Native-born white domestic workers in northern cities in the early 1800s avoided the term "servant," preferring to be called the "help" to distinguish themselves from free Blacks in the North and mark a difference between slavery and the household work that they were temporarily hired to do. As Faye Dudden noted, "... blacks could not lay claim to that title [help] and remained servants indefinitely."[80] Blacks also could not easily disassociate themselves from the title "servant" because it was predicated on notions of enslaved Black labor. Unlike native-born white women, Irish immigrant women were not always successful at distancing themselves from the notion that domestic service was Black work. Although Irish serving women were not always provided with adequate accommodations and wages that compensated them fairly for their arduous labors, there was still the prevailing notion that they relied on benevolent white Protestant families for food, lodging, and moral instruction. While Irish women's circumstances were not identical to the working and living conditions of enslaved Black servants, the perception of domestic service as dependent labor rooted in the institution of slavery marked the women who did it as racially inferior.

The entrance of poor, immigrant, female outsiders into U.S. homes, who were devoted to a suspicious religion and hailed from an "uncivilized" country that resisted Anglo-Saxon rule, did not rest comfortably with WASPs, and they expressed their uncertainties and discontent through racial epithets of Irish serving women. Working in a Black niche of labor made Irish servants susceptible to comparisons with the free Black women they displaced. As Marjorie Howes explained, "Often implicit in discussions of domestic servants were comparisons with laborers who were even more viciously exploited: slaves and free Black women."[81] Local writers drew comparisons between Irish immigrant and Black servants in the North. In 1855, *Eliza Leslie's Behavior Book* issued the following advice to white families who were served by Black and Irish immigrant women: "Refrain from all conversation in their presence that may grate harshly on their feelings, by reminding them of their unfortunate African blood. Do not talk of them as 'negroes,' or 'darkies.' Avoid all discussions of abolition, (either for or against) . . . When the domestics are Irish, and you have occasion to reprove them for their negligence, forgetfulness, or blunders, do so without any reference to their country."[82]

Employers sometimes expressed their discontent with Irish servants by reminiscing about the days when "Dinah," or northern-born Black women servants, dominated domestic service before Irish immigration. The trope "Dinah" was adopted from the family cook character in *Uncle Tom's Cabin*.[83] And employers wrote most warm-heartedly about Dinah's cooking. As an employer from New York explained:

> Thirty or forty years ago, there was a set of servants, mostly Blacks, attached to Knickerbocker families in New York and New Jersey who were as near perfection as men and women can become. Those were the days of Dutch kitchens, Dutch dishes, Dutch neatness, and Dutch housewifery, now long past and never to return. With them faded away that old faithful race of servants, who honored and respected their employers, and were honored and respected by all . . .
> I remember one of them now,—a negress named Diana,—with whose culinary art no French cook could compete, and with whose merits as a woman fewer white women could compare.[84]

The author declared that what determined the difference between good and bad servants was regional and national affiliation. While Black serving women were by no means considered American citizens, employers were suspicious of "outsiders," or the new crop of Irish servants who displaced "Diana."

Journalists and cartoonists captured these perceptions of Irish immigrant women in their construction of the troublesome "Bridget." The mythical dirty, clumsy, and domineering Irish servant emerged in print media and popular literature in America when Irish immigrant women entered domestic service in record numbers during the height of Irish immigration in the mid-nineteenth century. Saint Brigid was a revered saint in Ireland and many families named their daughters Bridget in honor of her. The name Bridget, however, took on a racial connotation for the daughters of Erin after they emigrated to the United States. Bridget, or "Biddy," along with the less frequently used names Mary, Kate, Norah, Katy, Maggie, and Peggy, were common nicknames in the United States for late-nineteenth and early-twentieth-century Irish immigrant domestic servants.[85] The meanings behind the names were not always endearing, although some employers boasted that the best servants were the Bridgets from Ireland. As historian Faye Dudden put it, "The Irish 'Biddy' became the stereotype of the servant, and Biddy jokes celebrated her inadequacies."[86]

The mythical Irish Bridget was a composite of WASP patriarchal, racist, and anti-Catholic beliefs. Sociologist Judith Rollins noted, "All immigrant servants were considered inferior to native white Americans, but the Irish were particularly despised as 'vulgar,' 'childlike,' 'barbaric,' 'ignorant,' 'unclean,' and, worst of all, not Christian."[87] Employers and writers accused Irish immigrant women of displaying more loyalty to the pope than their employing family because they were Catholic. Protestant employers confessed to local news-papers that they feared that Irish servants would take their children to the local Catholic Church and secretly baptize them. Periodicals deemed Bridget the sole representative for all Irish immigrant women in the occupation and thereby domestic service was synonymous with "her." As evidenced in the 1855 image (see Figure 1) entitled "Mr. Simpkins's Experiment in Housekeeping," Bridget was a masculine, stout, drunken, brutish, and belligerent servant who did not operate household appliances properly and outright defied the male head of the household. The perceived way that Irish domestic servants did household work carried a negative stigma that was distinctly attributed to the Irish. Bridget, like the other Irish immigrant women she was intended to rep-resent, was clearly unqualified for domestic service.

As the largest group of workers employed in domestic service in north-eastern cities, Irish immigrant women also influenced how the occupation was defined. Domestic service in northern cities was viewed as not only Black work, but Irish immigrant women's work. By the latter half of the nineteenth century, ubiquitous representations of the cantankerous Irish "Bridget" had become engrained in the American imagination so much so that she informed representations of the women who hailed from Ireland even when her name was not present in the image itself.[88] It was enough to include a woman in an image whose last name sounded Irish for the reader to assume that her first name was Bridget and that she was a domestic servant. Historian Peter Flynn explained, "No other ethnic group epitomized the servant class in America more than the Irish, and the Irish servant girl was synonymous with female domestic help . . ."[89] The Irish stigma of domestic service had become so pro-nounced that native-born white women refused to re-enter the occupation during periods of unemployment. As Hasia Diner put it, ". . . it [domestic ser-vice] was not just demeaning, it was not just degrading, but it bore the Irish label and as such was something no [white] American girl would touch if she could avoid it."[90]

The cult of true womanhood undergirded the disparaging racialized repre-sentations of Irish servants and their household labors. Native-born whites had adopted the "cult of true womanhood" from their British cousins overseas to mark racial and class differences between white and enslaved Black women. As Phyllis Palmer noted, "The United States received the ethos of female fragility from Europe, especially England, and added its own unique system of gender differentiation developed in the institution of black slavery."[91] According to this prevailing ideology of domesticity that spanned the nineteenth century and over half of the twentieth century, what constituted the respectability of

Mr. Simpkins's Experiment in Housekeeping.

Mr. Simpkins applies at an Intelligence Office for a sober, tidy, respectable servant.

The Keeper sends him one, with first-rate recommendations from her last place.

Mrs. Simpkins wonders why Bridget will always draw corks with her teeth.

The cork-drawing mystery is solved—not to Mrs. Simpkins's satisfaction.

Mr. Simpkins insists that Bridget shall leave the house at once.

VOL. XI.—No. 62.—S*

Attempting to carry his order into execution, a slight misunderstanding ensues.

FIG. 1 "Mr. Simpkins's Experiment in Housekeeping," *Harper's New Monthly Magazine* 11 (1855): 235. Credit: *Harper's Magazine.*

white middle class and elite Christian women was that they were "'pious, pure, obedient, and domestic.'"[92] As with ideologies of domesticity in England, dirt was often associated with working-class women to describe them as inherently immoral, lazy, ignorant, and of a deviant sexuality to "justify social ranks of race, class, and gender."[93]

Ladies were native-born, Protestant, married, and did not work for wages. They were clean. Their hands avoided contact with dirt and "dirty" substances including household waste and bodily fluids. They were devoid of sexual desires and pleasure, and their primary duties consisted of satisfying the sexual desires of their husbands, supervising servants, and instilling Christian morals in their children. They also never traveled without the company of their husband, father, or other men in their family. White northerners relied on these Anglo-Saxon based ideologies of race and domesticity to evaluate the unmarried Catholic Irish newcomers who traveled to the United States alone and did servile and "dirty" manual labor.

Although Irish women on both sides of the Atlantic were portrayed as dirty, lazy, domineering, and incapable of doing household work, the circumstances by which they were racialized by the British in Ireland were distinct from the conditions from which the Irish "Bridget" emerged in U.S. racial discourse. The battle between Protestants and Catholics for power in the name of religion, Britain's refusal to release Ireland and its other colonies from its stronghold, and the struggle over territory between the Gaelic Irish and Norman invaders since the reign of Henry II of England had set the Irish and British apart as separate races since the twelfth century. The racialization of the Irish in the United States had nothing to do with land, but had everything to do with political territory, jobs, religion, and, most importantly, slavery and American citizenship. In addition, native-born whites aligned themselves with the English, thereby shaping their views of Irish immigrants. As historian Nell Irvin Painter noted, "The American was the same as the Englishman, who was the same as the Saxon . . . Thus 'Saxon' supplied the key word exiling the Celtic Irish—white though they may be—from American identity."[94]

Disparaging depictions of Irish immigrant servants were also rooted in white supremacist movements to protest the abolition of slavery as well as the arrival of Irish immigrants to northern U.S. cities. White nativist political groups emerged nearly overnight to protest the arrival of the Irish newcomers during the famine years. As historian Thomas Gassett noted, "race was by far the most powerful source of objection" to immigrants in the late nineteenth century.[95] The Know Nothings, a nativist anti-Catholic group, were determined to bar Irish immigrants from the privileges of whiteness. Between 1845–1860 the group pushed for legal stipulations requiring a longer process for Irish immigrant men to become American citizens and earn the right to vote. They also demanded that local city governments bar all immigrants from public offices. Nativists argued that the Irish were not ready for American citizenship because "the famine had produced an Irish 'race' incapable of freedom." The concentration of Irish immigrant women and men in menial low-wage jobs that had once been occupied by free Blacks further convinced nativists that the Irish were more akin to Negroes than free and independent white American male workers.[96]

By emancipation, however, Irish immigrant men had become unquestionably white, which meant that they could "avoid many forms of violence and humiliation" and had "access to citizenship, property, higher wages, political power, and social status, among other privileges."[97] They had established a white working-class identity for themselves by supporting the Democratic Party, a major political party that supported slavery. Irish immigrant men also attacked Black men working in trades the Irish newcomers considered only befitting for white men. They harassed Black men they worked alongside on the ports of New York City and Boston, and Black male porters, tobacco stemmers, waiters, barbers, cooks, construction workers, and longshoremen.[98] The Draft Riots of 1863 in New York City was the most violent and widespread attack on Blacks. In March of 1863, the federal government entered all male citizens between the ages of twenty and thirty-five and all unmarried men between the ages of thirty-five and forty-five into a military duty lottery. Black men were exempted from the draft because they had not yet been granted American citizenship. On Saturday, July 11, 1863, the first lottery was held. Two days later, Irish rioters took to the streets, initially taking out their anger on military and federal government buildings, and then on Black women, men, and children.[99]

They spearheaded a week-long violent spree destroying Black-owned businesses, homes, and institutions, as well as white-owned businesses that served Blacks. Their attack on the Colored Orphan Asylum, established to provide education, medical care, and housing for Black children, was a testament to the ferocious manner in which rioters confronted Blacks. After the riots ended, Irish immigrant men continued harassing Black men with whom they worked on the docks. In addition to violent attacks on African Americans, Irish immigrant men gained political influence by becoming leaders of labor unions that campaigned for labor rights for white male industrial workers.[100] Irish immigrant men advanced in politics and in the labor sector as whitened unionized workers who could vote.[101] Irish and other European immigrant union members whitened themselves by opposing Black membership in labor unions after emancipation.[102]

Irish immigrant women remained concentrated in the lowest-wage and racially stigmatized women's occupations of the nineteenth century. They could not vote and did not have a labor union. As such, the racial and gendered implications of anti-Irish sentiments and exploitative low-wage household work lasted longer for Irish immigrant women than their male counterparts.

The ubiquity of the Irish Bridget and visual representations of her well into the late nineteenth century signaled that Irish immigrant women had become a standard medium by which to evaluate race, domestic service, and women migrants in northeastern cities for several decades after emancipation.

Conclusion

The relegation of Irish women to tenant farming and domestic service in a British-controlled labor system stratified by race, class, and gender sustained British colonialism in Ireland for nearly a century. Race was inherent to notions of womanhood and women's labors in the British political economy. As such, what women did with their hands indicated and reinforced both their racial and gender status. Respectable white ladies did not come into contact with "dirty" substances; therefore, manual labor was considered only befitting of racially inferior women. In the British colonial context, those workers were working-class Irish and English women as well as enslaved Blacks.

In the United States, Irish women were also concentrated in domestic service and thereby constructed as the stark contrast to the pious white Anglo-Saxon Protestant mistress. WASP employers in the United States and England relied on mediums of race, ethnicity, and religion to determine their representations of and interactions with Irish immigrant women well into the nineteenth century. Whereas Irish immigrant men established social distance from their African American male counterparts after emancipation by entering trades defined as suitable for white working-class men, Irish immigrant women remained concentrated in a Black women's niche of labor into the early twentieth century.

Working in domestic service during slavery certainly intensified the racial backlash towards Irish immigrant women. They had entered a country where the ruling white Anglo-Saxon Protestant class regarded domestic service as degrading labor, and thereby Black women's work. When Irish women arrived in the United States during the famine era, slavery was legal in the South and Blacks had labored for over a century as enslaved house workers in both the U.S. North and South. Thus, any group of women that entered domestic service was racially defined in relation to blackness and slavery. Scholars have argued that Irish immigrant women were the butt of jokes and complaints about domestic servants because they dominated the occupation. I argue that Irish women confronted this dilemma more intimately than any other European group of women in the occupation because of race. They were concentrated in a racially stigmatized niche of labor, their own colonial and racial history in the British colony of Ireland, and the racial political landscape of the northeast. Native-born whites, who prided themselves on their British ancestry, adopted British attitudes towards the Irish women who worked in their homes.

Although domestic service was "Black" work in the United States, what made domestic service distinct in the North from that in the South was that it was fraught with racial, gender, and immigration politics because "cantankerous" and "domineering" Irish immigrant women dominated it. Only Black women, many migrating from the South after emancipation, posed a serious challenge to the Irish monopoly in domestic service. While Black women's household labors during slavery influenced the racialization of the work Irish serving women did, southern Black women who migrated to northern cities after emancipation were integrated into regional debates about race, women's migrations, and labors that were spurred by Irish women's immigration and their entrance into domestic service. In northeastern cities, domestic service was stigmatized labor because it was simultaneously touted as Black work and an occupation only suitable for inferior "foreign" women.

Similar to Irish women in Ireland, southern Black women were relegated to domestic service and agricultural work in a stratified labor system that sustained white supremacy through the exploitation of their manual labors. Whereas Irish women were considered a race apart from the British, southern Black women were deemed in a permanent state of racial inferiority that ranked even below the despised Irish immigrants in the United States. Touted as subservient manual labor unbefitting for native-born white women, domestic service marked southern Black women as racially inferior. Simultaneously, domestic service was degrading labor because it was women's manual work and Black women were concentrated in it. Chapter 3, the next chapter of this book, uses the racialized and gendered political economy of the U.S. South as a starting point to trace how representations of Black women household workers and the actual exploitation of their domestic labors were integral to the reconstitution of white supremacy after emancipation. It also examines how emancipation and Irish immigration shaped public perceptions about southern Black women migrants in northern cities.

3

Southern Mammy and African American "Immigrant" Women

————————————————◄o►————————————————

Reconstituting White Supremacy after Emancipation

The labor exploitation of Black women determined the very definitions of race, womanhood, and citizenship since the inception of the United States. Southern Black women had been relegated to domestic service and agricultural work in a stratified labor system that sustained white supremacy since slavery. Black women's manual labors in fields and in the homes of slaveholding families marked them as racially inferior and the antithesis of respectable (read: white) ladyhood and U.S. citizenship in a country that had sustained the British colonial institution of slavery and adopted British notions of womanhood and respectability.

Simultaneously, domestic service and agricultural work were considered degrading labor because Black women constituted the majority of the workforce. Emancipation thereby posed a serious challenge to the racial, class, and gendered divisions of labor, and consequently native-born white rule over Blacks in the South. In the words of historian Elizabeth Clark-Lewis, ". . . nothing threatened whites more than the loss of control over African Americans."[1] According to white southerners, the abolition of slavery destroyed the natural order of the races and they turned to the "home" to reinforce racial, class, and gender hierarchies in the South that were established by the institution of slavery. As with the stratified labor system in Ireland that sustained British colonial rule over the Irish, white southerners reproduced a political labor economy stratified by race and gender to keep white supremacy intact.

Southern Black women asserted ownership over their own labors by migrating to northern cities in search of better working and living conditions than what was available to them in the South. Their very movements into northeastern cities intensified the regional debates about race, labor, and immigration that Irish women's immigration had fueled since the mid-nineteenth century. Newspapers routinely described southern Black women as "refugees" and "immigrants" when they reached northeastern cities. Northeastern whites considered southern Black women "foreign" because they were not "Dinah," or northern-born Black women who had worked in "Yankee" homes since slavery in the North.[2] Southern Black women also migrated from a region ruled by "uncivilized" and "barbaric" whites, according to northern-born whites and some northern-born Blacks, to a region that had not settled the race question for immigrants, or "outsiders." The region was also ambivalent about racial and gender equality for U.S.-born Blacks and denied Black membership in labor unions. I argue that these markers of foreignness were attributed to the native-born southern women because of their race, gender, southern identity, and entrance into a niche of labor defined by slavery, anti-Irish immigrant sentiments, and white nativist fears about newly emancipated Black women working in northern white homes.

To underscore the significance of southern Black women to the race and labor questions in both the U.S. North and South, I begin this chapter by tracing the recapturing of Black women's domestic labors to maintain white political, social, and economic power in the South. I argue that representations of Black women as household workers and the actual exploitation of their domestic labors were endemic to the reconstitution of white supremacy after emancipation. Just as the British used constructions of Irish women servants and Irish domestic life to justify British colonial rule in Ireland, white southerners used representations of Mammy and southern white domestic life, as well as actual laws, to sustain political and socioeconomic control over Black women in the absence of slavery and amid Black women's resistance to labor exploitation in domestic service. In the second part of this chapter, I document the impact of southern Black migrant women's movements into northern cities on constructions of race, household labor, and citizenship in the region. More specifically, I argue that white nativists in the North constructed representations of southern Black women as "foreign" to reconstitute white supremacy in a region where Irish women's immigration had complicated gendered constructions of whiteness.

Controlling Black Women's Labor through the "Home"

No archetype was as ubiquitous and encompassing of late-nineteenth-century white supremacist projects than Mammy. She was a mythological representation of enslaved Black women who worked inside the homes of slaveholding families that first appeared in antebellum literature, travel narratives, and religious propaganda as baby nurse, cook, and all-around domestic help. Although the skin color and body size of Mammy varied from the 1820s–1850s, what she always represented was that Black women household servants brought racial harmony to the slave plantation. Mammy believed "within her heart in the rightness of the established order of which she [was] a part."[3] Her undying loyalty to white families and the protection and wisdom that whites received under her care naturalized slavery and, more specifically, the exploitation of Black women's labors. The special charm, nurturance, and stability that Mammy brought to white families ensured a racial order in their homes that reverberated throughout the South.[4]

Contrary to these romanticized portrayals of domestic life during slavery, peaceful coexistence rarely occurred in homes where Black women were under the constant supervision of white families and at their beck and call twenty-four hours a day. Enslaved Black women who did household work were vulnerable to labor and sexual exploitation. Their work was highly scrutinized, and they were always vulnerable to the most dehumanizing punishments. Slaveholders sometimes banished household servants at a moment's notice.[5] Most Black women rarely—and others, never—developed emotional attachments to white children that were deeper than their love for their own children. Black women household servants were even susceptible to abuse at the hands of the male children whom they raised.[6]

Despite the actual experiences of enslaved household workers, white southerners complained that the abolition of slavery disrupted the harmony and order of their homes, and this domestic disorder resounded throughout all aspects of Southern society. According to southern whites, slavery protected Black women from their natural propensity to exhibit immoral behavior. Rather than showing deference to whites, which was the moral and rightful thing to do according to white planters, Black women had become defiant and lazy after being freed. They demanded an end to their workday and left their places of employment when their expectations were not met. Although both Black women and men engaged in acts of resistance, some planters viewed Black women as the primary conspirators. Charles Colcock Jones Jr., son of a Georgian slaveholding planter who died in the war, expressed his frustration with trying to manage his inherited property and having to pay former slaves wages by complaining that they refused to work. He also noted that he thought the women were the "controlling spirits" that fueled the resistance.[7]

As Black women resisted labor exploitation after slavery, whites reproduced representations of Mammy because "she was the centerpiece in the antebellum Southerners' perception of the perfectly organized society."[8] In their writings about "Mammy" after the Civil War, Deborah Gray White explained, "The descriptions are written with a certainty and definitiveness that seem to defy question."[9] According to these white authors, Mammy was undeniably the best servant. She cooked meals, cleaned the home, and cared for white children with such precision and perfection that "she" naturalized the belief that only Black women could and should be servants in white homes. Scholars have made the important argument that Mammy was used in the latter half of the nineteenth century to reaffirm white southern womanhood and patriarchy in the absence of slavery.[10] If read against the backdrop of Black women's resistance to labor exploitation and the laws that southern governments passed to control domestic workers, it could be concluded that the authoritative tone of Mammy representations also signified whites' assertion of ownership over Black women's household labors to sustain white power. After all, as Grace Elizabeth Hale put it, after the Civil War, "the [actual] relationships between white southerners and black women domestics became crucial to the reproduction of white supremacy."[11]

The pervasiveness of the stubborn desire to recapture white supremacy through domestic service is reflected in constructions of Mammy and idyllic representations of plantation life in the literature of the wives, daughters, and granddaughters of Confederate veterans. After the Civil War, Mammy signaled that Black inferiority was natural and that Black women's rightful place was in the home and under the supervision of white women and men, as it had been during slavery. According to Kimberly Wallace-Sanders, her large black body, round smiling face, raucous laugh, and self-deprecating wit all pointed to her implicit understanding and acceptance of her inferiority and devotion to whites.[12] In postwar literature, Mammy was undeniably overweight, tall, broad-shouldered with skin nearly black in color, and she wore an apron and a scarf. Her personality and demeanor reeked of deference to the white family that she worked for. She took better care of white children than her own. Her children were usually dirty, and their only value was that they were appropriate playmates for her white surrogate children. These depictions were significant to the assertion of white rule because Black household workers had been significant to white supremacy since slavery. During slavery, whites relied on Black household servants to "miraculously make a household white" by "washing away" the "unspeakability of [white] women's work," and these social expectations and practices persisted after emancipation.[13] After the Civil War, some employers experimented with hiring white servants, but they felt uncomfortable with hiring people of their own color.[14]

Daughters of the Confederacy made concerted efforts to assert authority over Black women domestic laborers. As Grace Elizabeth Hale noted, the

"Daughters of Confederate heroes" were vital to ensuring that "traditional race and gender roles were not altered but 'remade'" through depictions of plantation domestic life.[15] The depictions conveyed their desires to return Black women to the days of slavery when they were "loyal" and submissive servants. Virginia-native women's suffragist and daughter of a Confederate Army veteran, Mary Johnston was among the most well-known novelists who wrote romantic tales about faithful house servants in colonial Virginia and during the Civil War. Her books broke publishing records, attesting to the popularity of Civil War literature.[16]

Descendants of Confederate soldiers made a concerted effort to memorialize plantation homes as historic landmarks. The Owens-Thomas House in Savannah, Georgia, was declared a National Landmark after the granddaughter of planter, lawyer, and mayor of Savannah during the nineteenth century bequeathed the property to the Telfair Museum. Historian Leslie Harris explained, "Sites such as the Owens-Thomas House were concerned only with the fine objects the wealthy had left behind, and visitors—largely white—fantasized about owning the mansion, the comfortable bedrooms, and the luxurious dining rooms; they never imagined themselves as the enslaved and free laborers who made such living possible."[17]

As late as 1905, nearly forty years after emancipation, the United Daughters of the Confederacy (UDC) lobbied Congress for a national monument in honor of Mammy to be erected in Washington D.C. until their efforts were squelched two decades later after the House of Representatives opted to build the Lincoln Memorial instead.[18] The UDC wanted the monument built to attest to what they believed were loving relationships between slaveholders and the Black servants who worked in their homes.[19] In his explanation of racist caricatures of Black men after emancipation, Richard Follett explained, ". . . vigorous black resistance gave way to racially soothing stereotypes, images of servitude that could be controlled, confined, and ultimately mastered."[20] Mammy, too, was a way of avoiding recognition of Black women's resistance to the terms of domestic service that had changed very little since the days of slavery. As Trudier Harris put it, Mammy had "difficulty envisioning a world other than one of white masters and black servants, white power and black submissiveness . . ."[21] Mammy also communicated that white men and women were the rightful owners of Black women's household labors. She was a part of their families and that made her and other serving Black women the property of the white men and women who employed them. This sentiment also informed the refusal of southern governments to transform the labor economy of the South into one that offered Black women equal access to occupational opportunities outside of domestic service. While Mammy in the late nineteenth century signified a white middle-class construction of domesticity, Black women worked for white families of all classes. They were employed in the homes of the white elite, middle, and working classes.[22] Hence, the social construction of whiteness in the South relied on having "negro" domestic help.[23]

Black women's labor resistance and migrations certainly challenged white supremacy. Hence, the faithful female slave mythology, as David Blight put it, revealed "more about tensions in the Jim Crow South than it does about antebellum history."[24] Unlike Mammy, actual Black women left the plantations where they were enslaved to seek domestic service employment. Black women also resisted labor exploitation by migrating from rural farms to small towns and then to cities, constantly in search of better wages and living conditions.[25] Some women "abided by a 'code of ethics' or established a sort of blacklist to collectively avoid working for employers who proved unscrupulous, abusive, or unfair."[26] Black women also left their jobs when employers did not adhere to their expectations of living wages, manageable workloads, and standard work hours. To make sure employers felt the impact of their decision, some household workers quit shortly before their employer hosted an important social event.

Quitting jobs could be risky in a southern economy where employers did not always have the resources to pay Black women exactly what they expected and where the cost of rent and food for both African Americans and whites had risen after the war. Black women's decisions to leave their places of employment sometimes overrode the financial circumstances of their households. They believed it was important to assert themselves as independent workers and humans. In the words of Jacqueline Jones, "freedwomen perceived freedom to mean not a release from back-breaking labor, but rather the opportunity to labor on behalf of their own families and kin within the protected spheres of household and community."[27]

Southern governments passed the black codes in the fall of 1865 to recapture control over Black labor by curtailing its political power. After Abraham Lincoln was assassinated, President Andrew Johnson's administration undermined the promises of Reconstruction.[28] As a white southerner born into poverty in Raleigh, North Carolina, Johnson's vision for reuniting the Union after the Civil War was to restore old Confederate government leaders. He approved their reelection to Congress and supported southern governments' decisions to pass the black codes, a series of oppressive laws that restricted the mobility of the formerly enslaved, restored property ownership to former slaveholders, and relegated Blacks to low-wage, exploitative work.[29]

The black codes were abolished when Republicans passed the Civil Rights Act of 1866. Johnson challenged the Act and Republicans responded by passing the Reconstruction Acts of 1867, which encompassed the Fourteenth and Fifteenth Amendments.[30] The amendments extended citizenship rights to Blacks and specifically granted Black men the right to vote and hold political office. During this short-lived period of political advancement in the 1860s and 1870s, Blacks were allowed to sit on juries, vote, hold elective offices, and serve as magistrates, bailiffs, sheriffs, and justices of the peace.[31] Southern Black communities also established public school systems, colleges, churches, stores, social clubs, and bargaining resources between laborers and planters.[32] These developments, however, did not translate into labor rights for Blacks.[33] The amendments did not mandate the redistribution of land. Whites remained in control of the land and refused to sell their property. With limited capital and property of their own, Blacks remained confined to low-wage labor systems managed by former slaveholders.[34]

Reconstruction was cut short with the Compromise of 1877, when the federal government withdrew federal troops from the former Confederate states before Blacks could amass enough economic and political power to resist white supremacy on their own.[35] African Americans were left to fend for themselves against former Confederate soldiers, politicians, and their families for nearly a century. Confederate Democrats took over city governments relying on the Ku Klux Klan (KKK) and White Leagues as their strong arm.[36] The KKK threatened to lynch Blacks who exercised their Fifteenth Amendment right to vote. Democrats also imposed unsurpassable reading and skin color tests that made it all but impossible for Black citizens to vote, and passed a series of laws establishing racial segregation to assert political, social, and economic control. In 1896, the Supreme Court's *Plessy v. Ferguson* decision further entrenched white supremacy by legalizing racial segregation.[37] Except for the very few southern towns that Blacks established and controlled, Blacks were barred from political and civil service positions and could only use institutions and public spaces and live in residential neighborhoods that had been marked for the "colored."[38] Northern and midwestern states also sustained the South's Jim Crow efforts by refusing to serve Black customers in restaurants and hotels, establishing racially segregated neighborhoods, and prohibiting Blacks from being hired into safer and better paying jobs.

With very little capital and no political power, Black women were denied jobs working in small manufacturing plants that hired working-class white women to produce candy, textiles, paper boxes, bookbinding, and straw goods. Only a few Black women could find work as teachers and seamstresses. The vast majority worked as sharecroppers, tenant farmers, laundresses, or domestic servants in white homes.[39] Black women sharecroppers and tenant farmer workers were considered "debased, degraded, and masculinized" because they did what was perceived as men's work.[40] Processing sugarcane required mass field labor. Black women worked alongside men in their communities planting, cutting, and harvesting in the sugarcane fields of Louisiana. Tenant farming women and their children in other parts of the South cultivated other crops along with the men in their families, and sometimes on the same property where they had been enslaved.[41] They also reared the children, cooked the daily meals, cleaned the home, and washed the laundry for family members in the household. Women also made important labor and financial decisions for the household. They decided which members of the family would work and who they could work for.[42]

While Black women's daily routines consisted of domestic chores, including cooking breakfast for male farmers and children in the household, they also worked alongside men planting, chopping, and harvesting cotton; stripping quarter; and harvesting potatoes and peas on small plots of land. White landowners held Black families in perpetual debt with exorbitant prices for the tools, seeds, and fertilizer needed to harvest crops, and with strict rules that required families to pay rent in the form of a fixed amount of cash rather than a portion of the harvest. Weather conditions posed a serious challenge to sharecroppers meeting these steep demands since crop yields were always vulnerable to droughts, heavy rains, and boll weevil attacks.[43] Black workers in the fields resisted by organizing labor strikes, labor organizations, insisting on taking the weekends off, and setting their own hours for the workday. Some workers also expressed to white landowners that they expected certain working conditions that included food, housing, clothing, clean water, wood, and medical care. [44]

The household was a site from which Black women most loudly articulated their views on labor exploitation. Household workers engaged in labor organizing across the South. In Jackson, Mississippi, domestic workers and laundresses sent a letter and petition to the mayor in 1866 that called for higher and uniform wages, and they organized a strike when their demands were ignored. In 1877, servants and laundresses in Galveston, Texas, organized a strike insisting that their wages increase to $1.50 a day, or $9.00 per week. Twenty laundresses in Atlanta, Georgia, formed a Washing Society in July 1881, and shortly afterwards enlisted nearly three thousand members through door-to-door canvassing. The society organized a ten-day strike pushing for higher wages, and they picketed in front of Chinese-owned commercial laundries accusing their owners of stealing Washing Society members' clientele.[45] The strike ended because the city arrested and fined the protesters. Although the society did not receive higher wages, it set a precedent for Black women's labor activism that persisted for nearly a century. African American women throughout the South continued resisting exploitation in laundry work by occasionally refusing to deliver their patrons' clothes when not paid on time.[46]

Tera Hunter notes that the striking laundresses were possibly joined by Irish immigrant laundresses in an "unusual display of interracial solidarity." Little information is known about the Irish women allies, however, because local newspapers refused to identify them to protect them from public scorn.[47] African Americans, both women and men, who worked inside of their employers' homes also engaged in acts of resistance to assert ownership of their labors. As Eric Foner explained, "Butlers refused to cook or polish brass, domestics would not black the boots of plantation guests, chambermaids declared that it was not their duty to answer the front door, and serving girls insisted on the right to entertain male visitors in their rooms."[48]

Southern whites resorted to incessant complaining when household workers insisted on boundaries in the workplace and better working conditions. In 1880, the financial situation of white southerners worsened as the per capita wealth of the South, based on estimated true valuation of property, fell to $376 as compared with $1,186 per capita in Northeastern states.[49] Southern employers justified their inability to pay living wages by complaining that Black women abandoned their work ethic after emancipation. The "labor problem" was not only an economic issue; it was a racial one. The "problem" was rooted in the conflict between whites' "determination to preserve the old forms of domination" and the desire of the formerly enslaved to "carve out the greatest possible independence for themselves and their families."[50]

This tension was reflected in the complaint of a Texan employer who wrote the following on a questionnaire for historian Lucy Maynard Salmon's study on domestic service: "Their [Black women's] idea of freedom is to come and go at will, and they expect full wages for light work." Another employer from South Carolina complained, "The colored servants don't like to be kept at steady employment."[51] A disgruntled employer in New Orleans declared in 1889, "There are too many low-grade cooks, dirty nurses and lazy house girls. They have demoralized the better class of negro servants, to be found here before the war, and at that time one of the features of the Southern households . . . If we could ship annually some 10,000 or even 100,000 negro servants North it would be better for all hands." [52]

Employers' expectations of domestic workers were similar to those that slaveholders had of house servants. Such practices, which were meant to suppress domestic workers' autonomy, persisted from the latter half of the nineteenth century well into the twentieth. A child-nurse asserted in 1912 that Black women in domestic service were still "literally slaves." Although primarily responsible for caring for her employers' three young children, she was also expected to water the lawn, sweep the sidewalk, cook, and mop the porch and hallways. She worked fourteen to sixteen hours a day and was required to sleep in her employers' home. She could only go to her own home to check on her children once every two weeks. As she put it, "you might as well say that I'm on duty all the time."[53] Some male employers used rape to assert their dominance over live-in domestic workers. To help their daughters avoid this fate, Black women made a point of warning them about the possibility of sexual assault before they accepted a live-in position. They directed their daughters not to stay in a room by themselves with the father or sons of the household. They also told their daughters to run away from the home if they even suspected they would be assaulted.[54]

Local governments passed laws to control the mobile class of women laborers and suppress their resistance to low wages and deplorable working conditions. Although the laws and intimidation were not always effective, the attempt to control the movements of Black women by force and by law signaled that their domestic labors were political and their refusal to adhere to labor exploitation threatened white supremacy. The laws also racialized Black women as deviant to justify state surveillance and exploitation of their labors. The city government in Atlanta passed laws in the 1880s requiring employers to seek references from previous employers before hiring domestic workers in an effort to stop them from moving from house to house.[55] The city government also allowed the Ku Klux Klan to threaten domestic workers who "gave too much lip," or talked back to their employers.[56] Challenging racial boundaries, which were inconsistently defined, could also land Black women in prison. Beginning in the last decade of the nineteenth century as the prison industry expanded in the South, Black women were arrested at a moment's notice and sentenced to prison labor for minor offenses such as picking up a piece of coal (with no evidence of malice intentions), throwing dirty water into the street, arguing with white women, and "keeping a house of ill repute."[57]

Sarah Haley revealed in her poignant study that by the early twentieth century, Black women and girl inmates in the Georgia penal system were subjected to a convict-leasing system in which they were required to do chain gang labor for prison industries as well as household work in white homes as part of their sentences.[58] Southern labor economies were inherently racialized and gendered. Thus, the vast majority of Black women worked in domestic service outside of the penal system. Contracting out Black women inmates to work in household service, however, sustained white supremacy under the direct control of the state. In the words of Haley, the domestic service assignments "helped to maintain the notion that a white woman's social and economic role was as domestic manager, a position perceived to be necessary for capitalist expansion," and the consolidation of Jim Crow.[59]

Until the early twentieth century, white southerners relied on other methods of social control to assert power over Black women laborers. The discovery of the tubercle bacillus in 1882, also known as tuberculosis, came at a convenient time for white southerners who were disgruntled by Black women's mobility and resistance in domestic service. Southern scientists dubbed tuberculosis the "negro servants' disease," which diverted attention from the infrastructural sources of the epidemic. They argued that slavery supported the natural hierarchy of races that kept "Black" diseases at bay and the tuberculosis outbreak proved that domestic workers needed to be monitored by city governments. This erroneous flawed scientific explanation had more to do with anxieties about race and labor after the war than the actual disease itself. As historian Tera Hunter explained, "The disease became a medium for 'framing' tensions in labor and race relations . . . The fact that tuberculosis was primarily an urban disorder fueled the correlations between disease, emancipation, and rural-to-urban migration."[60]

Child-nurses and laundresses were among the most targeted workers in domestic service. Nurses were accused of spreading illness to children when the youngsters became sick and laundresses were accused of using unsanitary water and equipment to wash clothes in bacteria-ridden homes. In Macon, Georgia, the city passed a law that required laundresses to surrender to sanitary inspections of their homes. Subjected to long work hours and low wages, household workers were not always able to purchase nutritious foods to build healthy immune systems. Their work, however, protected white homes because it required serving women to sanitize furniture, linens, plates, clothes, and utensils. Due to the unstable financial circumstances of some white households in the South it might have been possible that they did not have well-balanced diets themselves. Hence, white employers more likely contracted illnesses from weakened immune defense systems due to nutritional deficiencies.

City ordinances and rumors of the "negro servants' disease" did not fully suppress political organizing among Black domestic workers. While Black women could not hold political offices during the Reconstruction Era, they were politically active.[61] Domestic workers took off on election days as well as to attend parades, rallies, and Republican Party conventions. They voted, asserted their opinions on laws, and organized their communities from the meeting rooms of Black churches across the South. According to historian Elsa Barkley Brown, Black women remained politically active after the civil rights of the Black community were curtailed when former Confederate generals took over southern governments. By the 1880s and 1890s, Black women created "their own pulpits from which to speak—to restore their voices to the community."[62] From these pulpits, Black women asserted their right to basic, fundamental rights as American citizens. They wanted physical and political protection under the law, access to formal education for themselves, their sons and daughters, and future generations. They asserted the right to vote, own land without harassment and legally contest the threat of having it unfairly stripped from them, access to secure employment at fair and living wages, and work without being fired at a moment's notice.

Black women asserted ownership of their own labors and their right to live better lives through their decisions to migrate. Migrating North was an audacious decision because it was an affront to southern white supremacy. As Carol Anderson explained, "Black labor was the foundation of the region's economy, and African Americans were also the sine qua non of the South's social and political structure," thus African American migrations threatened the "entire socioeconomic structure of the South."[63] They understood that the North was not an ideal place to live, yet they took their chances and migrated to northern and western cities in search of a better future. Black women and girls who left the South during the late nineteenth century charted a path for the mass exodus of southern Blacks to the urban North during the First Great Migration from 1910–1940.[64] Migrating to the North was an audacious decision.

Determined to escape the exploitative tenant farming system, racial violence, and inhumane working conditions of domestic service, southern Black women trickled into northern cities in the 1870s and 1880s primarily settling in neighborhoods along the eastern shore, including Washington D.C., Philadelphia, Baltimore, and New York City. Some women traveled alone while others sought assistance from the pastors of their churches who put them in touch with Black clubwomen committed to ensuring the safe arrival of southern migrants and helping them find domestic service employment.[65] They maintained strong ties with their family members in the rural South by sending money and letters telling them about life and work in the urban centers.[66]

Black women migrated from southern cities where they had been central to the reconstitution of racial hierarchies after emancipation, and in northern cities they became integral to regional debates about race, labor, and immigration rooted in the reinforcement of white supremacy due to white nativist fears about European immigration and Black migration. Since the mid-nineteenth century, Irish immigration had posed a serious dilemma to establishing clear racial boundaries between native-born whites, immigrants, and Blacks in northern cities. The increasing presence of a southern and formerly enslaved class of Black women laborers intensified these already existing debates. Northerners kept their attention on the home to remedy the disruptions to racial hierarchies that not only Irish immigration, but also southern Black women ushered in. In the words of psychiatrist Robert Coles, "For decades a steady trek of blacks from the South [. . .] increasingly brought race as a local, volatile problem to the North . . ."[67]

An Immigrant Prelude to Southern Black Women's Migrations

All newcomers to northeastern cities had to deal with the Irish in some way. As historian James Barrett noted in his study of the influence of Irish immigration on the "Americanization" of European immigrants, "Immigrants who arrived in American cities around the turn of the century found it difficult to avoid the Irish . . ."[68] They were the first largest ethnic group of European immigrants to emigrate to the United States in the nineteenth century. By the late 1800s, more than three million Irish immigrants had arrived in the United States, and by 1900, approximately five million of their first and second generations were settled in the country.[69]

The sheer demographics and political organizing of Irish immigrants made a significant impact on the political and social scene of New York City and other northern cities where the Irish and their descendants were concentrated. According to Barrett, "new immigrants" from eastern and southeastern Europe who arrived in the United States between 1890–1920 encountered Irish influences in their daily lives. Irish immigrant male leaders had established several Catholic parishes and saloons and had entered local politics and the labor market as ward politicians, contractors, foremen, bishops, union officers, firemen, and policemen.[70] Reaping the benefits of their predecessors' labor organizing, Irish American had a prominent presence in the public school system as teachers as well. Hence, "whether 'new immigrants' wanted to save their souls, get a drink, find a job, or walk around the corner," the newcomers often had to deal with entrenched Irish Americans."[71] There was also a strong possibility that the children of European immigrant women were taught by Irish American women.

Southern migrants, too, were not immune to Irish influences on the political economy of northeastern cities. When they migrated in the latter half of the nineteenth century, labor unions that were primarily led by Irish immigrant men had amassed enough power to define the distinctions between black and white working-class jobs, and between black and white wages within the same occupations. Hence, the Irish-influenced labor economy shaped the job prospects and experiences of southern migrants. The Irish began molding the racial stratification of the northern labor markets during the height of Irish immigration in the mid-nineteenth century. When the Irish arrived in the United States, they were concentrated in "nigger" work, or the same "unskilled" manual trades as free Blacks. To distance themselves from African Americans and diminish job competition, the Irish worked at redefining their jobs as white labor. As David Roediger explained, "They had to drive all Blacks, and if possible their memories, from the places where the Irish labored," through orchestrated violence against and refusal to work alongside Black male laborers.[72] The Irish also "consistently argued that African American workers were lazy, improvident and irresponsible."[73]

The Irish reproduced characterizations of African Americans that were similar to white nativist portrayals of the barbaric Irish immigrant. Such racialized immigration discourses were rooted in native-born whites' disdain for free and enslaved African Americans, as well as the Irish newcomers. White nativists constructed both Irish immigrant men and women as racially inferior to native-born whites by comparing them to Blacks. As historians have argued, Irish immigrant men whitened themselves by intentionally becoming coconspirators in white nativist discourses that supported slavery and denigrated free Blacks. By emancipation, Irish immigrant men had developed a white working class that dominated labor unions that denied Black membership and protected the interests of only white workers.

When Black southerners settled in northern cities in the latter half of the nineteenth century, there was already a racially segmented labor sector shaped by the Irish that created greater job opportunities for white European immigrants. In Boston, for instance, the formerly enslaved found themselves in a place where the poverty between Blacks and the Irish was no longer equal because Irish immigrants had experienced social advancement by the end of the Civil War.[74] According to David Yentis's study on Black migration in New York City, the directories revealed that there was hardly "any great differences among the Negroes themselves, nor ever, at least before the civil war, as between the Negro and the Irish and German immigrants." The "range of Negro occupations was so definitely circumscribed" because the "incoming Irish and German immigration deprived them even of the street and unskilled occupations."[75] In the words of W.E.B. DuBois, the color prejudice in Philadelphia was so strong that the "Negro workmen may not often work side by side with white workmen . . . Because of these difficulties which virtually increase competition in his case, he is forced to take lower wages for the same work than white workmen." DuBois also noted that the color prejudice impacted women workers such that a "Negro woman has but three careers open to her in this city: domestic service, sewing, or married life."[76]

Southerners also entered northeastern cities with an established discourse of marking nonwhites and immigrants as "outsiders" and racially inferior. I argue that the discourse of "uncivilized" immigrant "outsiders," which was then over a decade old, was mapped onto Black migrants because it was rooted in native-born and white immigrant disdain for Blacks that persisted beyond the mid nineteenth century. In addition, southern African Americans hailed from a region of the country that was looked down upon by white northerners, and their citizenship remained contested after slavery because of their race and the looming presence of "slavery's ghost."[77] Thus, descriptions of the native-born southerners as immigrants and refugees were simultaneously rooted in the history of slavery, white northern sentiments about white southerners, and regional public discourses about immigration.

Furthermore, the history of slavery, and particularly Irish women's immigration, shaped the actual migration and labor experiences of southern migrant women. Southern migrants were concentrated in domestic service with their Irish counterparts. Black women were also targeted by labor programs and unscrupulous employment agencies that bore similarities to those that targeted Irish women and girls in the mid- and late nineteenth century. Southern migrants were concentrated in domestic service and thereby faced job competition from Irish immigrant women who had established a monopoly in the occupation since the mid-nineteenth century. When the terms "immigrant" and "refugee" were not explicitly used, Black migrant women were portrayed similarly to how Irish immigrant women were characterized: backwards and uncivilized, willing to accept low wages for strenuous work, helpless, shiftless, ignorant of modern American culture, and threats to the moral fiber and health of the urban city. What also fueled Black women's association with immigrants into the twentieth century was that they had migrated to cities where not only the Irish, but southern and eastern European immigrants and British West Indian immigrants as well, had settled in the North.[78] These simultaneous movements of native born Black women and non-native born white and Black immigrant women into urban cities forced a constant redrawing of racial boundaries and solutions to the labor question, of which African American women were implicated.[79] The racialization of southern Black migrant women and their labors within the larger women's immigration context in which they lived and worked are further explored in the next section of this chapter.

Southern Black "Foreign" Women

The framing of Black migration from the South as a political and social problem, even when expressed benevolently, fueled depictions of southerners as foreigners. These sentiments were articulated in a letter that the governor of Kansas and former Lieutenant of the Union Army John Piece St. John wrote to the Colored Republican General Committee of New York City in 1880. He thanked the committee for donating $250 to the state of Kansas to help support southern migrants who arrived there. According to him, the "refugees" were "in a destitute condition, being very scantily clad, and without bread or the means to obtain it" and it was up to northerners to make up their "mind to stand by this down-trodden people." This would be "the second emancipation" that could make "blacks absolutely and forever free."[80] A year later, the New York Times reported in an article entitled "The Colored Refugees" that the Relief Committee of the Young Men's Colored Christian Association met at the Shiloh Presbyterian Church on 167 West Twenty-Sixth Street to devise a plan to locate shelters and raise money for a total of 144 "distressed refugees" from Arkansas who "fled from Southern persecution."[81]

The southern newcomers were both familiar and foreign. Leading up to the Civil War, white northerners had used the enslavement of Blacks as evidence that they were superior to their barbaric counterparts in the South. New Yorkers, for instance, boasted that, in comparison to southern slavery, their slavery was a relatively mild and benevolent institution.[82] According to northerners, southern Blacks had been trained under a brutish system and as a result, their characters could not be trusted. The formerly enslaved from the southern region could be either submissive or rebellious towards whites. Ex-slaves were also "foreign" to white northerners because they had a newfound sense of freedom. During slavery, southerners escaped to freedom in northern cities through the Underground Railroad. After the Civil War, the southerners traveled in ways that they could not have done before emancipation, and they asserted their right to livable working conditions in ways that would have been punishable even in northern courts during slavery.

Southern Blacks also hailed from a region that was looked down upon by white northerners. By the end of the nineteenth century, the South had disproportionately high rates of mortality due to malaria, yellow fever, and hookworm that were difficult to contain in a region that was still recovering from the financial and physical damage of the Civil War.[83] White northerners attributed these social ills to laziness and other abnormal traits of white southerners. As Tera Hunter put it, "White Southerners were increasingly considered a backward and inferior breed of Anglo-Saxons" in the late nineteenth century.[84] The Yankees proclaimed that Black migration to the North was a clear indication that white southerners continued to mismanage their region of the country with brutish treatment of African Americans. According to northerners, southern Black migration was a southern problem imposed on the North. As a race of inferior people that had been under the rule of lazy, uncivilized, white southerners for over a century, white northerners concluded that southern Blacks were also stuck in a primordial past that was foreign to modern Americans in the industrialized North. Considered outside of the boundaries of American citizenship, southern migrants were perceived as "refugees" and "immigrants" unfit for self-government.

The federal government also designated the formerly enslaved as outsiders in their Bureau of Refugees, Freedmen, and Abandoned Lands (the Freedmen's Bureau) program. While designed to integrate the formerly enslaved into U.S. institutions as "new" citizens of the country, "refugees" was in the very name of the program. The very description of African Americans as "refugees" negated their legal status as U.S. citizens, and more specifically native-born U.S. citizens. The federal government led the charge to end slavery based on the argument that Blacks were human and deserving of American citizenship, yet their Reconstruction efforts were not fully committed to the arduous work that it took to achieve true racial equality. As Edward Baptist put it, ". . . many white northerners celebrated emancipation as one of their collective triumphs. Yet whites' belief in the emancipation made permanent by the Thirteenth Amendment, much less in the race-neutral citizenship that the Fourteenth and Fifteenth Amendments had written into the Constitution, was never that deep."[85] Their ambivalence over racial equality was reflected in Reconstruction era projects that marked African Americans as excess populations. After the Civil War, the federal government created the first program that sponsored internal migrations of formerly enslaved women from the South to work in domestic service in northern cities. The purpose of the program was twofold. The government wanted to remove Black women from federal relief services in the South to reduce the financial burden of Reconstruction, as well as create job opportunities for the freedwomen in what the government believed was a region less hostile toward Blacks. Some employers welcomed the idea of southern Black women working in their homes because they were perceived as hard workers that accepted low wages, unlike unruly and cantankerous Irish immigrant women. White New England families sent requests for "colored girl servants" to Boston representatives of the Bureau of Refugees, Freedmen, and Abandoned Lands (the Freedmen's Bureau), who forwarded their lists to the bureau's headquarters in Virginia and Washington D.C.[86] The bureau became an employment agency for domestic servants as it arranged job placements and covered the transportation costs for the southern newcomers who boarded steamers to work their new jobs. The bureau also promised to pay for their return fare, if they found their job unsatisfactory.[87]

To be clear, the bureau's project was never to create opportunities for southern Black women to access political and economic resources afforded to whites, and the bureau's program was distinct from the assisted migrations of Irish immigrant women. The programs that assisted Irish women's emigration to the United States operated under the assumption that the daughters of Erin would eventually become self-sustaining citizens in the United States. The Freedmen's Bureau's labor program, however, reproduced slavery-era beliefs that Blacks were inherently incapable of becoming independent self-sustaining U.S. citizens, and Black women in the program encountered the brunt of this myth because of their race and gender. Black women were the primary caretakers of their children, and they had been racialized and gendered as hypersexual since Europeans' first encounters with African women in the nascent years of the transatlantic slave trade to justify the enslavement of African-descended women and their children.[88] Adopting these two-century-old myths, the bureau viewed Black women as most likely to become dependent on federal government resources indefinitely.

Determined to remove Black women and their children from federal relief services in the South, the bureau sponsored domestic service training for young mothers and orphans. The bureau paid for approximately one hundred orphans and young mothers between the years of 1866 and 1868 alone to receive domestic service training at the Cambridge Industrial School in Massachusetts.[89] Another labor program was developed in the Appalachian region that sponsored the transportation of approximately 350 formerly enslaved from Kentucky to work in private homes in Springfield, Ohio.[90] These federally funded programs, however, ended before the end of the nineteenth century. The newly freed became suspicious of the programs after hearing stories of migrants who were exploited by their employers and domestic service training instructors.[91] In addition, not enough employers were committed to exclusively hiring the southerners and not hiring European immigrant women. In the northeast, this might have been due to the large percentage of Irish immigrant women who remained in domestic service.

The white supremacist desire to control and profit from Black women's labor persisted after the Freedmen's Bureau program ended. In Boston, for example, an employer recruited 250 ex-slaves from Richmond, Virginia, to work as cooks, housemaids, and dining room servants in Boston.[92] As with labor agencies designed to recruit "cheap" immigrant women's labor from Ireland, unregulated employment agencies offered compensation to white and black men in the South who could convince African Americans to work in the North. The agents made aggressive attempts to recruit Black women laborers to northern cities. They ran ads in local Black newspapers throughout the South and traveled to southern Black neighborhoods to appeal to Black women in person with promises that plentiful and better domestic service jobs awaited them in the North.[93] Agents and journalists used language imbued with references to immigration and slavery to describe the native-born southern workers. They characterized African American migrants as cheap labor that could be transported across state lines to serve in the homes of white families. William Walton, a writer for *The Daily Register Call* in Central City, Colorado, advertised in 1879: "I hereby request all citizens who wish to employ colored refugees from the South, to write the name, address, number of male or females needed, kind of labor to be performed, or the number of children they would like to bring up . . ."[94] In 1879, the San Francisco's *Daily Evening Bulletin* reported that William Hughes, an "intelligent man," gardener, and shoemaker of "their nationality," had been to Richmond, Virginia, twice to recruit the "immigrants" bringing "a dozen or more at first and the last installment in June" to New York City."[95]

Characterized as "immigrant" labor with Mammy qualities, there were proposals to transport Black women from the United States to supply homes overseas with traditional southern cuisine. An 1892 article published in *The Daily Inter Ocean* reported a proposal to transport Black women to the British colony of Australia. The report read:

> As there seems to be a delay on the plantation managers to employ negro field labor, Mr. Gardner, who came to the Island [Australia] for the purpose of supplying that class of labor, has yielded to the requests made by a number of householders and will supply them with colored house servants direct from the South. Only bona-fide orders will be filled, and the number depends entirely upon the orders handed into him before his departure from Australia. The servants will include cooks, coachmen, yard-men, and nurses. Anyone who has traveled in the South remembers with pleasure the delicious fried chicken and corn bread.[96]

While it is unknown whether these plans were actually executed, the article articulated the enduring sentiment that Black women were not free and independent workers. What is also striking about the proposal to send Black women to Australia is that British colonists had devised a similar plan to transport Irish girls to work in private homes in Australia during the famine era.[97]

The labor schemes rarely served the best interests of the southern migrants and the agents typically targeted Black women. With false promises of domestic service employment in the North that paid higher wages than what was available in the South, agents convinced the southern women to pay placement fees and sign contracts full of loopholes that gave employers absolute power to exploit them. After the transaction, Black women traveled to the North anticipating decent employment that would enable them to support themselves and their families back home. Southern migrants were placed in homes where they sometimes did not receive wages for as much as three months and in some cases, no wages at all. Most women did not have the financial resources to return home and continued working in domestic service or turned to sex work to make a living for themselves and their families.[98]

Black women used resistance strategies in the North that were similar to those they employed in the South to negotiate the terms of their employment. They moved from house to house in search of better wages and working conditions, although they rarely found fully satisfying jobs. Some opted to leave household service and work in their own homes as laundresses for better pay and to have more time for themselves and their children. Daycare nurseries were not common, and Black women found it difficult to look after their small children when working the long hours that private household work required. Laundry work allowed Black women to work at home and keep a more careful eye on their children and other domestic matters. Despite the relative independence of laundry work, it was exhausting and strenuous labor. Working in a commercial laundry was a rare opportunity since employers preferred to hire white immigrant women for those positions. Doing laundry work without the machinery in commercial laundries bound Black women to the oldest and most laborious cleaning methods. They had to wash large loads of clothing piece by piece over washboards in small and poorly ventilated apartments.[99] Black women also lacked the protections of labor regulations working alone and in their own homes. Most decided that domestic service was better suited for them because of the inconsistency of laundry work, although they were vulnerable to labor exploitation in both occupations.

In some cases, Black migrant women sought legal justice against labor exploitation by suing their employers. The Halligan family convinced Livinia Pickney to leave her home in Savannah, Georgia, and work for them in their home in Brooklyn. Pickney testified during her trial that the Halligans refused to pay her wages, and when she tried to return to Georgia, they threatened to call the police. The *Brooklyn Eagle* reported that each member of the Halligan family testified that "the girl was not worth more than her board and clothes, and that the agreement was that she would have no more than that."[100] The jury favored Livinia despite the Halligan family's false testimonies and awarded her $300 in compensation before she returned to Savannah, Georgia. Edward Pickney, Livinia's brother and a medical student, later commented that the Halligans coerced his sister into going to Brooklyn. Edward asserted, "Neither my father nor any person or persons ever bound my sister out to Mr. Halligan, either orally or in writing, and I now challenge Mr. Halligan to produce any such writing or stand convicted of falsehood before this community as well as attempting to enslave my sister." [101] While Pickney won her case, this was not a common outcome for most Black women who were either coerced into migrating or migrated under false pretenses.

The belief that southern arrivals were outsiders impacted their daily lives and interactions with northerners, even outside of their places of employment. Thieves, con artists, and slum landlords often targeted the "green" southerners, cheating them out of their possessions and charging them exorbitant rent prices. According to Elizabeth Clark-Lewis, some Black northerners believed that migrants were "educationally inferior" and "crude and 'country' in their social graces."[102] At times, northern-born Blacks distanced themselves from the "gullible" and "unrefined" southerners by creating benevolent societies that foregrounded their northern regional identity. As Elizabeth Pleck explained, "In New York City hostility toward southern migrants and a heightened pride in northern heritage led to the founding of the Sons of New York in 1884."[103] According to these northerners, they did not want to become associated with Blacks that spoke in unrefined dialects, wore colorful clothes, and practiced superstitious rituals such as voodoo.[104]

Southern migrants embraced their distinctiveness in ways that defied the negative depictions of them in newspapers. They established their own social organizations to assert their personhood and pool resources for survival in overcrowded cities where they had been shunned from existing social organizations, labor unions, and higher-wage occupations in favor of European immigrants and sometimes Caribbean immigrants and northern-born Blacks.[105] The names of the southerners' mutual aid societies reflected the importance they placed on regional identity and their proud assertion that they were in fact distinct from their northern-born and immigrant counterparts. As historian Irma Watkins-Owens explained, "Membership in these associations provided practical mutual aid but also helped to establish an individual's social position and identity in a large, impersonal city."[106] The southern societies based in Harlem, New York, for example, not only called for recognition of the cultural distinctions between African Americans and their immigrant counterparts, but also the regional distinctions among African Americans. Harlem's residents lived and socialized across ethnic and regional lines, yet the names of organizations, including the Sons and Daughters of Florida, the Sons and Daughters of

Virginia, and the South Carolina Club, made clear that the particularities of regional and state identities were important to southern migrants.[107] Association members drew on mutual aid from their organizations when they were wrongfully terminated from their jobs or could no longer work because of illnesses or injuries. Members also borrowed from their associations when they were unable to cover the funeral costs to bury family members with the low wages they received from their jobs.[108]

While southern migrants might have experienced complex social and political interactions with northern Blacks, European immigration determined their positioning in the labor sector. Labor union organizing, primarily led by Irish immigrant men, had a significant role in determining the employment prospects for southern Blacks when they arrived at their destinations. Irish and other white European immigrants earned higher wages than Blacks while working in the same occupations. Although Irish immigrant men remained concentrated in dangerous manual work, they had greater access to job mobility and thereby higher wages than their Black counterparts. Blacks were concentrated in menial jobs for several generations while Irish immigrants and other white immigrants could work alongside working-class native-born whites in skilled trades, clerical jobs, and factory work by the latter half of the nineteenth century.[109]

Women's occupations were also racially segmented. White employers barred Black women for several generations from jobs in garment factories and retail stores, offering these jobs to native-born white women and European immigrant women and their daughters, who sometimes refused to work alongside Black women. Late-nineteenth-century directories of New York City show that Black women worked in candy stores, dry goods stores, and oyster saloons; and as embroiderers, dressmakers, milliners, hairdressers, teachers, and midwives; yet most were employed in domestic service.[110] Although Irish immigrant women had greater access to factory work than Black women, they remained a generational step behind white native-born and immigrant women in occupations outside of domestic service. Hence, southern Black women entering the ranks of domestic service did not immediately drive out the 54 percent of Irish immigrant women who remained in domestic service in the latter half of the nineteenth century.[111]

Black women, however, faced competition with Irish newcomers for the higher-paying positions in domestic service. It was difficult for Black women to land service jobs in large businesses that paid higher wages than those offered by middle-class families in the domestic service industry. Employers of large service staff in first-class hotels, restaurants, and wealthy family homes preferred to hire European immigrants over both Black women and men. This discriminatory employment pattern dated back to the height of Irish immigration in the 1850s.[112] David Yentis explained in his study of Black women laborers in late-nineteenth-century New York City that socially elite families in Brooklyn preferred Irish servants. According to Yentis, Black women were mostly hired as day workers or laundresses because "the Negro was decidedly in bad taste as a household servant, among the leading families" in Brooklyn Heights.[113] When Black women were hired as household servants, the white staff refused to eat with them. To avoid racial conflicts, employers dismissed the Black servants, while other employers vowed never to hire southern migrants.[114] As Yentis put it, "The competition with white women of the immigrant class was so strong that the majority of Negro women listed in the directories have no occupation ascribed to them."[115] The majority of "cooks of the Heights, for several generations were of Irish birth and parentage."[116] Although Irish immigrant women occupied the lowest stratum of the white race, when they had the option employers preferred white immigrant servants over Black servants.[117] Most Black women in places like Brooklyn who could find domestic service employment worked in middle-class homes rather than those of the socially elite.[118]

Immigration also determined how the occupation of domestic work differed in the North and the South. Black women occupied all the ranks of domestic service in the South, and thereby the "servant problem," or employers' claim that there was a declining quantity and quality of "efficient" and "loyal" domestic servants was integral to whites' concerns about free Black laborers after emancipation. The servant problem in northeastern cities was inherent to native-born white concerns about European immigration. The advancements of the Irish community after the Civil War did not eliminate white nativist resentment towards Irish immigrant women. Although active members of male-led labor unions and social organizations, Irish immigrant women held virtually no political power on their own because they were women, and their concentration in domestic service was a testament to their limited social status.[119]

Irish women were the only immigrant group that symbolized the typical American servant in the North.[120] Irish immigrant women had dominated domestic service in the North since the mid-nineteenth century, and by the latter half of the nineteenth century characterizations of the belligerent Irish serving women were ubiquitous. As Vanessa May noted, "Cartoonists frequently portrayed the Irish domestic as apelike and aggressive, towering over the demure, Protestant lady who employed her."[121] The darkening of Irish servants in print media coincided with the increasing percentage of southern Black women in the occupation in the North.[122]

The challenges that white immigrant women, like the daughters of Erin, posed to the racial status of native-born whites sometimes shaped Black women's interactions with their employers. Velma Davis, interviewed by historian Elizabeth Clark-Lewis for her study of Black migrant women in domestic service in Washington D.C., recalled: "At home [in the South], they [employers] was white and they knew it. Wasn't no need to be on you to make them feel more white. Up here they knew they was white too, but they seemed to need you to make-up to them to keep minding them how white they are." [123] When Black women migrated to the North, they were also integrated into the larger debates about race, immigration, and labor such that they were routinely characterized as "immigrants" and "refugees." Although the same terms were used to describe southern Black men, the terms held specific meaning for Black women who migrated in the Progressive era of women's social reform in the urban city and worked in domestic service.

"Green" Black Women and White Women's Social Reform

Late-nineteenth-century white women social reformers were among the most vocal orators of the Black "immigrant" women discourse, extending it into the early twentieth century. The reform movement emerged from women's concerns with the growing corruption and poverty of the industrial era. Nineteenth and early twentieth century middle-class reformers "emphasized the home to national preservations" and declared that they had the "moral authority to enact social change."[124] Industrialization during the late nineteenth century widened the economic gap between the upper class, middle class, and working poor of whites, immigrants, and African Americans.[125] The white Protestant elite constituted less than 1 percent of the U.S. population, yet owned the factories, financial institutions, and transportation companies in the country. The Vanderbilts owned the railroads that stretched from the East Coast to the lands the U.S. acquired through western expansion. The Rockefellers owned oil refining companies and banks, and Andrew Carnegie owned steel manufacturing businesses. The working classes responded to the glaring class inequalities by engaging in social reform and political activism from roughly the 1870s to the 1920s.[126] As historian Nell Irvin Painter explained, "Comparing the lavish lives of the aristocrats who did not work with the poverty of the working masses, many thoughtful observers questioned the existence of immutable natural laws and worried instead that their society was out of joint."[127] Middle class Black, Native American, and white women argued that they were the most qualified to take on the noble endeavor of correcting society because they were innately capable of bringing a strong moral perspective to reform as respectable women.

White women reformers were especially eager to fix corruption in the nation by creating social programs and advocating for services to help poor and working-class white immigrant women and Black women. By the 1880s, they had created settlement homes for European immigrant women in the major industrial cities of Chicago, New York City, and Boston and in several smaller cities. The primary objective of these homes was to assimilate the residents into middle-class American culture by providing classes in U.S. art, literature, and history, and by offering job assistance and public kitchens and baths to reduce poverty. Settlement homes like Jane Adams' Hull House in Chicago were centers for social and political activism among white women reformers. Adams was a leading voice for legislation to reduce poverty among women and labor exploitation of European immigrant women in the industrial trades. According to reformers, settlement homes also provided a refuge from what they considered were immoral influences of urban slum living in tenement homes. Although southern Black women also needed support transitioning into urban life, white women reformers concentrated their efforts on European immigrant women because of their own racial biases.

Some white women reformers, however, found it difficult to ignore the needs of southern migrant women because they sometimes lived in the same neighborhoods and tenement home buildings as poor European immigrant women. In nineteenth-century Boston, Black migrants lived near the Irish, Germans, British, Jews, and a few Italians. In some neighborhoods in Boston's South End area, Blacks and the working-class Irish and British lived on the same streets and comingled in gambling rooms and saloons.[128] Bostonian social reformers found these communities the center of dirt and vice in the city because poor Blacks and European immigrants were concentrated in them. Blacks and immigrants also made up most of the Columbus Hill neighborhood in New York City. Although they lived segregated social lives, southern migrants, "foreign born whites", and British West Indian immigrants lived in the same tenement buildings in the community.[129]

In addition to Black migration, the domestic servant problem, or the belief that there was a decline in the quantity and quality of domestic workers, was of ultimate importance to social reformers. They believed that the home was the anchor of American civilization, and it was vital that it remain stable and harmonious. According to white women social reformers, the entry of immigrant and southern Black women, unschooled in modern American culture, into white private homes, introduced instability that reverberated across the country. Reformers perceived domestic workers as impoverished residents of tenement housing and believed that they introduced urban vice into their employers' homes.[130] Unlike the reform agenda to push for higher wages and safer working conditions for women industrial workers, reformers rarely argued that higher wages and better working conditions for domestics could alleviate the servant problem. Instead, they focused their efforts on creating training programs and societies for domestic servants and middle-class housewives to address complaints that housewives aired about Black women and immigrant women servants.

Progressive-era reformer Frances Alice Kellor, co-founder of the New York Association for Household Research, specialized in the study of women immigrant workers in the United States while advocating for household reform on behalf of southern Black migrant women.[131] As a sociologist, Kellor believed that social scientific studies of domestic workers' living and working conditions could transform society into a better place for housewives and the women they employed.[132] Kellor frequently made comparisons between the living conditions of European immigrant women and southern Black migrant women in her research on the working conditions in domestic service. As Andrew T. Urban put it, "Kellor's work bridged the concerns that middle-class Americans in northern cities had about 'new' immigration from Eastern and Southern Europe with the like-minded apprehensions that they directed at the increased number of black migrants arriving from the South."[133] Kellor drew comparisons specifically between southern Black women and European immigrant women more frequently after the association merged with the Woman's Municipal League and became the Inter-Municipal Committee. Kellor, who became general director of the Inter-Municipal Committee, believed that the United States could become a less corrupt and better place if the elite and politicians were more attentive to the needs of working European immigrant and Black women. [134]

The parallels that Kellor drew between European immigrant women and Black women are evidenced in her 1905 article, "Southern Colored Girls in the North: The Problems of their Protection," in the journal *Charities*. The journal featured stories about immigrant populations and the problems that they posed in New York City. The placement of the article in this particular periodical attested to the overlapping concerns of immigrants and southern Black women in the city. It followed a story about overcrowded hospitals in the city due to immigration and preceded an article about the "anti-tuberculosis movement" in Washington D.C. that targeted both immigrants and Black migrants.[135] Kellor compared the fates of southern Black women and immigrants to argue that the predicament of the southerners was actually worse than that of immigrants. She asserted, "Ellis Island has its missionaries who guide and direct the immigrant women; the stations have agents, but there is no one to extend a helping hand to the country girl from the Southern port." Kellor was unaware of, or chose to ignore, the extensive organizing and work that Black clubwoman Victoria Earle Matthews and her colleagues had done since the late nineteenth century to establish the White Rose Mission Home and a traveler's aid society to address the exploitation of southern Black women.[136]

Although Kellor claimed to act in the best interest of southern migrating women, she certainly believed that German, Irish, and Swedish immigrant women were inherently more capable than Black woman of becoming self-sufficient and productive citizens in northern cities.[137] While advocating for more employment opportunities for Black women who were "supplanted with whites" after being "unquestionably shut out from many lines of occupation" in domestic service and the hotel industry, she also accused the southerners of losing their jobs because they were "increasingly inefficient" and had a "desire to avoid hard work." According to Kellor, Black women's laziness made them more susceptible to being duped by corrupt employment agencies that preyed on "green helpless negro women" and "led them into immoral habits, vice, and laziness," or prostitution with "promises of easy work, lots of money, and good times."[138] Kellor's article thereby made "a strong case for the creation of an alternate set of institutions to police the actual migrating bodies of black women."[139]

White women social reformers and employers accused southern Black women of bringing immoral habits into the urban city and such complaints echoed those about Irish immigrant women.[140] While there might have already been a blueprint for these sorts of complaints about immoral women that was shaped by Irish women's immigration, disparaging descriptions of southern migrant women were also deeply rooted in the history of slavery and thereby a more enduring myth than that associated with Irish immigrant women. Nineteenth-century white physicians during slavery claimed to have sound scientific evidence that Black women were inherently hypersexual since the antebellum period. Such claims justified slaveholders' labor exploitation and rape of enslaved Black women and upheld the ideology of white female respectability.[141] These perceptions of libidinous Black women resurfaced in the North to explain white anxieties about southern Black women's migrations. As Hazel Carby explained, "The movement of black women between rural and urban areas and between southern and northern cities generated a series of moral panics. One serious consequence was that the behavior of Black female migrants was characterized as sexually degenerate and, therefore socially dangerous."[142] The resurgence of the Jezebel myth justified white anxieties about the growing southern Black migrant female population in overcrowded urban areas that lacked the infrastructure to support new immigrant and African American residents.

Depicted as rural southern women stuck in the pre-industrial past of slavery, Kellor insisted that Black women were unaccustomed to more efficient modes of production. Her proposal for ridding the city of shiftless Black women and corrupt employment agencies was to establish training schools that could teach "colored women" how to "be made more efficient."[143]

To tackle the exploitation of southern migrants, Kellor co-founded the National League for the Protection of Colored Women (NLPCW) with her colleague and African American clubwoman Sarah Willie Layten.[144] The League provided traveler's aid services and domestic service training classes for African American women migrants. Layten replaced Kellor as general secretary of the League in 1910 and founded the Mary S. Tribbitt Home for Girls in Philadelphia in the 1920s. It is important to note that Layten's approach was distinct from that of Kellor's in that she described migrant women as skillful and important workers in need of help. In her article "The Servant Problem," she proclaimed to her Black middle-class readers, "Few of us recognize the possible power of our people in domestic service . . . while our brilliant orators plead eloquently the Negroes' rights, their voices are seldom heard by the powers that be, but while those who serve acceptably and well, filling helpful positions or trust as domestics, are capable of creating a sentiment favorable to the Negro in his struggle for opportunity and a just verdict."[145]

Kellor's beliefs about "lazy" Black women shifted over time, signaling that perhaps her working relationships with Sarah Willie Layten and other Black women reformers might have prompted her to rethink some of her views. By the end of the first decade in the twentieth century, Kellor turned her attention to reforming domestic service itself and not the women employed in it. As historian Vanessa H. May noted, "Kellor depicted African American women, along with European immigrants who made up the majority of domestics in the early twentieth-century New York, as victims of urban vice rather than agents of it."[146] Kellor also argued, however, that immigrant and Black women were more prone to immoral behavior if they were exposed to urban vice, which she believed was unavoidable in tenement homes. Thus, she advocated for the development of training programs and employment agencies for domestics that were separate and apart from the tenement agencies.[147]

Similar to Kellor, some women's reform organizations did not notice many differences between "negro" and immigrant women and they proposed plans to develop domestic service programs to train both immigrant and Black women to becoming more efficient workers. The Woman's Municipal League of the City of New York, formed in 1898 "to promote among women an intelligent interest in municipal affairs" and "secure good government for the City of New York," sent a similar message to the city twenty years later about southern Black women in domestic service.[148] As late as 1907, a *New York Times* article announced: "The Woman's Municipal League thinks that the chief need for lightening the domestic problem is to furnish training to both negroes and immigrant girls . . . they must be in an elementary way Americanized before they can properly go into American homes."[149]

While the League had issued a recommendation to the city of New York to "Americanize" Black women, some white employers welcomed the influx of what they imagined to be cheap southern Black labor that had already been properly trained by the institution of slavery on the decorum of domestic service. As Marcy Sacks explained, "Prevalent stereotypes of Black 'mammies,' suggesting an eagerness to serve white families and cook hearty meals, confirmed for white people that Black domestic workers would well care for whites' homes and children."[150] Other employers, however, feared that the Black "immigrants" from the South would bring into their homes diseases and harbored resentment toward whites from stories passed down to them about slavery. Fears about the "domestic servant problem" were compounded by persistent anxieties about the domineering Irish Bridget who was believed to have already disrupted white American Protestant homes.

Conclusion

Southern Black women migrated to a region of the country that had yet to settle the race question for women that Irish women's immigration had posed to the U.S. North since the mid-nineteenth century. Characterized as refugees and immigrants, Black women's migrations from the South further complicated the construction of racial boundaries between native-born whites, white immigrants, and Blacks. Although white northerners boasted that they were more progressive than white southerners in both industry and race relations, they, too, relied on mythical representations of southern Black women on plantations to construct racial hierarchies amid European immigration and Black migrations. Taking a cue from their southern counterparts, white northerners created reconstructionist tales of southern Black women who cooked delicious fried chicken and pancakes to justify the labor trafficking of Black women into private homes. Black women were also integrated into women's reform missions created to civilize the immoral and untrained Black and immigrant new arrivals in urban cities.

By virtue of their concentration in a racially stigmatized niche of labor, as well as their racial histories in the U.S. South and Ireland, southern Black women and Irish immigrant women fueled debates about race and women's migrations in the U.S. North—and informed how northerners viewed the women themselves—when they moved into the most intimate confines of white America. Chapter 4, the next chapter of this book, examines how white domestic service employers, journalists, and reformers evaluated the "Irishness" of the daughters of Erin and the "southernness" of Black women to draw racial differences and similarities between the Irish and southern arrivals in the North. Discerning the similarities and distinctions between them was deemed critical to solving the race and (im)migration question inherent to the "domestic servant problem" in northeastern cities.

4

Too Irish, Too Rural, Too Black

<hr>

aka "The Servant Problem"

Southern Black women and Irish immigrant women migrated to northeastern cities amid native-born white anxieties about race ignited by emancipation, western expansion, and European and Asian immigration. An illustrator for *Frank Leslie's Illustrated Newspaper* captured the unsettledness of race in an 1870 image entitled "Our Goddess of Liberty." In the caption, the illustrator posed the following questions: "What is she to be?" "To what complexion are we to come at last?" What is striking about *Frank Leslie's* image is that it reveals how citizenship, nation, and race were heavily debated and represented through images of women. After emancipation, native-born whites no longer attributed society's ills solely to the men of "degenerate" races.[1] In the image (see Figure 2), the cartoonist captured the social Darwinist argument for women of the late nineteenth century. Indigenous, Irish immigrant, African American, and Asian women—the "degenerate" races—surround the native-born white woman at the pinnacle of Americanness—"Liberty" herself, the superior woman who would prevail at the end of this evolutionary period of socioeconomic and political change. The image, in turn, reasserted white supremacy among women.

In this chapter, I trace how the two similarly drawn women at the top of the illustration became central to debates about race, labor, and the "home" that emanated from socioeconomic and political shifts in the late nineteenth and

OUR GODDESS OF LIBERTY.
WHAT IS SHE TO BE? TO WHAT COMPLEXION ARE WE TO COME AT LAST?

FIG. 2 "Our Goddess of Liberty," *Frank Leslie's Illustrated Newspaper*, 16 Jul 1870. Credit: Library of Congress Prints and Photographs Division.

early twentieth centuries. While some representations portrayed Irish immigrant women as unintelligent, yet jolly and fun-loving servants, the negative depictions portrayed them as more animalistic than ever before. Irish servants became darker in print as southern Black women began entering domestic service after the Civil War. On one hand, the southern newcomers were portrayed as uncivilized servants who could not possibly know how to maintain modern homes because they had been under the rule of brutish white slave-owners. On the other hand, southern Black women were considered ideal servants because they were presumed to be more submissive than Irish servants and knowledgeable about cooking the best southern cuisine. I argue that these fluctuating racialized representations of Black and Irish immigrant women and their household labors became a medium by which to gauge and define racial hierarchies to preserve white supremacy while the United States was undergoing significant political and socioeconomic change.

Incompetent Bridget or "Green" Colored Southerners?

Irish immigrant and southern Black women's deliberate decisions to migrate and work in white homes in the North intensified questions that the country had debated since emancipation: Were African Americans citizens of the United States? In the absence of slavery, what was the difference between white labor and Black labor? Were women, Blacks, and immigrants ready for American citizenship? How could the "home" serve as a stabilizing force to re-establish racial and moral order amid labor strikes and massive European immigration and Black migrations? Native-born whites debated these questions from the congressional floor to large public gatherings to their own private homes.

The question of who was best qualified to care for their homes was of ultimate importance to solving debates about race, gender, American citizenship, and labor. While the "home" was constructed in the American imagination as a woman's domain separate from politics, it was a focal point for debates about the political, social, and economic shifts in the country.[2] The prevailing belief was that order in the home would impact the nation and repair its fissures. According to social reformers, the "failings of the American home" led directly to "poverty, disease, alcoholism, unemployment, and all the other social miseries apparent at the turn of the century."[3] Journalists, employers, and social reformers turned their attention to domestic workers to determine who was best qualified to care for the home.

According to these observers, the nation was not in order because the home was not, and domestic workers were to blame. Middle-class employers lamented that the country had a domestic servant problem, more specifically, a lack of employable native-born white servants who were always reliable, clean, hardworking, honest, and loyal to their employers.[4] In the words of David Katzman, household positions in cities of the Northeast "were filled by immigrants from Ireland" and "black women from the South."[5] Employers resented having to rely on immigrant and "foreign" southern Black women to do household work. As Irish immigrant and southern Black women entered white homes in the latter half of the nineteenth century, the country confronted larger questions of race and American citizenship. The pressing question always boiled down to whether the familiar Irish Bridgets from Ireland or the "green" negro plantation women from the rural "backwards" South were better qualified to care for the home. While engaging in public discussions about this subject, white northerners used their perceptions about the "southernness" of Black women and the "Irishness" of Irish immigrant women to create racial order through the home.

By the late nineteenth century, Irish immigration to the United States had declined due to a series of immigration restriction acts, yet the persistence of British colonialism sustained violent conflicts between Irish nationalists and British soldiers, and the economic devastation caused by the potato famine continued to plague Ireland. To make matters worse, Ireland faced a series of crop failures from the late 1870s until the 1880s that fueled continuous Irish immigration to the United States, although not in the same record numbers of the famine era. Between 1885 and 1920, nearly 700,000 women emigrated from Ireland to the United States and over half of Irish-born women in the country during this time period worked as domestics.[6] In places like New York City between 1899 and 1910, 40 percent of Irish immigrant women were still in domestic service. Only 14 percent of Irish immigrants in New York were classified as having "no occupation," a category that consisted mostly of children and homemakers.[7] By 1900, according to the United States Immigration Commission, 71 percent of Irish immigrant women in the labor force were classified as "domestic and personal" workers; 54 percent of those women were specifically classified as "servants and waitresses"; and another 6.5 percent were laundresses.[8]

Despite the massive influx of immigrants from eastern and southern Europe after 1900, Irish women remained a dominant presence in the occupation along with much smaller populations of German, Dutch, and Finnish women. The waves of immigrants that entered the United States during the late nineteenth and early twentieth centuries were primarily Italians and Eastern European Jews. They did not pose a threat to the jobs of Irish servants because they primarily worked in textile factories. Although the working conditions were no better, Italian and European Jewish women had the option of working in occupations that could be more easily unionized than domestic service.[9] Irish immigrant women had mostly worked in some form of domestic labor in Ireland and did not hold the same reservations about domestic service as Italian and Eastern European Jewish women.[10] In 1900, Irish-born women comprised a majority of servants in Boston, Cambridge, Hartford, New Haven, Providence, and Springfield. They were 42 percent of the servant population in New York City and 38 percent in Philadelphia.[11]

Only southern Black women posed a challenge to Irish dominance in domestic service. As Faye Dudden noted, "After emancipation and increased migration to the North, black patterns of service would begin to have a significant effect on service as a whole."[12] From the last decades of the nineteenth century until the early twentieth century, the presence of southern Black women in domestic service rose exponentially. Between 1870 and 1910, an average of 6,700 southern African Americans migrated to the North annually in search of employment. As early as 1905, one-quarter of all adult Black women in New York lived alone or in lodging houses, and 90 percent of Black women in the city were domestic workers. Although Black women were native-born Americans, English speakers, and Protestants, they were barred from clerical and sales jobs. When they worked in factories, they were often hired for lower-paying jobs than those offered to European immigrant women. Hence, the southern newcomers remained concentrated in domestic service like their mothers, sisters, and aunts in the South.

Comparisons between Irish immigrants and the new southern arrivals became more pronounced as southern Black women migrated to northern cities in greater numbers during the latter half of the nineteenth century. Female migrants were young, single, separated, or widowed, and their primary destinations were Philadelphia, New York, Chicago, or Boston.[13] The percentage of Black domestic workers steadily increased in the North from 41.9 percent in 1900 to 54.9 percent by 1930.[14] Irish immigrants had reason to worry about job competition with southern Black women. The southerners could not be displaced like the northern-born Black women that Irish women had outnumbered in the mid-nineteenth century. They were more numerous than northern-born Black women, and employers thought they had inherited from slavery a southern charm of submissiveness. As an employer reported to the *New York Times* in 1893, she preferred to hire southern Black women over northern-born Black women because "the Northern darky has a strong predisposition to grow 'fat and sassy' in a good place."[15]

As the historical narrative goes, native-born white employers shunned Irish male workers from jobs dominated by native-born white working-class men. Irish immigrant men created job security for themselves by attacking and driving out men in African-American-male-dominated occupations. There is little archival evidence that violent conflicts occurred between Irish and Black women in domestic service. The *Brooklyn Eagle*, however, reported that white servants, probably mostly Irish, expressed concern about job competition with southern migrant women. According to the article, "Colored servants constitute a very large proportion of the domestic laboring population of the North . . . Underbidding is one of the chief causes of complaint, since competition in this field tends to reduce the wages paid as the supply increases. So, it is with that class who do domestic and other service of the kind. Domestic servants already in New York expressed their concerns to the Central Labor Union, which reported that it planned to 'say something forcible about this proposition to supplant white with colored labor, and the formation of a servant girls' union is not improbable.'"[16] Although concerned about the new southern arrivals, white servants had a degree of privilege that made their serving jobs more secure than those of African Americans. Consequently, there was no room for error among Blacks in service occupations. Just one accusation of dishonesty could result in the dismissal of the entire Black staff. As the *New York Globe* reported:

Time was when colored people largely monopolized such positions as coach-men, footmen, valets, chambermaids, chefs, and waiters; but they have been slowly superseded in these employments by foreign white help . . . They can only hold their own against the great odds by being constant in their employments, strictly honest, punctual and reliable, and studied in neatness of dress and man-ners. A case of one dishonest colored servant in this city recently, resulted in a whole sale discharge of the colored help in that flat and the substitution of white help . . . it behooves all of us, all and each, to do well what our hands find to do.[17]

Employers could dismiss Black servants with ease because while they wel-comed the idea of "new" cheap labor, they had also become accustomed to hir-ing Irish immigrant women to work in their homes. An employer articulated this sentiment when she declared, "Harriet Beecher Stowe, in 'Uncle Tom's Cabin,' immortalized the negro 'Mammy,' . . . but the faithful Bridget, whose tender care has endeared her to the members of innumerable Northern house-holds, needs not the eulogy of a novelist to establish her unclaimed right to be remembered for motherly devotion to the children of her mistress."[18]

White northerners, however, were not always keen on hiring Irish immi-grant nor southern Black women, and they expressed such sentiments as early as the 1860s. According to David Katzman, "With the Civil War and eman-cipation, the image of the servant girl as a black woman began to appear in the North."[19] White northerners voiced concerns about the possibility of both Irish immigrant and southern Black women working in their homes in antici-pation of southern Black women migrating North to escape the South after the Civil War. According to northerners, southern Black women, like their Irish sisters and southern white slave masters, were stuck in a pre-modern past and thereby unable to care for modern homes. New York City physician and writer Robert Tomes wrote the following commentary a year after President Lincoln issued the Emancipation Proclamation:

> Most of the negroes, however, even those who are called domestic servants, brought up as they have been in the slatternly households of the South and Southwest, would be as out of place in the better-ordered homes of the North as a bull in a china-shop. As for the old negro servants, once so common in our Northern kitchens and halls, they have become almost extinct through inherent weakness or the force of external pressure . . . [20]

As Tomes indicated, northerners thought of southern Black women as an exten-sion of the "uncivilized" rural white southerners. It was no coincidence that Tomes commented about Irish immigrant women in the same article because white northerners had adopted similar beliefs about Ireland. Perceptions of Ireland as an "uncivilized" rural country informed their complaints about the

Irish serving women. Thus, portraying Black women in a negative light did not always elevate the status of Irish immigrant women. Tomes asserted:

> Housekeepers complain bitterly of Bridget's ignorance and awkwardness, and will tell you, with tears in their eyes, how she cut off the tender and eatable parts of the asparagus and served up the tough stalks; how she washed her feet in the soup-tureen; how, in her zeal for a shine, she rubbed off the coat of bronze from the tea-urn; how she scrubbed the family portraits with soap and water . . . The ignorance of Bridget is, no doubt, tormenting to the careful housekeeper . . . but what else can we expect? Where has she had an opportunity to learn? Surely, not in her native Connaught. Born and bred in a mud hovel, in the companionship of boorish peasants like herself . . . she can know nothing of the simplest elements of civilized life.[21]

After emancipation, comparisons between Irish immigrant and southern Black migrant women became more pronounced. A writer for the *New York Times,* commenting on the perceived similarities between the rural backgrounds of Irish and Black women, wrote: "It is obviously irrational to expect that a girl who has spent her early life in an Irish cabin, or a negro's . . . should be expected to be either gentle-spoken or deft-handed, or neat in dress and habits, or scarcely anything else that the house-servant of a respectable family should be."[22] According to the writer, Irish and Black women did not "know how to take care of fine china" because they lived in rural dilapidated homes where they ate from a "tin platter." The newcomers from the South and Ireland had also been exposed to "rude wit" and "coarse language" and were thereby unfamiliar with civilized language and behavior.[23] The perception that Irish immigrant and southern women were stuck in a primordial past justified beliefs that they were incapable of operating household appliances.

As evidenced in an 1870 advertisement for the Eureka mop (shown in Figure 3), white employers believed that Irish immigrant and African American women were not prepared to manage modern industrialized homes in the North. It shows an Irish immigrant and an African American servant at the far left engaged in a competition with what appears to be a German servant and a native-born white American woman. The white woman dressed in yellow warns the others that "there's no use" in them trying because they will lose the competition to her because "she's got a Eureka." While the German woman isn't able to clean the floor, the Irish immigrant and African American servant appear to have the most trouble with their mops. The Black woman fell on the floor, and the Irish immigrant woman appears to have knocked over the bucket of water and is still trying to figure out how the old mop works. The white woman prevails in the end, which she confirms by telling the servants "I told you so!"[24]

FIG. 3 "The Great 'Scrub' Race," 1870. Eureka mop advertisement. Credit: Library of Congress Prints and Photographs Division

It is clear from the comparison between the Irish immigrant and African American women that domestic service remained inferior work and bore consequences for them. Although white women, Irish immigrant women were considered racially inferior because they were concentrated in the occupation of domestic service. As David Katzman explained, "Nearly all studies of household labor and servants' memoirs agreed that in the urban United States white servants had very low status."[25] Domestic service in the northeast was simultaneously "Black" and immigrant work, thereby making African American serving women susceptible to comparisons with Irish immigrant women. Employers viewed African American and Irish immigrant women as either the best, worst, or equally worst domestic workers in United States history.

Periodicals routinely expressed the sentiments of northerners who were confounded by the race question and the domestic service problem amid southern Black migrations and Irish immigration. Employers touted the English as the only employers who had figured out how to effectively manage servants. To make sense of the racial shifts in domestic service, northern employers turned to England. In an article entitled "Housekeeping, English and American" in the Boston-based *Every Saturday: A Journal of Choice Reading,* the anonymous author compared Black servants in the United States with English servants. The author lamented that Boston was plagued by inefficient Black and Irish servants. And what made emancipated southern Black women particularly incompetent was that they were no longer under the surveillance of slaveholders. The article stated, "Perhaps, the best servants we have had in America during the past twenty years were the black slaves in the South; but they are exceedingly lazy, wasteful, and expensive . . ."[26]

The author was not completely in favor of Irish immigrant women either. Southern Black women's history as enslaved laborers led to comparisons with Irish immigrant women, whom native-born whites branded as enslaved by their own unfortunate ancestry as a people who would never appreciate the advancements of modern civilization. In the same article, the anonymous author explained, "The Irish go from the emigrant ships to the "intelligence offices," or the servants' agencies; and often they have places,—that is to say, are hired—the next day after they leave shipboard . . . Coming from homes destitute of every comfort,—from straw thatched cabins, where the only housekeeping consists in piling peat upon the fire,—from hovels where all the meals are cooked in the same pot, and gaunt Poverty casts its curse on the scanty fare."[27]

Clearly, not all cartoonists and domestic service employers were convinced that Irish immigrant women had ascended to a higher stratum of the white race like their husbands, uncles, cousins, and fathers. Although Irish women had dominated domestic service in New York City since the mid-nineteenth century, they were still considered foreign invaders in white American homes. Representations of Irish serving women routinely portrayed them as domineering, lacking intelligence, untrustworthy, dirty, and incapable of operating household appliances, all of which proved that they were the antithesis to their genteel lady employers, and they remained a threat to the stability of the home and thereby the nation.

Complaints about Irish serving women were partly rooted in white supremacist beliefs that there was a culture of pathology in Irish immigrant communities. According to native-born white social reformers, Irish immigrant households were inherently dysfunctional because they were typically managed by Irish matriarchs who had "succumbed to madness, drunkenness, and other anti-social or masochistic behaviors," neglected their own children, and were too lazy to work and thereby provide a better life for their children outside of dirty and overcrowded tenements in the city. [28] The immigrant identity of Irish women certainly complicated their social status as mothers. It was one thing to be an Irish woman, but it was another to be an Irish immigrant woman in the midst of white anxieties about heightened European immigrations and Black migrations to urban cities. Some social reformers, in fact, praised Irish women back in Ireland and reserved their most disparaging comments for the newcomers. Charles Loring Brace, native-born white social reformer, and founder of the Children's Aid Society, praised Irish women living in Ireland but criticized Irish women in America. Brace declared: "It is another marked instance of the demoralizing influence of emigration, that so large a proportion of the female criminal class should be Irish-born, though the Irish female laboring class are well known to be at home one of the most virtuous in the world."[29]

Brace attributed crime in the urban city to Irish immigrant mothers who failed at raising their children according to white patriarchal domestic ideals. He strongly believed that drunken and promiscuous Irish immigrant husbands left their wives to raise their children alone as they frequented the local bars and engaged in multiple marriages. Social commentators also declared that Irish immigrant women were prone to drunkenness, prostitution, and criminality.[30] Brace concluded that the inherent immoral characteristics of Irish-born women and the absence of husbands in Irish homes made it difficult for Irish immigrant women to control their own children. Irish mothers, Brace claimed, lacked the morals and discipline to provide a positive example for their sons and daughters. He stated, "The boys get beyond her control . . . they become wild and vagrant, and soon end with being street-rovers, or petty thieves, or young criminals. The girls are trained in begging or peddling, and, meeting with bold company, they gradually learn the manners and morals of the streets, and after a while abandon the wretched home, and break what was left of the poor mother's hope and courage, by beginning a life of shame."[31] Brace sought to rescue and civilize the children of Irish immigrant women by sending them out West on orphan trains to work as farmhands for Anglo families.[32] Brace felt these families were well-equipped to teach Irish children the value of honest labor and Christianity.

Social reformers integrated African American and Irish immigrant mothers into debates about citizenship and race when Black men were granted the right to vote after the Fifteenth Amendment was ratified in 1870. Emancipation and passage of the amendment disrupted definitions of race that had established the requirements for American citizenship since slavery. Illustrations of Irish immigrant and Black women as mothers to their own children revealed native-born white concerns about Reconstruction and Irish immigration. In an 1871 *Harper's Weekly* image, a southern Black mother tells her children not to play in the mud. Otherwise, they would be mistaken for Irish children.[33] In the North, Blacks were considered more fit for American citizenship than Irish immigrants. James Barrett explained, for example, "Citizens of Rhode Island debated whether the Irish should be excluded from the provisions of the Fifteenth Amendment, as they appeared to be a distinctly different race from African Americans and the 'white' mainstream."[34]

The image "Effect of the Fifteenth Amendment" (shown in Figure 4) suggested that being a "good" mother meant that Black mothers should teach their sons how to live up to the expectations of the amendment by instructing them on how to become productive American citizens. According to the image, this sort of lesson required Black women to discourage their sons from adopting the "dirty" behaviors and physical appearance of Irish boys. Although an Irish immigrant mother does not appear in the cartoon, it implies that they were not "good" mothers since Black women needed to tell their children not to behave like Irish boys. The child sitting on the fence in his leprechaun-style hat and the feet of the son who has already tumbled over the fence suggest that despite the mother's warning, there was no clear distinction between Irish and Black boys, thereby raising the question of whether either group should truly be granted American citizenship. The cartoon, however, signaled that Black mothers might have a better chance of Americanizing their sons than Irish mothers. As the mother told her sons: "Cum in out of dat Mud right straight! Fust ting you'll know you'll be took for Irish Chil'en!"

The belief that Black women were slightly better at managing their own homes in comparison to Irish immigrant women was also reflected in employers' concentrated efforts to solve the domestic service problem by recruiting southern Black women after emancipation. Thus, the migration of southern Black women to northern cities during the late nineteenth and early twentieth centuries did not always bode well for Irish immigrant women and the way that they were portrayed in the media. Late-nineteenth-century newspaper reports about unruly Irish immigrant women in service explained why employers sought Black labor from the South. An article that appeared in the *Brooklyn Eagle* in 1872 read: "The great demand for reliable servant girls in

FIG. 4 "Effect of the Fifteenth Amendment," *Harper's Bazaar* magazine (New York), 4 Mar 1871. The Miriam and Ira D. Wallach Division of Art, Prints and Photographs: Picture Collection, The New York Public Library.

this section of the country has led to another scheme for the relief of housekeepers. It is now proposed to bring a large number of colored girls from the Southern States to the North." Employers believed that formerly enslaved Black women would accept lower wages than their Irish counterparts who were already settled in the North. A New York employer commented, "... they [southern Black women] are so unconscious of the indignity of fully earning their wages that they are likely to do twice the work of other kinds of servants without regarding themselves overtaxed."[35] Some northern employers believed that the southern construction Mammy reflected the real sentiments of Black women. They assumed that southern Black migrant women and their descendants would be as loyal and nurturing to their children and entire family as the mythological Mammy figure had been to slaveholders. A New York employer asserted, "In the not universal quality of kindness to children, they are simply excellent by the laws of their gentle, cheerful, grateful natures. These colored people ... at least take pride in considering the household their family."[36]

Other employers reserved their most disapproving remarks for Irish immigrant and Black serving women. An employer writing under the penname "M.E.P." complained to readers of the *Brooklyn Eagle* that she had given up trying to find reliable servants. She had hired two German women who left after only working for two days and a Swedish woman who never appeared for the first day of work. Then she tried hiring a Black woman whom she later fired because her previous employers in Rhode Island said that she was a "thief and a liar." Finally, she hired an Irish immigrant woman about whom she concluded: "I should have known better and will never have another in my house if I have to crawl and get the meals . . . Dirty, impudent, careless, wasteful and for incompetence they take the premium . . ."[37]

The strongest preference for southern Black women was most evident in Philadelphia where the Black population nearly matched that of white immigrants. As more Black women migrated to Philadelphia so, too, did complaints about Irish serving women. In 1899, W.E.B. Du Bois was invited by sociology professor Samuel McCune Lindsay at the University of Pennsylvania to conduct a study on the southern migrant population of Philadelphia. As part of the study, Du Bois employed Isabel Eaton, member of the College Settlement Association, who had been awarded a fellowship to live and work in Philadelphia's Seventh Ward, to research the labor experiences of southern and Philadelphia-born Black women in domestic service.[38] According to employers that Isabel Eaton interviewed for *The Philadelphia Negro,* Irish immigrant women were unrulier than ever before. One study participant explained:

> When my sister was ill, the Irish maid I had at the time refused to carry up the breakfast tray because she said, "it was not her business to do nursing," and she "wouldn't do it for ten dollars." The employer remembers that she was then forced to take the trays herself until the "colored girl, who came soon after, volunteered to do the work." She told the employer: "Let *me* take up the breakfast tray Mrs. W—. You look ready to drop." Ever since, Mrs. W—never had a white girl in the house.[39]

Another employer explained her preference for southern Black women:

> We had white servants for seven winters, and always employed the best Irish servants we could get; but they were so unsatisfactory that we gave them up and tried colored servants. Our experience of them is that they are infinitely cleaner than the white Irish, both in their work and personally; they are more self-respecting and better mannered—more agreeable in manners; indeed, I have found them capable of the very highest cultivation of manner.[40]

Employers believed that southern Black women's ties to the history of slavery made them more subservient to their employers than Irish women. Although white northerners boasted about not participating in slavery, they reproduced the myth that Black women had been trained to submit to white authority as enslaved laborers. Northern employers also assumed that southern Black women had extensive training caring for the needs of white families.[41]

Irish serving women were not always popular among native-born white domestic workers either, who even expressed the belief that they were so uncivilized that there was no place for them in domestic service. In 1895, an anonymous white servant submitted a letter to the *New York Times* to describe her negative experiences working in the same home with Irish women. She declared:

> My employers were very nice to me, but the other servants were unbearable. When I first went there to live I found an English cook, a German chamber-maid, and a Swedish laundress. They were all so kind to me that I never felt so happy in my life. But, alas! The chambermaid and laundress married and the cook went to England for a vacation. Three Irish girls took their places; three of the dirtiest and most grossly ignorant people I ever met.[42]

Drawing from republican ideology, the servant associated independence and "good" work ethics with the "white" English, German, and Swedish women while reserving "nonwhite" descriptions of dependence and poor work ethics for the Irish women. The author also proposed a solution to the influx of Irish women into domestic service that fit within the colonial history of Irish immigration. Just as the British government devised a labor scheme that transported poor Irish women to work in Australia, Canada, and the United States, the servant proposed that the United States government "annex Hawaii and then on the 17th of March charter enough steamers to send all the Irish servants in New York out there and leave them where they could fight among themselves, which they would do until they were exterminated. The servant question then might be settled."[43]

A New York City butler who proudly identified himself as a white American man articulated similar disdain for Irish immigrant women in a letter that he submitted to the *New York Times.* The butler wrote:

> Maggie is such a thorough cleaner, you know. Maggie's thoroughness is when she sweeps the parlor, and then, with a feather duster, flicks the dust from one place to settle in another, and yet this is cleaning. Let the lady make a visit (unexpected) to the servants' bedrooms, then she will see some of Maggie's thoroughness. She will see all the national traits that have clung to her since she left Ireland.
>
> There she will find water pitchers half filled with dirt, water that is reeking, and which compels men servants to take their towels down stairs, where they can get running water to wash with. The tenement house cannot compare with some of the top floors of the Fifth Avenue for filth. . . .

The butler also accused employers of giving preferential treatment to Irish immigrant women, which threatened the employment security of white American workers who remained in the occupation. The butler continued by accusing the Irish maid of theft, "Nothing happens in a house unless Maggie figures in it. For instance, a gentleman says, 'John, my cigars go very quick.' John says, 'Yes, Sir.' If you were over on the west side where Maggie's cousin Patrick lives, you could detect the same smell as you can in the smoking room of your own house, and yet Maggie gets the benefit of the doubt and John gets his discharge. Why is it that these ignorant people are given so much power over educated and competent servants and upheld by their mistresses?" [44]

Race and the Servant Problem across the Pond

Comparisons between Irish immigrant and southern Black women were not left to the white American imagination alone. An anonymous middle-class British husband and father of two daughters wrote a manual entitled *Our Jemimas: Addressed to the Middle Class by a Victim* that documented the many difficulties he experienced trying to find a suitable servant for his home. He lamented to his U.S. readers that England also had a domestic servant crisis. Like other British employers, the author complained about working-class English servants and their growing resistance to employers. Although British employers complained about England's working-poor, they thought that Irish servants were the worst because they were beyond discipline and civility. Thus, he could not offer any solutions to readers across the pond who hired "Bridget." All he could do was reassure employers that the problem was with Irish women and not with them.[45]

In a chapter entitled "Celt and Saxon," he explained in detail his horrific experiences living in his home while it was under the care of Bridget Hanlan. The author recounted that he and his wife Sabrina were dissatisfied with English servants and decided to "import a girl from Ireland." He described this as the worst decision that they could have ever made. He used a range of signifiers such as dirt, language, physical characteristics, and nationality as evidence that Bridget was a horrible servant and a race apart from his family. As such, she was ill-equipped to handle domestic affairs. Before Bridget could pick up a broom or wash any clothes, the author was put off by Bridget's physical appearance when she first arrived at his home. He described her as a "brawny Irish girl, the picture of rude health—dressed in raiment flowing as to its draperies . . . and with a brogue as long as my arm. Five foot ten in her stockings—which, by the way, she preferred to walk about in of a morning, probably scorning the Saxon show as an emblem of oppression."[46] Her physical appearance seemed to reflect that she was out of place in a middle-class British home. Bridget "had no conception of what proper boiling signified" and "she was entirely ignorant of the meaning of roasting a joint, she destroyed vegetables utterly." The author also accused Bridget of badly influencing the children. She refused to bathe the children and dirt in the home "accumulated till it became utter filth." Bridget also neglected the children and taught them "to lie audaciously."[47] By the end of the chapter, the author vowed to never hire an Irish woman again.

What is particularly striking about *Our Jemimas* is that its title referenced a term that was in wide circulation in the United States and resonated with the term "Aunt Jemima," which referred to a character in minstrel shows and was introduced to capitalist consumer culture through pancake mix boxes in 1889. Aunt Jemima was the ideal Black cook who was happy and loyal to the white middle-class families for whom she worked. Aunt Jemima and Bridget were tools designed by native-born whites to "clean up" the boundaries of whiteness that had been muddied by emancipation. As April Schultz explained in her comparative study of Mammy and the Irish Bridget, "Cultural representations, particularly the exaggerations found in cartoons and advertisements, serve to illuminate anxiety about and perceived threats to hegemonic security and well-being. White immigrant Irish and Black female bodies were set in opposition to elite white women in separate dramas that demonstrated unease about ethnicity, religion, and race . . ."[48] Unlike Mammy, Aunt Jemima in particular was a product of northern white anxieties and attempts to re-establish racial boundaries after slavery. Both Aunt Jemima and Bridget were custom-designed carving tools that northern whites created and used to mold, protect, and reaffirm the boundaries of white femininity and white supremacy more broadly. These representations of Black and Irish immigrant women as domestic servants played a significant role in affirming the illusion that race and gender were biological, and white supremacy was the natural and logical order.

The author of the English domestic service manual might have used the phrase "Our Jemimas" to communicate his perceptions of Irish immigrant women in England since the term "Jemima" had already begun circulating in the United States when this manual was published. The British author seemed to imply: You have your "Jemimas"; now, let me tell you about our "Jemimas," i.e., Irish immigrant women. The British author, however, took his complaints a step further by inserting Irish immigrant women into the American lexicon of race by referring to them as "Jemimas." While *Aunt Jemima* was not cantankerous like the Irish *Bridget*, both archetypes clearly conveyed the idea that Irish immigrant and Black women were inferior to their white employers.

Political unrest in England and Ireland over Irish home rule fueled complaints about Irish servants in England and the United States well into the late nineteenth century. The male author of *Our Jemimas* blamed Bridget Hanlan for all that destabilized racial, gender, and class hierarchies in England. By the late nineteenth century, working-class English women who worked in factories and private homes had developed a strong political voice that challenged class and gender hierarchies. In 1888, women factory workers left their machines in droves to organize a massive labor strike after the publication of social reformer Annie Besant's "White Slavery in London."[49] The English elite and middle class were fearful of these protests along with growing resistance to British colonial rule in Ireland, the rise of poverty and disease in overcrowded London, and Irish immigration to England. As women who worked in the cradle of British civilization, Irish servants bore the brunt of English fears about the political and social climate of late nineteenth-century England and Ireland.

Irish resistance to British rule also made U.S. employers skeptical. Irish women in the United States had developed and earned the reputation of being defiant, which defied British-derived ideals of domesticity. As Hasia Diner explained, "Irish women adhered to a behavioral code that deviated markedly from the celebrated 'cult of true womanhood' . . . Irish women viewed themselves as self-sufficient beings, with economic roles to play in their families and communities."[50] Irish women's struggle for independence in the workplace and in Ireland also shaped representations of them as domestic servants in U.S. periodicals.

Irish and Black Contagions in the Home and Urban City

Employers drew from erroneous scientific findings about race to convey the belief that the Irish struggle for independence brought instability into white American homes through Irish serving women. An image that appeared in *Puck* in 1883 entitled "The Irish Declaration of Independence" indicated that Ireland's movement for independence from Britain in the late 1800s informed perceptions in the United States of Irish servants as domineering people who could not be trusted.[51] Employers feared that Irish serving women might take a cue from their fellow countrymen and women in Ireland and rebel in their homes.[52] Consequently, as Andrew T. Urban put it, "Nineteenth-century authors and cartoonists frequently highlighted what they considered to be their Irish servants' crude qualities, savage disposition and masculine physique." Bridget was a "rebellious subject" and "quick to resort to physical intimidation and violence in order to get her way," like her fellow nationalist countrymen in Ireland."[53] Depictions of violent Irish immigrant women racialized and gendered the particular women in the images and Irish immigrant women more broadly. As Andrew T. Urban also explained "Violence was a common trope in Anglo-American employers' racialized portrayals of Irish immigrants as a people whose primitiveness meant that they had not yet evolved civilized gender distinctions."[54]

The Bridget in the image "The Goose that Lays the Golden Egg" (see Figure 5) is so uncivilized and racially inferior that she is an animal. Irish Fenian Leader Jeremiah O'Donovan Rossa is spoon-feeding her a promissory note that reads: "Pay the Bearer $5 When Ireland is Free." The golden eggs in the hat

FIG. 5 "The Goose that Lays the Golden Egg," *Puck*, 22 Aug 1883. Credit: Library of Congress Prints and Photographs Division.

on the floor are labeled "Money from Bridget" in support of the Irish rebellion. A bowl sitting on the table to the left is filled with eggs labeled "Irish Contributions from Servant Girls." The coins from the servants' contributions are pouring out of broken eggs on the floor, and the caption to the image reads: "Rossa:—'Begorra, we'll never kill her while her appetite lasts.'"[55]

Irish women's reputation as politically active informed such racialized representations of them as servants. In 1879, Irish women formed the Ladies' Land League, a political alliance between women farmers, the Sinn Feín, and the Irish Parliamentary Party that protested the high rents charged by Anglo-Irish landlords. The league was militant and effective at pressing landlords to lower rents until the British government disbanded it less than two years later.[56] By 1876, two women's suffrage societies had been established, one in Belfast and another in Dublin. And less than a decade after "The Goose that Lays the Golden Egg" was published, Irish women had already formed full-fledged labor organizations that advocated for better wages for domestic and factory workers.[57] Employers were suspicious that servants were sending money to support Irish nationalist campaigns against Anglo-Irish rule. The Irish Land League was subsidized by Irish-American dollars to persuade Parliament to pass the Land Act. The Act was intended to curtail Anglo-Irish landlords' exploitation of tenant families.[58]

United States employers might have also heard about Irish immigrants Leonora Barry and Mary Harris Jones and Irish American Leonora O'Reilly, labor organizers and national agitators who demanded better wages and working conditions for white working-class women, which included working-class Irish American and Irish immigrant women.[59] While these labor organizers rarely spoke about the particular circumstances of Irish women in domestic service, they certainly projected the sense that working-class Irish women were coming into their own in the political arena and demanded respect as wage workers.

As racially inferior immigrant women from a "rebellious" country, Irish women were hyper-masculinized in U.S. publications well into the late nineteenth century. Cartoonists borrowed from physician Samuel Morton's flawed scientific conclusions about race to illustrate Bridget's masculine body and Africanized face to imply that Irish servants were more masculine than working-class African American and Irish immigrant men. In his book *Crania Americana,* Morton ranked the world's races by cranium measurements. According to Morton, the Caucasian race had the "highest intellectual endowments" of all races, and some groups from Africa that he classified as Negro were of the "lowest grade of humanity."[60] Morton's erroneous beliefs persisted well beyond his death in 1851, influencing late nineteenth century drawings of Irish immigrant and African American women and men.[61] Author H. Strickland Constable published an 1899 drawing comparing the heads of white, Black, and Irish men that was widely circulated then and remains so in print and online today. The caption to the image read: "The [Irish] Iberians are believed to have been originally an African race, who thousands of years ago spread themselves through Spain over Western Europe."[62] The image conveyed the belief that Blacks and the Irish shared an African ancestry, and that both races were inferior to white Anglo-Saxons. Interestingly, depictions of Irish and Black males resembled the Irish immigrant and African American servants in the "Great Scrub Race" (see Figure 3 earlier in this chapter) and "Our Goddess of Liberty" (see Figure 2 earlier in this chapter). Academics also reproduced masculine portrayals of Irish immigrant women. Historian Lucy Salmon noted in her study of domestic service that Irish immigrant women were "a most numerous and important class engaged in domestic employment" because their "physical strength formed a partial compensation for their lack of skill and ignorance of American ways."[63]

Housewives were not exempt from complaints about the presumed instability of the American home. In the last quarter of the nineteenth century, teachers, writers, and housekeepers married science and housework in a Progressive Era that touted science and technology as the solution to all the nation's flaws. As an anonymous author declared in *Progressive Housekeeping:* "No woman is fitted to be a wife or mother, or to preside over a home, who has not a practical knowledge of household science."[64] These self-proclaimed experts on the "home" launched a major domestic reform movement that began in the Northeast and spread quickly to other parts of the country. Domestic science instructors placed the burden of the servant problem on housewives. Although they insisted that widespread poverty, disease, alcoholism, and unemployment were rooted in the immoral habits of working-class women, housewives could put a stop to their immoral influences.[65] They preached that if housewives learned the science of homemaking, then they could manage servants more efficiently, and they could also have the option of managing their own homes alone, if they were unable to find a reliable and efficient servant. By 1899, white housewives in several cities in the United States had either attended or heard of cooking schools and domestic-science conferences and had read domestic science magazines instructing them on how to keep a clean and virtuous home. By 1900, domestic science had become integrated into school curricula as home economics courses. Home economists believed that the courses would "raise the homemaker to a position of power and dignity by modernizing her as well."[66]

Housewives transferred some of the pressure they felt from social reformers to run a technologically sound and perfectly scientific home to the servants they supervised. And housewives' complaints about servants became more intensely focused on their perceptions that Irish and southern Black women could not adapt to the modern home. Northern perceptions of the U.S. South and Ireland as regions that had not been advanced by industrialization curtailed Irish immigrant and Black women's abilities to do housework and operate household appliances. An advertising circular for the Whitson Refrigerator circa 1880 stated that using the new appliance was so easy that it would please incompetent Irish and Black servants. The ad predicted that housewives would get the following response from an Irish maid: "Shore an I'll leave the place if they take it out." The housewife would also please a Black maid who would say, "After getting in day box everything comes out right."[67]

In a Progressive Era of social reform, northern employers were skeptical of all "outsiders," especially non-native-born white women. Despite the efforts of some Irish immigrants to distance themselves from Blacks in domestic service and distrust of the southerners in particular, some employing families and social reformers considered both Blacks and Irish immigrants to be similar in character and equally responsible for contributing to the domestic service problem. According to these public commentators, Irish and southern Black serving women migrated from the most underdeveloped places in the western hemisphere and they came to the North ignorant of the one subject in which all respectable women were well-versed: hygiene. They declared that the key to managing and protecting northern white homes from diseases and sexual vices was to keep an eye out for "dirty" Black and Irish immigrant servants and teach them the importance of cleanliness in body, spirit, and work.

Led by reformers Frances Kellor, Lucy Maynard Salmon, and Jane Addams, white women's organizations in the Progressive Era promoted policies to increase working-class women's wages and improve their working conditions. Salmon also urged the federal and state governments to provide resources for domestic workers like those available to servants in Germany. As she reported, there were "everywhere homes for aged servants, homes for servants out of work, unions for providing servants with recreation, and schools and homes where they taught household employment.[68] Reformers shifted their sympathetic views about the working class, however, when it came to labor regulation in private homes. In their quest to solve the "servant problem," reformers resisted government intrusion in their own households, yet pushed for intervention into the private lives of working-class women who worked in their homes.[69] They pressed state governments to crack down on working-class women from dilapidated overcrowded tenements who allegedly brought social and health problems into middle-class homes. While loudly voicing their concerns to state governments, they also took matters into their own hands by establishing immigrant girls' homes and settlement homes to provide basic services for domestic workers while also instructing them on how to cook, clean, and shed any immoral habits. Southern Black migrant women were also accused of bringing moral decay into the urban city. As Hazel Carby explained, "The movement of black women between rural and urban areas and between southern and northern cities generated a series of moral panics. One serious consequence was that the behavior of black female migrants was characterized as sexually degenerate and, therefore, socially dangerous." [70]

In the late nineteenth century and first decade of the twentieth century, Irish immigrant women and southern Black women were targets of the medical community. Black women were blamed for spreading tuberculosis to their employers in the South and both Irish immigrant and southern Black migrant women were blamed for epidemics in the urban North.[71] Anxieties over race in domestic service were most loudly articulated in depictions of the "dangerous" Irish and Black classes who were accused of bringing diseases into white homes. The circle of blame for disease outbreaks in Philadelphia began with southern Black women. W.E.B. Du Bois sought to dispel these scientific myths in *The Philadelphia Negro,* based on the research he'd done for the study he was invited to conduct by Samuel McCune Lindsay at the University of Pennsylvania, referred to earlier in this chapter. The movement of southern Blacks into Philadelphia sparked anger from whites who accused the southern newcomers of compromising the moral fiber and health of the city. Professor Lindsay expected the research data to confirm whites' beliefs that the migrants were biologically prone to disease. Contrary to Lindsay's predictions, Du Bois considered the study a prime opportunity to disrupt scientific myths about race that were fueled by prevailing views on Social Darwinism. After conducting extensive interviews with Philadelphia-born and southern Blacks in Philadelphia, Du Bois concluded that Blacks were more susceptible to contracting diseases because they were relegated to overcrowded tenement houses due to discriminatory housing laws rather than due to any innate weakness or degeneracy. He shared details of the tenement buildings he visited:

> Many share the use of one bath-room with one or more other families. The bath-tubs usually are not supplied with hot water and very often have no water-connection at all . . . the bad sanitary results are shown in the death rates of the ward. . . . over 20 percent and possibly 30 per cent of the Negro families of this ward lack some of the very elementary accommodations necessary to health and decency . . . Here too there comes another consideration, and that is the lack of public urinals and water-closets in this ward and, in fact, throughout Philadelphia. The result is that the closets of tenements are used by the public.[72]

Du Bois's findings revealed that the North had not developed the infrastructure to accommodate southern migration and European immigration. After analyzing the data collected from Isabel Eaton's interviews with domestic service employers, Eaton and Du Bois concluded that Black women could not move out of tenement buildings because they could not afford better housing, thus disproving skewed scientific evidence that southern Blacks were inherently prone to disease. The spread of diseases in urban Philadelphia was a structural problem and not a matter of racial biology.

Irish immigrant servants were deemed the source of disease epidemics in New York City. Those who did not live in their employers' homes lived in overcrowded tenement homes in the poorest areas. In New York City, these neighborhoods included the First, Fifth, and Sixth wards where these women contracted chronic and terminal illnesses from dangerous and unsanitary living conditions. Prevailing scientific claims about Irish immigrant women and their close proximity to their employers amplified fears that Irish serving women were the cause of sickness in white American households.

The frenzy began with the infamous case of "Typhoid Mary." Mary Mallon was born in County Tyrone, Ireland, in 1869 and immigrated to the United States in 1883 when she was about fifteen years old.[73] She worked as a cook for several affluent employers when typhoid fever struck New York. In 1906, prosperous banker Charles Henry Warren hired Mallon as a cook in his summer rental home when typhoid fever had already struck six of the eleven people in his household. The owners of the house, Mr. and Mrs. George Thompson, hired civil engineer George Soper to investigate the outbreak and determine its source. Although contaminated water supplies were the actual source of the disease, Soper concluded from his findings that Mallon was responsible for the outbreak.[74] By that time, Mallon had already left the Warren home and was working as a cook for a family on Park Avenue. Soper tracked Mallon down and accused her of spreading typhoid fever to her employers through the food that she prepared. Mallon was transported to a hospital where doctors forced her to give them blood, stool, and urine samples. After testing the fluids, doctors concluded that she was in fact a carrier of typhoid bacilli, and she became known to the city as "Typhoid Mary."

Although Mallon was a carrier, doctors believed that she was infected and insisted that she cure the disease by undergoing an operation, which Mallon refused.[75] A New York City judge ordered her to spend three years in isolation on North Brother Island for refusing to comply with the doctors' orders. Mallon responded by filing a lawsuit against the city and its Health Department for $50,000 because the media attention severely curtailed her prospects of getting another job. She lost the case.[76] Before her release from North Brother Island, she had to vow that she would never work as a cook again. She tried working as a laundress, but it paid less than domestic service, so she decided to return to her original line of work. After New York City health inspectors discovered that she was working as a cook again, she was quarantined a second time on North Brother Island in 1915 and was later transported to Riverside Hospital where she remained until she died on November 11, 1938.[77]

To this day, "Typhoid Mary" is used to describe someone who either knowingly or unknowingly spreads illnesses and diseases. Although Mallon may have spread typhoid fever to the people for whom she worked, she was not the source of the outbreak. There were other carriers in the city, and the bacteria could have been contained had there been better health and sanitary regulations and resources to accommodate the city's large population.[78] For decades, newspapers featured numerous renditions of the story, some true and many others fabricated. Some reports, for example, indicated that Mallon had infected over sixty people who died because they encountered her.

Mallon was probably one among hundreds of asymptomatic, healthy typhoid bacilli carriers in the city. As Judith Walzer Leavitt explained, Mallon was targeted because of her "gender, class, marital status, and foreign birth" that left her with few options but to hire out her domestic services to wealthy New Yorkers."[79] In addition to Leavitt's argument, I argue that the racialization of Mallon's status is why she became the face of the typhoid epidemic. Since the famine era, employers had lamented that the domineering, dirty, untrustworthy, and thereby socially dangerous Irish Bridget had invaded their homes. Such descriptions of the Irish were grounded in race, and Irish immigrant women like Mallon were most susceptible to the consequences of these scientific racist beliefs because they worked in the homes of native-born whites. "Biddy" was a more immediate danger to American homes than the loud, drunken "Paddy" who did not work alongside, nor always live in the same neighborhoods, as WASP men. These depictions of Irish serving women persisted well into the early twentieth century and informed public opinion and medical studies about Mary Mallon.

Local government officials did not acknowledge until the 1970s that the infamous typhoid fever epidemic in New York City was caused by the city's lack of sanitation policies.[80] In response to the Mary Mallon story, several states passed laws requiring restaurant workers to be examined, but no serious efforts were made to pass laws regarding domestic workers until Black women dominated the ranks of domestic service in New York City in the 1930s.[81] Ironically, disparaging representations of Irish immigrant servants facilitated the process in which they could transition out of domestic service and become whiter women. Rebellious and repugnant acts of the Irish "Bridget" contributed to notions that Irish immigrant women were inherently incapable of working in domestic service or simply not willing to work as domestic servants. These depictions of defiant Irish immigrant women unwilling to adhere to social decorum and hierarchies contrasted with representations of southern Black women as submissive to their employers. Irish immigrant women were constructed as rebellious to social hierarchies whereas southern Black women accepted them as a natural part of life. As such, the volatile Irish Bridget supported the belief that Irish immigrant women were not in a permanent state of racial and gender inferiority and could eventually become productive U.S. citizens, unlike their Black counterparts.

Conclusion

Irish immigrant and southern Black women's movements to the U.S. North intensified the race and labor questions for women of the late nineteenth century. As Catholic immigrant women who performed racially stigmatized labor associated with slavery in a Protestant country, Irish women occupied the lowest stratum of the white race and were routinely depicted as nonwhite and masculine in late-nineteenth-century periodicals. They were also touted as contagions to the urban city, spreading disease, sexual immorality, and political disruption. Emancipation seemed good to northerners in theory until African Americans migrated in record numbers to northern cities in the latter half of the nineteenth century. While some employers welcomed what they thought would be cheap Black labor, others went into a frenzy declaring that the southern newcomers compromised the morals and health of the urban cities, and, more importantly, private homes.

Chapter 5, the next chapter of this book, examines the women behind the racialized servant tropes. Irish immigrant and African American women had their own perspectives about the race and labor question of their time. They worked at redefining the meanings of race, gender, and women's work to access better working conditions in the occupation while asserting their personhood and significance of their household labors to labor reform movements. Irish immigrant women demanded protection from exploitation in the home by making themselves whiter. They did so by borrowing from the cult of true womanhood and discourses developed by white reformers and white working-class labor organizers to argue that they were entitled to labor rights in the home because they were respectable white working-class ladies who had been subjected to "white slavery."

African American women had the larger task of redefining what it meant to be southern, migrant, and wage-earning Black women in northern cities hostile to Blacks, "foreigners," and southerners with a not-so-distant history of slavery. African American women kneaded together labor reform, women's suffrage, and racial equality movement discourses to declare that they were independent workers and U.S. citizens entitled to living wages, safe working and living conditions, and protection from corrupt employment agencies that preyed on southern Black migrant women.

5

Irish Immigrant Women
Whiten Themselves,
African American Women
Demand the Unseen

———————————————————◄o►

African American and Irish immigrant women molded race through their resistance to labor exploitation in domestic service. As non-WASP women in a racially stigmatizing occupation in a country that did not recognize domestic service as productive and respectable work, they asserted their own definitions of race and household work and argued that they deserved living wages and safer working conditions. These women inserted themselves into Progressive Era movements by kneading together discourses about racial equality, respectability, and industrial labor reform. Some of these discourses were borrowed, but they shaped them in their own distinct ways to address labor rights among working-class women in their particular racial communities.

In this chapter, I put into conversation the labors of resistance in which Irish immigrant and African American women engaged, sometimes from different social classes, to change working conditions in domestic service. I use the term "labors of resistance" to emphasize the actual work that it took for these women to redefine race in the process of challenging labor exploitation. I also define labors of resistance broadly to encompass any form of action that women took to address labor exploitation in domestic service, including writing and delivering speeches, letters and books, labor organizing, participating in strikes, creating settlement homes, and building educational institutions for wage-earning women. It is through this work, I argue, that Irish immigrant and African American women molded race.

Unlike Irish immigrant men who whitened themselves in violent opposition to Black male workers, Irish immigrant women rarely physically attacked African American women. They did make a point, however, of insisting that they deserved higher wages and safer working conditions than African Americans because they were white women subjected to "white slavery." "White slavery" was a discourse that reified the belief that African Americans were inherently inferior and did not deserve legal protections in the workplace like white workers. To situate themselves firmly within the parameters of respectability and white womanhood, Irish immigrant women also redefined what it meant to be a "lady." As historian Evelyn Higginbotham argued, race is a metalanguage, or a "powerful, all-encompassing effect on the construction and representation of other social and power relations, namely gender, class, and sexuality."[1] Although *white* was rarely placed in front of the word *lady*, the term *lady* had been reserved for non-wage-earning middle- and upper-class native-born white women since slavery. The inextricability of race and gender, combined with Irish serving women's roles as breadwinners in their families, meant that they had to redefine what it meant to be a lady in their struggle to be recognized as white American citizens and women workers who deserved better treatment in their places of employment. They asserted working-class Irish immigrant women as respectable workers by inserting themselves into a whitened Progressive Era discourse of "working ladyhood."[2]

African American women imagined, hoped, and fought for the Unseen.[3] They racialized and gendered Progressive Era labor reform discourse to address the specific labor exploitation of African American women in domestic service. They did this by inserting racial and gender equality, and uplifting goals and language into the Progressive discourse that only recognized the labors of white working-class men and women. Improving working conditions for southern migrant women also required African American women to disentangle perceptions about domestic service from the history of southern Black women's enslavement immortalized by Aunt Jemima, Civil War novels and rituals, racially segregated institutions, and laws that denied them American citizenship. Black women worked at severing the ties between domestic work and servitude by declaring the modern value of Black women's domestic labors and the significance of their household work to industrial capitalism. As such, Black women commanded a radical shift in racial and gender ideologies that had deemed them noncitizens and in a permanent state of racial and gender inferiority since slavery. Hence, African American women's late-nineteenth-century racial project of domestic service reform was twofold and lasted longer than that of Irish immigrant women.

Irish Domestic Workers Construct White Slaving Ladyhood

The vast majority of Irish immigrant women remained concentrated in domestic service in the latter half of the nineteenth century, while a smaller percentage worked alongside European immigrant women and native-born white working-class women in factories and mills. To address labor exploitation in domestic service, Irish domestic workers labored at constructing their own working-class identity that was distinct from that of men in their communities. They based their demands for better working conditions and pay on the claim that they were intelligent, hardworking *ladies* who deserved respectable wages and working conditions.

Irish immigrant men had achieved a white male working-class identity and contingency with significant political power by emancipation. As such, their demands for better pay and working conditions in the working-class male occupations in which they labored received more recognition from labor organizations and state governments than Irish immigrant women's demands for higher wages and safer working conditions in the feminized occupation of domestic service. Irish immigrant men had entered prominent leadership positions in the Democratic Party through Tammany Hall in New York City, the most influential Irish-controlled political machine in the late nineteenth century. Tammany Hall representatives waited at the docks with food and water for the ships that hailed from Ireland while encouraging the new male arrivals to vote for Democratic candidates. In exchange for the Irish male vote, the political machine supplied Irish neighborhoods with food, coal, and housing.[4]

Tammany Hall was responsible for getting Irish immigrant men hired into secure city jobs including factories, the police force, fire departments, and other city and federal government occupations. Irish men were hired into the police and fire departments more than other European immigrant men. Their entrance into the police department gave them the power to shape the way that racial and class boundaries were drawn and enforced "on the ground." Although policing and firefighting were and remain dangerous jobs, they offered Irish immigrant men and their families the benefits of secure employment and a pension, which were privileges and resources denied to most African American workers. Tammany Hall also distributed vital city contracts to Irish-owned businesses, which in turn hired Irish male workers. As historian Ed O'Donnell explained, ". . . Irish politicians rewarded Irish contractors, who in turn employed thousands of Irish workers of every rank and skill."[5]

The Democratic Party provided political backing for labor unions spearheaded by Irish male workers who demanded fair wages and safer working conditions. By the early twentieth century, over half of the 110-member unions of the American Federation of Labor (AFL) were led by men of Irish descent. Irish immigrant men were hired by Irish contractors to construct buildings, streets, mass transit systems, and sewer, water, and gas lines. Irish male work-ers were also instrumental in the construction of the IRT subway line and the Brooklyn Bridge in New York City; the Transcontinental Railroad and the Erie Canal; and the National Road, a highway that connected Pennsylvania and Ohio. Few labor organizations addressed labor exploitation in domestic service, although some Irish immigrant domestic workers had joined women's auxiliary groups in white labor unions.

Irish immigrant women took matters into their own hands to expose exploitation in domestic service. They wrote letters to their local newspapers exposing exploitative employers, especially those who had been unfair to their fellow Irish sisters. Irish servants used local newspapers to insert themselves into white respectability by taking to task both male and female employers who complained about Irish servants. The cult of true womanhood guided the social expectations of domestic service. Housewives, or ladies, were expected to evaluate and manage the labor of domestic servants. Irish servants placed housewives under a microscope and determined whether or not their actions truly measured up to what was expected of a lady. By positioning themselves as the judge of employers, servants inserted themselves into and expanded the definition of ladyhood to include themselves.

In 1897, an Irish immigrant woman submitted a letter to the *Brooklyn Eagle* under the penname "Brave Irish Girl" in response to a letter submitted by a white woman employer in an earlier edition of the newspaper. The employer, writing under the penname C.O.P., criticized Irish girls for being the laziest servants that she had ever employed. Brave Irish Girl responded by discredit-ing the employer's claim on the basis that she and other Irish servants were more ladylike than the employer could ever be, that is until she had been schooled by Irish women about managing a home. Turning upside down the ideology of domesticity that touted native-born white women as the managers of servants, Brave Irish Girl concluded that the employer could learn a thing or two from Irish serving women about housekeeping. She wrote:

> I pity the poor, innocent Irish girls who meet with such as 'C.O.P.' I don't consider her a lady. I guess 'C.O.P.'s' girl must have been starved when she too ate the bread. I hope she did not eat the soap. 'C.O.P' is more of a servant herself than the lady help that worked for her. I guess 'C.O.P.' is one of those ladies who pay $5 a month and expects everything done first class . . . I have lived with a lady who always stole my shoe blacking to polish her shoes with. She would not give me a cake of soap in my room. She said she could not afford it . . . You can see how deceitful she was. So many of the ladies are. —A Brave Irish Girl[6]

Brave Irish Girl inserted the domestic worker that C.O.P. lamented about, and other Irish serving women, into her own discourse of white working-class female gentility by referring to her fellow Irish sister as the "lady help." Native-born white employers used the term "help" to describe the native-born white servants who primarily worked in neighbors' homes and on farms throughout the northeast prior to the famine-era Irish immigration.[7] Employers also used the term "help" after the mid-nineteenth century to refer to native-born household workers to distinguish them from immigrant and African American household workers who were often referred to by the least respected title of "servant." Brave Irish Girl made it abundantly clear that the domestic worker in question was white by inserting "lady" in front of "help." Lady was a term reserved for native-born white middle-class and elite housewives.

Brave Irish Girl's definition of white femininity also asserted that the title of lady had to be earned and thereby worked for. Women were not simply ladies by virtue of being native-born white American housewives. Ladies were hardworking, wage-earning, and honest women who treated other women with respect and dignity.[8] Hence, employers who did not treat servants with respect were more servants themselves than ladies. Describing an ex-employer who reminded her of C.O.P., Irish Brave Girl continued, " She [the employer] wanted me to wear a cap and collars and cuffs in the kitchen, but I told her it would be more becoming to herself, for she was more suitable for the kitchen than I was."[9] Brave Irish Girl's letter's hit at the heart of ladyhood as evidenced by C.O.P.'s response to the letter. C.O.P. wrote that Brave Irish Girl "should beg her pardon, as she has made a very grave mistake." She was a "very liberal provider" and her husband made enough money to pay the two domestic workers in their home $10–$12 a week. The servants were "faithful girls that would do anything that she would ask of them," and former servants "would like to live with her again, had they not homes of their own."[10] C.O.P.'s response was embedded in what was expected of her as a respectable white housewife. She reasserted her whiteness by referring to servants as "girls" while also explaining that she was an excellent manager of servants as evidenced by the fact that most "girls" wanted to continue working with her. According to C.O.P., she was also married to a man who could easily afford to pay domestic workers competitive wages.

C.O.P. was not the only Irish immigrant woman to air her frustrations with employers in the *Eagle*. A servant writing under the penname "Plucky Irish Girl" submitted a letter in response to a housewife who complained to readers about Irish servants. According to Plucky Irish Girl, a good housekeeper, or lady, knew exactly how to teach servants the necessary skills for domestic service. Hence, the housewife must have been at fault because she had failed to properly train the Irish newcomer in housekeeping. As the outspoken Irish author declared, it was thereby "disgusting for her [the employer] to say that she was a housekeeper." Plucky Irish Girl predicted that the employer had difficulties with the servants she hired because she was not willing to do the work that it took to manage the home. The Irish servant believed that good housewives were committed to maintaining order and cleanliness in the home, which meant that they worked just as hard as servants. Disorder in the home was thereby a reflection of the employer's poor work ethic. As Plucky Irish Girl predicted, ". . . she must have gotten a bicycle and bloomers to keep her busy instead of teaching a girl what to do . . . the very best remedy I can give to housekeepers is to pawn the bicycle, take off the bloomers, and go to a cooking school."[11]

Plucky Irish Girl also called into question the middle-class respectability of the employer. She accused middle-class employers of "getting so poor that they send their girls away and then say that they went of their own accord." The opinionated Irish letter writer also took the employer to task for stepping across gender boundaries by criticizing her for riding a bike and wearing bloomers rather than learning how to cook. Plucky Irish Girl also criticized the employer for mentioning that her husband complained about the servant. The author noted that housewives maintained proper gender boundaries in the home such that they kept their husbands out of housekeeping affairs. If the housewife failed to establish that important boundary, then she had failed at not only managing the home, but also choosing a proper husband. As the author put it, "If your husband goes into the kitchen looking after the cooking he can't be worth much . . ." She concluded her letter by defending the character of Irish servants as being superior not only to native-born white women employers, but also to European immigrant women whose whiteness had never been called into question. Plucky Irish Girl asserted, "Irish girls are thorough, honest, splendid workers, and nothing would comfort me more than to have these upstarts [housewives] depending on Swedes or Germans . . ."[12]

Other servants expanded the definition of white female respectability by challenging male employers and questioning their masculinity. Traditional ideologies of domesticity set the expectation that men were the breadwinners who left the domestic affairs to their wives to manage. The Irish letter writers proclaimed that men who complained about Irish servants were not in their natural place, which was the public sphere. Some Irish servants believed that if the husband of the house interfered in household management, then the lady of the home was responsible for telling him that he should refrain from instructing servants on how to clean and cook. The "brave" and "plucky" Irish women breadwinners assumed the lady's role in instructing the male employers who publicized their frustrations with Irish servants.

A male employer writing under the penname "J.S.G." sparked many reactions from Irish servants in the *Brooklyn Eagle*. J.S.G. asserted that Irish immigrant women were "dirty, impudent, careless, wasteful, and incompetent." He claimed not to have any shame in describing Irish women as such because he was an Irish man.[13] "Miss M.," an Irish servant, wrote to J.S.G. that he was a coward, and if he had any spunk left in him he would make his name and address public so that she could "have a talk with such an amiable gentleman." She announced that had she been a servant in his home, she would "season his soup with something better than pepper and salt" because she was "one of the Irish evils."[14] Another servant, "Irish Rambler," warned J.S.G. that if anyone "hits the Irish wrongfully," then you will "get hit rightfully." She challenged J.S.G.'s claims by asserting that Irish serving women were "bright, clean, willing, generous, and God loving people." She instructed the readers of the *Brooklyn Eagle* to discredit J.S.G.'s views on the basis that he was not a man who knew his proper place. Irish Rambler asserted that J.S.G. was "feigning gentility" and was in "great need of a rest from being queen of the kitchen."

To drive home her point, Irish Rambler employed the "white slavery" metaphor to frame J.S.G. as an exploitative employer. She concluded that if employers like J.S.G. continued paying low wages to Irish immigrant servants, "then we will have what Abe Lincoln never thought of—white slavery. It is very near that now." [15] "D.M.B.," another Irish servant, also employed "white slavery" to describe J.S.G. as a bad employer and explain why Irish immigrant women were better than other racial and ethnic groups of women in domestic service. D.M.B. asserted that Irish servants were white and ladies, and therefore refused to do masculine work and work that resembled [read: Black] slave labor. She continued, "'J.S.G.' says his girl has the liberty of the house and she lives on the best that money can buy. Let the lady treat the girl right and she will be rewarded for it. I have lived and am living with a family that would not have any other help but Irish. Certainly the Irish will not do such slavish work as others may do, and they are not to do a man's work."[16]

D.M.B. marked her racial superiority to African American domestic workers by referencing "slavish work," which was inherently racialized as Black work. By employing the "white slavery" discourse, she also drew from mid nineteenth-century racist scientific claims about racial and gender hierarchies. "White slavery" was a discourse rooted in the mid-nineteenth century discourse of "wage slavery." As Andrew T. Urban explained, proslavery commentators reaffirmed the status of free white laborers by using "wage slavery" to compare "the treatment of Irish servants to that of black slaves" to argue that the enslavement of Blacks "was a more 'natural' way of organizing the social relations of production that reflected innate and permanent differences in status."[17] D.M.B's distancing of Irish women from "slavish work" in a women's occupation marked them as white and feminine who were naturally deserving of better working conditions because they were white women.

Servants' construction of Irish working ladyhood also had roots in the transnational Irish struggle for independence from Great Britain. D.M.B.'s insistence that Irish servants were respectable workers who were equal, if not superior to their women employers echoed activist sentiments expressed in Irish nationalist periodicals. Such periodicals often boasted about the inherent

"Celtic nature" of the Irish to counteract British and WASP portrayals of the Irish as an inferior race. As an author for *An Gaodhal: A Monthly Journal Devoted to the Preservation and Cultivation of the Irish Language and the Autonomy of the Irish Nation* noted, "The maid who cooks and washes is as honorably employed as her mistress, who serves the public from behind the counter of some of our larger stores . . . We have known young women doing general housework in this city, whose ancestors were of the most respectable families in the old country. Does the nature of their employment detract from that respectability? Certainly not . . . True dignity is inherent in the Celtic nature, and all that is required to make it visible is a little polish."[18]

The Irish Rambler and D.M.B. also borrowed from the Progressive Era labor reform discourse of white slavery to make visible the dignity of Irish women's personhood and labors. The term white slavery was ubiquitous by the late nineteenth century and domestic servants like the Irish Rambler and D.M.B. could easily find references to it in popular labor organization magazines and newspapers. By evoking white slavery to explain the treatment of Irish immigrant women in domestic service, they inserted their Irish sisters into Progressive reformers' national outcry to protect white working-class women and girls from labor exploitation. Reformers rarely addressed the exploitation of domestic workers. They focused on the concerns of women factory workers because factory and millwork was at least recognized by the government as an industrial trade—or "real" work—whereas domestic service remained a labor niche that the government was not motivated to regulate for fear of invading the privacy of white middle- and upper-class men's homes. Domestic workers, however, saw themselves as part of the reform movement and latched onto it believing that it could be beneficial to them as well. Some Irish household workers went beyond writing letters to local periodicals and created domestic servant assemblies that organized collectively with women factory and mill workers against "white slavery."[19] Like factory and mill workers, servants wanted to be legally recognized as respectable working ladies who deserved livable wages and safer working conditions. Irish immigrant servants' insertion of their concerns into the larger labor reform movement eventually emerged into a transnational organizing strategy. Irish domestics in Ireland established a domestic workers union, although short-lived, within the Irish Women Workers' Union in 1909 as part of the larger women's labor reform movement in Ireland.[20] The union was formed by women laborers who had been excluded from the male dominated Dublin's trade union movement. The inclusivity of the union was reflected in its declaration that it welcomed women "whatever you are or wherever you work."[21]

Irish serving women in the United States were not wrong in their prediction that the labor and social reform movement would better their working conditions, although their particular concerns were rarely addressed in the movement. Irish women labor organizers, researchers, and institutions would buttress the goals of Irish servants by advancing the whitening of all Irish working-class women.

Labor Reformers and Whitening Working-Class Irish Women

Irish immigrant women became whiter and could transition out of domestic service by the early twentieth century because they reaped the benefits of Irish institutions and women organizers' participation in the national movement to protect white working-class women from labor and sexual exploitation. The United States economy expanded at a rapid rate in the latter half of the nineteenth century. Coal and steel production significantly increased, and the railroad system stretched across the country. Within thirty years, the United States had become a world economic leader. However, only elite white Protestant men reaped the financial benefits of this economic growth, leaving the working classes to bear the burden of rapid and dangerous production for little pay. Men who ironed clothing in garment factories earned $9–$10 a week, while women in the same occupation earned $7 a week. These low wages were not enough for a family to survive without all members in the household working. Children joined the workforce and became the most exploited workers in factories, receiving as little as $2 per week.[22] The white working classes began using references to slavery during the Gilded Age to mobilize support for ending labor exploitation in the industrial trades and demand legal protection in the workplace on the basis that they were white citizens. As historian Alex Gourevitch explained, ". . . if slavery [was] being subjected to the will of masters, then the category of 'slaves' [had] potentially enormous scope."[23] The manual laborers expressed that now that chattel slavery had been abolished, the time was ripe to remove the shackles from the white workers who toiled in dangerous industrial jobs and barely earned enough to support themselves, much less their loved ones.

By the 1880s, white women labor organizers expanded the concept of white slavery to include wage-earning European immigrant and native-born white women in factories and mills. While northern cities had gone into a moral panic over fears of southern African American women who were framed as incapable of shedding their immoral and unclean habits, there was a national push to restore the innate virtue and purity of white native-born and European immigrant women who had fallen prey to prostitution and unscrupulous employers. As evidenced by the archetype Bridget, all native-born whites were not convinced that Irish immigrant women were capable of reform. Irish American and Irish immigrant women labor organizers and writers, some of whom were active in Ireland's struggle for independence from Britain, were prominent leaders in the movement to protect white working-class women.

These Irish-descended activists deliberately inserted their fellow Irish sisters into the movement to end white slavery by foregrounding the labor exploitation of specifically Irish women.

Undercover investigator Helen Cusack-Cavarlho, writing under the name Nell Nelson, urged the country to rally behind working-class white women to end white slavery in "City Slave Girls," a series of editorial articles published by the *Chicago Times*. Nelson, whose birth name Cusack suggests Irish ancestry, exposed the poor working conditions of working-class women in Chicago to the American public in her newspaper series. Her first article featured the story of Martha Rafferty, an eighteen-year-old girl of Irish descent who had been cheated out of six months' pay by an employment agency that hired her to crochet mats.[24] Nelson also chronicled the experiences of other European immigrant women in her series, thereby consolidating the ethnic differences between the workers under the banner of white slavery. As Lara Vapnek explained, "In affirming the difference between white and Black working women 'City Slave Girls' rhetorically erased the differences in ethnicity that divided the city's industrial labor force . . . By referring to immigrants from Ireland, Germany, Sweden, Poland, and Russia and their American-born daughters as 'slave girls' and depicting them as victims with whom the public should sympathize, the series 'whitened' and Americanized an alien workforce."[25] Nelson also established European immigrant women as white workers in dire need of sympathy from and action on behalf of the nation. She did so by referring to all European immigrant women in her writings as white slaves and omitting stories about African American women in her crusade to end the labor exploitation of women factory workers.

Carroll D. Wright, an attorney, state senator, and colonel in the Union Army, helped popularize the term "working girls" for white women in his 1884 state-sponsored investigation of female industrial workers, "The Working Girls of Boston." His report set racial standards for federal interventions into the work of wage-earning women. His exclusion of African American women and domestic workers from his national study clearly prioritized concern for working-class white women in the industrial trades. While his omission of domestic service marginalized the significant percentage of Irish immigrant women in the occupation, Wright made little mention of ethnic differences between the European immigrant and native-born white women workers in the industrial trades.[26] In effect, the female industrial workers in his study (including Irish immigrant female factory workers) were white women. Hence, the term "working girls" had a racial undercurrent that referred primarily to native-born and all European immigrant working-class white women.

Women labor organizers, many of Irish descent, whitened themselves while establishing political alliances with native-born white women to organize against factory and mill owners who exploited women workers. Undoubtedly, white women labor organizers united across their distinct ethnic identities under the banner of protecting European immigrant women from white slavery. As historian Annelise Orleck explained, working-class women activists identified class and gender, not ethnicity or religion, as the primary sources of their oppression.[27] They collectively asserted that the government and factory owners should enact labor regulations to protect white working-class women in the workplace.

In the remainder of this section, I argue that influential Irish-descended labor organizers such as Leonora Barry and Leonora O'Reilly advanced the particular whitening of all working-class women of Irish descent. While these Irish agitators committed most of their energies to addressing the struggles of white immigrant women on the factory and mill floors, they were among the most vocal and influential leaders of the labor reform movement who pushed for the inclusion of Irish women newcomers into the Progressive Era agenda of abolishing "slavery" for white women. O'Reilly and Barry, with the backing of the Knights of Labor and elite native white women allies, had the resources to speak to a wider audience about respectable Irish working ladyhood than Irish servants who published letters in local newspapers.

While Barry is mostly remembered as among the first female labor organizers in the United States, she is less known for expanding whiteness and femininity to include working-class Irish women. She was born Leonora Marie in County Cork, Ireland, in 1849 and emigrated to upstate New York during the potato famine in 1851 with her parents, John and Honor Brown Kearney. Barry became active in the Knights of Labor's Victory Assembly after experiencing firsthand the low wages and dangerous working conditions of mill workers when she had few options but to work at a hosiery mill to support her two sons after her husband, William E. Barry, died from work-related lung disease.[28]

Barry ascended to a leadership position in the labor organization and was thereby influential in inserting Irish immigrant women workers into the white labor reform movement. The Holy Order of the Knights of Labor was founded by a small group of garment workers in Philadelphia whose mission was to "organize and direct the masses." It was the first major labor organization that mobilized black and white—both women and men—skilled and unskilled workers.[29] Terence Powderly, general master workman of the Knights of Labor, appointed Barry as head of the Department of Women's Work in 1886. Her primary charge as head of the department was to investigate the abuse of child and women workers in factories and mills across the country.[30] While she traveled to the South to support African American domestic laundresses in Florida who had already begun organizing their own local assemblies, Barry's most ardent desire was to solve the challenges that working-class native-born and immigrant white women faced in mills and factories. She documented their experiences from Philadelphia, Pennsylvania; Detroit, Michigan; Baltimore, Maryland; to Bellaire, Ohio, as evidence of slavery. As she explained in an 1887 report, "The abuse, injustice and suffering which the women of this industry endure from the tyranny, cruelty and slave-driving propensities of the employers is something terrible to be allowed existence in free America." [31]

While investigating the struggles of native-born and immigrant white women workers, Barry made a concerted effort to insert Irish women in the United States and Ireland into the Knights of Labor's movement to end white slavery. Barry saw Michael Davitt's meeting with Knights of Labor leaders in New York as a critical opportunity to denounce the slave-like working conditions of Irish women workers in Ireland and the United States. She asked the labor organizer and founder of the Irish National Land League at the meeting to tell women workers in Belfast, Ireland, that she, along with their fellow Irish sisters in the United States, stood with them in solidarity to end labor exploitation in British-owned factories. More specifically, she told Davitt, "The women of this country wish you to carry to their oppressed sisters across the sea who are noted the world over for their unwavering and spotless purity and honor our well wishes and sympathy. The women of Ireland deserve it. They need it. There are women working for mere pittance in the factories of tyrants; they are bound by chains of oppression. Say to them that we would aid them, that we would like to see the chains that bind them fall from their forms with a crash that would startle the whole world into sympathy with them." Barry also asserted that Irish women on both sides of the Atlantic needed to work together because their fates were connected. As she expressed to Davitt, "the same tyrants that own the mills of Belfast" used the "workingwomen of Ireland to break the backs of their sisters in America." [32] Barry did not end there. She also urged the men of the KOL to "turn their attention to the poor downtrodden white slave, as represented by the women wage-workers of this country [the United States]" and to assist with the "abolition of poverty" among women workers. [33]

Barry's gender politics posed a serious challenge to the patriarchal beliefs that male KOL leaders had about women's workers. While KOL leaders supported women's suffrage and equal pay for equal work, they also believed that women's natural and rightful place was in the home. It was only the evil force of capitalism that forced women to work outside of the home and engage with the politics of industrial labor. [34] The male constituency of the KOL tried to eliminate the women's department of the KOL shortly after Barry made this bold declaration. Terence Powderly, once her staunchest supporter in the organization, fell in line with the majority of men in the KOL and withdrew his support of her position. With the cards stacked against her, Barry announced her resignation in 1890. She continued organizing on behalf of working-class white women until her death in 1930.

Leonora O'Reilly's tenure at the organization overlapped with that of Barry and, like her, she too became frustrated with the male unionists in the organization and their chauvinist attitudes towards women workers. Born on February 16, 1870, to famine-era Irish immigrants Winifred Rooney, a garment worker and domestic servant, and John O'Reilly, a printer, Leonora O'Reilly was no stranger to working women's struggles. O'Reilly was inspired to join a local assembly of the KOL in New York City at sixteen years old after experiencing firsthand horrible working conditions as a shirtwaist factory worker. After leaving the KOL, O'Reilly joined and co-founded cross-class women's labor organizations committed to improving the working conditions of native-born and immigrant white working-class women.

While active in the organizations, she worked at leveling the social hierarchies between the working-class European immigrant women and native born white women in the organizations, which in turn helped whiten immigrant women. O'Reilly openly denounced the white nativist views of the upper class white women patrons of the WTUL who advocated for addressing the particular labor concerns of native-born white women before those of European immigrant women. Her frustrations with the nativist members led her to resign from the WTUL temporarily in 1905 and permanently in 1915.[35]

While critical of white nativist views, O'Reilly whitened and Americanized her Irish sisters who worked in factories by distinguishing them from recent immigrant women factory workers from southern and eastern Europe and aligned them with groups of unquestionably white women. O'Reilly proclaimed in her 1899 speech, "The Conditions, Limitations, and Possibilities of the Working Woman Today," in Philadelphia, that the recent European immigrant arrivals drove down the wages of native-born white, Irish, and German women who had been working for decades in factories before massive immigration from southern and eastern Europe in the late nineteenth century. She proclaimed, "These girls have no idea of the proper reward of labor and a small sum will naturally seem like a fabulous wage. As to the work done in sweat shops . . . It is done largely by foreigners—Russian, Jews, Poles, Hungarians, and Italians . . . Their ignorance is taken advantage of to supply our market with cheap goods . . . Russians and Jews come over here and take the place of the Irish and German girls in the shirt factory working harder and longer."[36]

O'Reilly also advocated specifically for the abolition of white slavery in trades in which Irish immigrant women were heavily concentrated. After finishing her studies at the Pratt Institute, O'Reilly attempted to elevate the sewing trade, which was considered "second to domestic service" and primarily employed Irish immigrant women.[37] In the 1880s, Irish immigrant women and their daughters took over the sewing trades, an occupation previously dominated by native-born white Protestant women. In 1865, only 19 percent of collar sewers were born in Ireland, but by 1880, 56 percent of sewers were either

Irish-born or the daughters of Irish immigrants.[38] Seamstresses were usually paid for piece work that they made either in mass producing warehouses or in their own homes. Seamstresses often worked eleven hours a day in buildings, whether residential or commercial, without proper ventilation, clean water, heat, and toilet facilities while earning an average of only $2 to $6 a week.[39]

O'Reilly attempted to elevate the sewing trade in her master's thesis by demonstrating to her readers that sewing was a form of art, and seamstresses were thereby intelligent, hardworking, skilled laborers guided by a core set of moral principles—all of which were the attributes of respectable white working ladies as outlined by white women reformers. As O'Reilly declared, "Sewing has a right to a place in the public school curriculum not only as a branch of manual training but as a useful art" because sewing was a "state of being in which the body and soul are united." [40] She also wrote that seamstresses were "better than others morally because the law of life is the law of labor. They obey that law and don't get into mischief. Vice is only another name for idleness . . . Our heads work together with our hands as we labor and we have become thinkers in spite of ourselves. As we are being taught through our fingers, our fingers are teaching our hands."[41]

While the Irish agitator mostly addressed the working conditions of white women factory workers and seamstresses during her tenure as a labor organizer, she also addressed women's labor struggles in an occupation that was closely associated with her Irish sisters by advocating for the federal regulation of private household work. She explained to an audience in 1907, "We think our civilization is near its meridian, but we are yet only at the cock-crowing and the morning star. The end of political struggle is to establish morality as the basis of all legislation . . . the reform that applies itself to the household must not be partial. It must correct the whole system of our social living. It must come with plain living and high thinking. It must break up caste and put domestic service on another foundation."[42]

Although O'Reilly passed away at the young age of 57 from heart disease, her activism played an influential role in advancing the labor concerns of all working-class Irish immigrant women. By the time of her death, Irish immigrant women and their daughters were whiter and had access to a wider range of employment opportunities than what was available to them from the mid- to late nineteenth century.

Whitening Irish Immigrant Women through Moral Reform

White women reformers also cultivated sympathy for European immigrant women sex workers. These reformers insisted that native-born and immigrant white women were victims of men who preyed on their innocence and poverty. They also made the argument that sex workers could return to their innate innocence, if sex trafficking were abolished. Asserting the moral sanctity of white women was a stark contrast to the prevailing belief that southern African American migrant women were a threat to the moral sanctity of northern cities regardless of whether or not they were actually laboring as sex workers. As writer Gloria Wade Gayles explained, "According to nineteenth century racist definitions, Black women were inferior members of the sex whom God himself had colored a distasteful hue and imbued with insatiable sexuality, phenomenal strength and limited intelligence."[43] Omitting African American women from their cause, white women social reformers declared that it was essential for the nation to mobilize resources to protect white women from sexual exploitation and forgive them for any immoral sexual acts that they committed.

As Clifford Griffith Roe and B.S. Steadwell explained in *The Great War on Slavery,* reformers were aggressive in their campaign to eradicate white slavery because they deemed it necessary to "protect the purity and sanctity of the home" and to "open the door of forgiveness to the prodigal daughter" in hopes that "the truth may be known throughout the world concerning the traffic in girls and women."[44] To eradicate white slavery, Progressive reformers warned wage-earning women not to "taste the pleasures of the public sphere," i.e., engage in prostitution. They also worked on the legislative front to protect working-class women by pushing for laws to raise the age of sexual consent from eighteen to twenty-one. Other reformers argued that labor reform was integral to protecting white women from sex trafficking. They advocated for a minimum wage law to increase the factory wages of white women to dissuade them from entering sex work.[45] Although some native-born middle-class and elite whites remained skeptical and unmoved by pleas to help the poor and working-class female victims of white sexual slavery, there was broad enough sentiment to capture the attention of influential politicians, lawyers, and religious institutions, and their support gave some credence to the cause. As Clifford Roe noted, "Educators are beginning to realize its vital importance as they never have before. Lawyers, doctors, business men and women are engrossed with it. The churches have cast aside the cloak of over scrupulous delicacy, and modesty, and are gradually assuming their responsibility."[46]

Catholic institutions helped bolster the white sanctity of Irish immigrant women by inserting them into the moral reform agenda of the Progressive Era. They boldly declared that it was their mission to protect the poor, young, and innocent Irish girls from the dangers of urban living as evidenced in the name of a church-sponsored temporary lodging place for new arrivals called The Mission of Our Lady of the Rosary for the Protection of Irish Immigrant Girls. Father John J. Riordan first opened the mission's doors in 1886 to Irish women who arrived at Castle Garden, the first official immigration center in the United States.[47] The mission was created in response to the earlier investigations of Charlotte O'Brien into the conditions that Irish women endured during their passage to the United States and their living conditions when they arrived. O'Brien convinced priests that a Catholic institution was needed to protect the daughters of Erin after she presented her findings on the many dangers that Irish women encountered during and after their voyage to New York City. The mission was highly visible to Irish women once they arrived in the city. A priest from the mission welcomed Irish immigrant women at the docks and offered them assistance with securing employment and a place to stay until they located family or friends, found their own housing, or left for another destination.[48]

Echoing the sentiments of domestic workers expressed in local newspapers, priests at the Lady of Our Rosary regarded Irish immigrant women in domestic service as honorable and respectable workers. The priests boasted that the mission was a worthy and important institution because it protected Irish immigrant women who had a long history of doing noble work in American homes. As Reverend Michael Henry of the mission wrote in 1900: "The Irish girls have had much to do with the building up of our great cities . . . As the honest, faithful and trustworthy helpmate in our homes for the last two generations she has had no equal."[49] The mission's support was part of the city's broad-based effort to end the exploitation of white women in general and western European immigrant women, like the Irish, in particular. As Andy T. Urban argues, the State government helped create a "commonsense policy" that Irish immigrant women, while viewed as dependents and undeserving of free movement as women, deserved regulation and protection."[50] By 1867, New York State had authorized Irish and German societies to offer services to newly arrived Irish and German women at Castle Garden, such as assistance with meals, money for travel, and finding jobs. While these assistance programs policed Irish immigrant women's movements in the city and the decisions they made about employment, the programs were supported by politically and economically influential white elites and were thereby significant in creating the discourse that Irish immigrant women could eventually assimilate into U.S. (read: white) society with patriarchal guidance from the State.

By the early twentieth century, churches, labor organizers, investigators, and immigrant societies had convinced the federal government that white women needed legal and moral protection from sex trafficking. In 1910, the federal government passed the Mann Act, which criminalized prostitution and sex trafficking across state lines. Dubbed the White Slave Traffic Act, the Mann Act was a response to a moral panic that emerged from the sentiment that white women needed protection. The Act was drafted with the premise that nativeborn and immigrant white women were inherently sexually chaste whereas Black women and men were never afforded the same consideration. While the Act censored the decisions that both Black and white women made about their bodies and made it harder for poor women with few employment options to engage in sex work to support themselves and their families, it also buttressed the racial privileges of white women, as it was frequently used to criminalize African American men who engaged in consensual sex with white women.[51]

While reformers and Irish domestic workers were building a national movement to protect Irish immigrant women from labor and sexual exploitation, African American women were, in the words of historian Deborah Gray White, engaged in nation-making, or stepping "forth to mold and direct the thought of their age" through organized labor resistance and community building.[52] Unlike Irish serving women and labor organizers who organized under the banner of white slavery, African American women, who were once enslaved, had to demand that the country recognize them as wage workers in their fight for better working conditions and higher wages in domestic service. Irish immigrant women shed their reputations of being inferior to WASPs by inserting themselves into white ladyhood and actually organizing with native born white women. Denied membership in the most influential labor unions and women's labor organization in northern cities because of their race and gender, Black women had the much larger task of redefining what it meant to be southern, migrant, and wage-earning Black women in a nation where Black women were defined as the very antithesis to ladyhood and American citizenship. Unlike Irish immigrant women, there was no national campaign to protect Black migrant women from the dangers of northern urban cities. Black women also labored in a region where whites were ambivalent about the South and where whites (both native-born and immigrant) were just as hostile to Blacks as white southerners.

"We Need a Bucket Brigade All Over This City": Black Women Assert the Urgency of Labor Reform for Black Women

African American migrant women faced prejudice, racial and gender violence, and poverty when they reached northeastern cities. They were also relegated to the lowest-wage unskilled labors and concentrated in the poorest residential sections of all urban cities. Domestic service employers rarely hired African American and European immigrant domestic workers to work in the same homes because of white attacks on Black workers, and they often preferred "foreign" white servants for higher wage domestic service positions over Black women. Poor living conditions and unstable low-wage employment resulted in death for many African American migrants. As Anna J. Cooper noted in her essay "What Are We Worth?," the 1880 census documented that the African American mortality rate was higher than that of whites in all sections of the country. The difference in the mortality rate among African American and white children was, as Cooper described it, "alarming." In Washington,

D.C., alone, for example, the mortality rate of African American children was double that of white children in 1899, although "the white population of the District outnumbered the colored two to one."[53]

African American migrant clubwomen and domestic workers found optimism for their future amid these glaring inequalities in the cities where they settled. They brought to northeastern cities their own recent histories of labor organizing in the South. Black laundresses in Florida had formed local assemblies to protest low wages across the state and laundresses organized against exploitative employers across state lines in the cities of Atlanta, Georgia; Galveston, Texas; and Jackson, Mississippi.[54] It would take until the 1920s and 30s when the overall population of Black women, and in particular domestic service, had increased significantly in northern cities when they developed their own labor movement to address the struggles of Black women in domestic service. Until then, southern Black women inserted themselves into the labor reform movements of the late nineteenth century through individual acts of resistance, institution building, community work, and scholarship. They demanded that the country see Black women in a way that they had never been recognized before. Black women across social class argued that migrant household workers deserved better working conditions and pay because they were citizens of the United States and their labors were critical to the national and global economies.

Unprotected by the racial privileges afforded to Irish immigrant women, African American domestic workers rarely aired their complaints in local newspapers. Openly challenging white employers, even in the North, could result in lynching, sexual assault, and other forms of violence. Instead, they engaged in less public acts of resistance by negotiating with employers for livable wages and refusing to work for employers who did not meet their demands. They also insisted on an end to their work day and left their places of employment when employers arbitrarily changed their work hours and assignments. Some domestic workers demanded assistance from the local courts to prosecute employers who subjected them to slave-like conditions, and sometimes the courts worked in the southerners' favor. Lavinia Pinckney, a Black woman from Savannah, Georgia, won her lawsuit against the Halligan family in the New York City case *Pinckney vs. Halligan* in 1877. Mr. and Mrs. Halligan met Pinckney during their trip to Savannah in search of cheap domestic labor. They promised her a live-in position with wages. Pinckney moved into their New York City home and left shortly afterwards when it became clear that she would not receive pay for her work. With the help of her brother Edward Pinckney, a medical student in Boston, she took the Halligans to court.[55] While the Halligans testified that Lavinia was "not worth more than her board and clothes, and that the agreement was that she would have no more than that," the jury ruled in Pinckney's favor and awarded her $300 in compensation.[56]

Some migrant women relied on the courts for protection because there were few other places for them to turn. They had been ignored by white social reformers who established several settlement homes across northern cities to help women newcomers from Europe. These institutions excluded African American women due to the prevailing belief that European immigrant women would not seek aid from homes that served African American women.[57] African American clubwomen inserted domestic workers' concerns into the reform movement by building their own settlement homes for the new southern arrivals. Settlement homes, clubwomen believed, were critical for the survival of their southern sisters in northern cities where their needs were ignored by local governments and labor organizations. African American clubwomen's settlement homes offered a range of resources to migrants, including clothing, food, shelter, employment assistance services, literary courses, domestic service training courses, and maternal health courses that provided information about how to best sanitize their homes in the overcrowded city.

Victoria Earle Matthews and Anna Julia Cooper were among the most outspoken clubwomen about the labor struggles of southern migrant domestic workers. I argue that they were more critical of systemic racial, gender, and class inequalities that impacted Black women's migrations and labor experiences than some of their late nineteenth century Black and white contemporaries. Cooper and Matthews' complex middle-class status and shared commitment to improving the lives of southern Black women in household employment begs a deeper and comparative investigation of their community work in relation to each other and to domestic service.

Unlike some clergymen, male civil rights leaders, and fellow clubwomen, Cooper and Matthews did not attribute Black women's concentration in poor neighborhoods and low-wage work to a lack of strong work ethics, sexual restraint, and knowledge of proper hygiene and cleaning methods. Cooper and Matthews were clear that migrants' futures depended on disentangling domestic service from the history of slavery. Through their scholarship, speeches, and institution-building, they asserted the urgency of transforming the working conditions of Black women into national labor and social reform discourses. They argued that migrants were now wage workers whose domestic service labors were critical to the United States, and global economies and were vulnerable to unscrupulous employment agencies that preyed on "green" southern women. Matthews's approach to labor reform had nationalist leanings, whereas Cooper's approach was nativist. Matthews believed that Black-centered education was vital to "uplifting" working-class Black women at the White Rose Mission Home, and Cooper argued that improving Black women's working conditions required the country to recognize that their struggles were more important than those of European immigrants because Black women were American citizens.

Across their distinct approaches, Cooper's and Matthews' keen awareness of southern Black women's labor and migration experiences, and their knowledge of the inequalities between wage-earning Black women and white women, ignited their passion to address the domestic service problem for Black women in northern cities.

Victoria Earle Matthews

In the late spring of 1898, Miss Hattie Morehouse, a white woman who taught at the Baylan Home in Jacksonville, Florida, knew the right person to contact to ensure the safe arrival of her student who was traveling to New York City in search of a domestic service job. Morehouse sent a letter to clubwoman Victoria Earle Matthews, co-founder of the White Rose Home for Colored Working Girls and White Rose Mission and Industrial Association, asking her to look out for a Black girl from Florida scheduled to arrive at the Old Dominion Steamship Company line at Pier 26 in New York City in a few days. Morehouse informed Matthews that the girl planned to wear a red ribbon in her shirt buttonhole so that she would be easily recognizable among the crowd of other Black women from the South who would also land at the pier. As a southern Black migrant herself, Matthews was already deeply committed to keeping other southern migrant women out of the claws of exploitative employment agents waiting at the dock to lure them into prostitution and unpaid domestic service positions. Matthews's experience with the Floridian, however, changed the course of her own life. As the board of directors of the White Rose Mission Home recalled, "The experience impressed upon Mrs. Matthews and other workers the need of being vigilant."[58]

Matthews was a few seconds late and, before she arrived at Pier 26, an agent immediately spotted the girl and lured her away from the dock. Matthews was determined to find the girl. She sent a message to her network of local clubwomen, clergymen, and residents to call her if they heard about a new girl in town from Florida. Matthews's extensive Black networks located the girl within three days and fortunately before she was harmed. Matthews found her and brought her to the White Rose Mission Home for lodging and food. Up until that point, the Home was a place that offered domestic service training classes to domestic workers and sent volunteers to Pier 26 to meet migrants.

After locating and helping the Floridian, Matthews concentrated her efforts on designing a more reliable and organized traveler's aid service to protect southern Black women. She developed an extensive and detailed system of spotting southerners on the docks and assigning volunteers from the Home to meet them at docks in Virginia to protect them from exploitative labor agents before they arrived in New York City. The Home also arranged for a group of volunteers to meet the southern travelers at Pier 26 in New York City to lead them to the Home before they were spotted by exploitative labor agents. News about the traveler's aid service reached women's networks across the African Diaspora. At times, women from Africa and the Caribbean sought out assistance from the Home after arriving in the city. The exact number of women that Matthews and her colleagues helped is unknown, yet the rescue stories documented by White Rose Mission volunteers and the eighty-six-year existence of the Home indicate that the traveler's aid and other services that it provided for Black women in the city were certainly important and helpful resources.

Matthews was sympathetic to the labor struggles of southern women before she founded the White Rose Mission Home because she was a migrant herself who had labored as a domestic worker. She was born to an enslaved mother and slaveholding father in Fort Valley, Georgia, in 1861. Her mother, Carolina Smith, won a court case to emancipate her two daughters, and they all settled in New York City where Matthews had to work as a domestic servant to help support the family. She taught herself to read from books in her employer's library that she read in between cooking and cleaning. She left domestic service by the age of eighteen in 1879 and became a local journalist and creative writer. By the early 1880s, she was immersed in the Black intellectual life and activism that flourished in the city during the late nineteenth century. Matthews worked with fellow clubwomen Susan McKinney and Josephine St. Pierre Ruffin to organize Black women's clubs in New York, Brooklyn, and Boston after hearing Ida B. Wells speak about her anti-lynching campaign.[59] By the 1890s, Matthews had established "The Inquiry Club," an organization that brought together Blacks in New York to discuss politics; become a columnist for the *Washington Bee*, an African American newspaper based in Washington, D.C.; and co-founded the Woman's Loyal Union (WLU), an organization that supported African American women political activists.

Matthews developed a strong interest in institution-building to address the exploitation of Black women after attending the Congress of Colored Women in the United States at the Atlanta Exposition in December 1895. While disturbed by the living conditions of working poor Black women and children in the South, she was convinced that southern migrant women's circumstances in northern cities were even worse because they did not have established networks of family and friends for support like Black women in the South. New York City had several settlement homes and organizations for white European immigrant women, but not one institution for Black migrant women. As Matthews explained, there were "all sorts of institutions" for the "young and unfriended [women] of other races" that guided them to safe housing and employment, but for Black girls and women, "there is nothing."[60]

Although Matthews's skin complexion, self-education, and marital status granted her entrance into elite and influential Black circles more easily than some of her contemporaries with darker complexions, she worked most closely with African American clubwomen who challenged elitist views about working-class women. While president of the WLU, Matthews developed a friendship with Amanda Miller, a Georgia native and member of the WLU who resigned from her position as chairwoman of the Woman's Business Club of New York City "on account of club members discriminating between domestics and those working in higher fields of labor." Miller told the club that "organizations formed by colored women to further their interests should not draw such a line."[61] Prior to the establishment of the White Rose Mission Home, Miller had already begun taking southern migrants into her own home when they arrived in New York City under false pretenses. She once offered her home as a place of refuge for a southern family who paid an agent for a ticket to Liberia because they intended to relocate to the African American settlement there, yet they were sent to New York City instead.[62]

On February 11, 1897, Matthews co-founded the White Rose Home for Colored Working Girls and White Rose Mission and Industrial Association with Amanda Miller and nine other clubwomen. While primarily servicing southern migrant women, Matthews insisted that the Home would welcome all daughters of the African diaspora, and she was true to her word. As one pamphlet detailed, the Home attendants offered lodging to a "refined woman" from Africa "who could not be admitted to a hotel because of her dark skin." Sympathetic Ellis Island officials who sighted Caribbean women who were not met by family members or friends at the dock called the Home and requested that the attendant help the travelers, to which the attendant replied, "All right. House pretty full, but we can make up some extra cots."[63] Frances Keyser, assistant superintendent of the Mission who took charge after Matthews's death, reported in a bulletin dated September 27, 1906, that the Home had also aided travelers from Honolulu, Bermuda, and Brazil.[64]

Matthews's mission was enormous and required both the "practical" work of creating the Home and traveler's aid service, as well as the ideological work of raising concern for the safety and working conditions of southern Black migrant women. A White Rose Mission and Industrial Association pamphlet (see Figure 6) contains a photograph of Victoria Earle Matthews, a boarding room in the home, and the reception area of the home. The photograph at the top is of White Rose Mission volunteers greeting a southern woman who arrived at the Old Dominion train station in New York. The volunteer wearing a light-colored jacket is believed to be Victoria Earl Matthews' sister Anna Rich.[65] The Home offered lodging and food to travelers, daily kindergarten classes for the children of working families in the neighborhood, and classes in sewing, woodcarving, cobbling, chair caning, basketry, clay modeling, dressmaking, millinery, and cooking for boarders and neighborhood residents.

Matthews asserted and put into practice her belief that wage-earning Black women should have access to a formal education based on a curriculum that

DO YOU REALIZE WHAT THIS
MEANS TO A STRANGE GIRL
IN NEW YORK CITY?

IF YOU were away from your home—your relatives—your friends—in a strange city—all alone
—and was fortunate enough to secure work—
would you not welcome a home where you
would really feel "at home?" That is part of the mission
of the *White Rose Industrial Association* in maintaining the
Working Girls' Home. It is the only institution of its kind
in New York City for colored girls—and we are coming to
you—hoping to interest you to the slightest degree in our
efforts. Just read our brief history—read between the lines
—you will appreciate just how much our work means—just
how necessary and important it is—we need help—just a
little from each one to whom this appeal goes.

Won't you help us ?

MRS. VICTORIA EARL MATTHEWS
Founder

White Rose Industrial Association

262 West 136th Street
New York City
TELEPHONE MORNINGSIDE 8407

Officers :

Miss M. L. Stone, President
Miss M. L. Lewis, 1st Vice-President
Rev. W. H. Brooks, 2nd Vice-President
Mrs. M. B. Pope, Recording Secretary
Mrs. Evelyn Connell, Cor. Secretary
Mrs. S. E. Wilkerson, Treasurer
Mrs. H. L. Ferrell, Superintendent

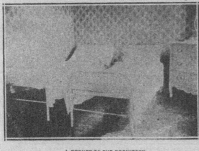

A CORNER OF THE DORMITORY

THE RECEPTION ROOM

FIG. 6 A White Rose Mission and Industrial Association, date unknown. Credit: White
Rose Mission and Industrial Association Collection, Schomburg Center for Research in
Black Culture, Manuscripts, Archives and Rare Books Division, New York Public Library by
permission of Mr. Kenneth Ambrose.

centered the scholarship and accomplishments of their own race. More broadly
and most importantly, the classes and educational resources that she provided at
the Home indicated her political view that Black women's worth extended far
beyond serving white families. Thus, racial uplift for Matthews meant improving the quality of life for southern migrant women through gainful employment and access to the cultural artifacts and scholarship of the Black race.

Matthews built a library at the Home that housed an extensive book collection authored by Black activists, poets, and educators. Matthews and her friend, poet, political activist, and journalist Alice Ruth Moore taught classes based on the library's holdings, including books by Phyllis Wheatley, Charles Chesnutt, Booker T. Washington, Paul Laurence Dunbar, and other Black writers who wrote about racial inequalities in the United States.[66] The library also included an 1859 volume of the *Anglo-African Magazine* that detailed the account of the Harper's Ferry rising and the trial and execution of John Brown. It also contained abolition literature such as the first edition of *Appeal in Favor of That Class of American Called Africans* by Lydia Maria Child, as well as rare letters, including one written by George Washington to Phillis Wheatley, and a slave narrative authored by Linda, an escaped slave. The curriculum for the race history classes were based on these holdings.[67] Matthews also contributed to the scholarship in the Home's library as the author of the short story collection *Aunt Lindy* and the editor of *Black-Belt Diamonds: Gems from the Speeches, Addresses, and Talks to Students of Booker T. Washington.*[68] In 1908, socialist Hubert Harrison, founder of the New Negro Movement and described by labor activist A. Phillip Randolph as "the father of Harlem Radicalism," offered Black history courses at the Home and presented lectures on Reconstruction.[69] The involvement of such a radical figure at the Home reflected the critical racial and class analysis that Matthews created as a foundation for the Home's programs and courses.

Matthews also did the discursive labor of making the argument that white women were not the only victims of labor and sexual exploitation. Black women, she argued, were in dire need of social programs to protect them from pimps and corrupt employment agencies after arriving in northern cities. She used local newspaper to challenge the myth that Black women were inherently immoral and did not deserve public sympathy and action on their behalf. As Matthews told a reporter from the *New York Telegram,* "cornfield hands" from the South were "changed into [the] dangerous women of the Tenderloin of New York." She also explained that representatives of employment agencies traveled to the South to recruit household labor for white northern families and deceived "good-looking Afro-American" girls from rural areas seeking to "fill honorable positions in respectable families." Migrants reached New York City "radiant in their youth and full of hope," yet they were quickly disillusioned after discovering that the "glowing accounts of life in New York" were false promises.[70]

Matthews demanded through her speeches that the country turn its attention to labor schemes that targeted southern Black migrant women. For Matthews, spreading the word about the injustices committed against southern Black women would achieve both ideological and practical outcomes.

Changing public perceptions about southern migrant women would produce more gainful domestic service employment opportunities for them in the face of job competition with white girls in northern cities. As she explained, "The trade which supplies southern girls as domestics to the disreputable has been carried to such an extent that many ladies refuse to employ colored help . . . until public sentiment has been created in favor of employing her along with respectable white girls."[71]

She delivered her most renowned speech on race, migration, and domestic service at the Hampton Negro Conference in 1898, a national gathering of Black civil rights leaders, clubwomen, clergymen, educators, and others who supported the "advancement of matters of interest to Negroes."[72] In her speech "Dangers Encountered by Southern Girls in Northern Cities," she challenged the prevailing slavery-era myth that Black women encountered problems in northern cities because they were inherently lazy, hypersexual, and immoral. On the contrary, Matthews argued, migrants were not the problem. The problem was structural. Similar to white women reformers who advocated for the sanctity of white immigrant women, African American clubwomen like Matthews argued that migrants were vulnerable in cities. As Beverly Guy-Sheftall explained, Black women agreed that their working-class sisters "departed from the ideal, but not because she was morally defective; rather, she was the victim of sexual abuse and exploitation, and could therefore not be blamed for circumstances beyond her control."[73]

Matthews detailed to the audience how agents traveled to rural areas throughout the South offering Black women and girl sharecroppers false promises of gainful domestic service employment in northern cities. Such promises were attractive to southern women who wanted to escape the isolation of rural life. As Matthews explained, ". . . it is reasonable to suppose that self-respect would deter hundreds from rushing into a life that only the strongest physically, spiritually and morally can be expected to stand. But the girls don't know: they feel stifled in the dead country town. Their very nature turns scornfully from the thought of supporting themselves in the home village by raising vegetables, chickens, making honey, butter, canning fruit or vegetables, putting up pickles and such like."[74] When they reached their destinations, they were forced to work in brothels or work for white families who refused to pay them. She noted that domestic service employment agencies "treat them as so many head of cattle" and "they are hurdled into dirty ill-smelling apartments, many feeling lucky if a pallet given them."[75] The food provided was of the "most miserable quality."[76] Agencies housed migrant women in boarding homes that charged them exorbitant rates for rent, making it impossible for them to climb their way out of debt. Some women were drawn into prostitution with promises that they would be able to pay their debts quicker by performing sexual acts. The agencies collected the women's earnings and shared them with the magistrates of the courts, the employment agency, and policemen while the women suffered from poverty and disease. Consequently, Matthews reported, "The poor butterfly [Black women] finally drifts, a mass of disease and yearning for death, to the city hospital on Blackwell's Island."[77]

Matthews insisted that more resources be dedicated to helping southern Black migrant women because simply asking them to return to the South was not always a viable solution. Matthews revealed that when she asked women why they did not go back home, they told her: "Go back! Never! I could not face the folks; I'd rather die."[78] Matthews argued that the shame of being taken advantage of discouraged some women from telling other Black women in the South who had dreams of "making it" about the perils in the North. Many of these stories that deserved to be told and could have helped other women remained buried in anger, shame, and disappointment.

Matthews urged the audience not to become passive listeners who would do nothing but shake their heads in disbelief after hearing about the women's stories. She told her audience that they were obligated to help their southern sisters now that they were educated on their experiences in northern cities. As Matthews proclaimed, ". . . now that this honored institution has enabled the message to come to you, no women here can shirk without sin the obligation to study into this matter, to the end that the evil may be completely exterminated, and protection guaranteed to the lives and reputations of the generations yet to come."[79] She demanded that the conference participants spread the word about the corrupt employment that preyed on southern Black women. As she predicted, "Could even some of the women see and hear these things, the condition of our people in the cities would soon change . . ."[80]

Matthews also challenged class divisions within the Black community by arguing that the exploitation of southern Black migrant women should not be thought of as only a problem for the poor. She believed that both educated and uneducated Black migrant women were at risk of sexual abuse and labor exploitation. She insisted, "Until the truth is known in every town and hamlet in the South, the youth of our race, educated and uneducated alike, will pay with their bright young lives."[81] She continued, ". . . particularly mulattoes and fair quadroons [from the South], are secured for the diversion of young Hebrews. These girls are led to believe they will get permanent work in stores and public service under the control of politics."[82]

Four years after the Hampton Negro Conference, Matthews appealed to the Black clergymen of New York City at the "Redemption of our City" conference organized by the Federation of Churches and Christian Organizations in New York City in 1902. She began her speech with an impatient greeting. She told the federation, "I do not want to take more than two or three minutes, for it means much to me to be somewhere else." The same year that Matthews spoke at the conference, members of the Federation had accused some of its own urban missionaries of addressing the needs of Chinese immigrants in the city while neglecting the needs of its Black residents.[83] It is likely that Matthews was also angered by the Federation turning a blind eye to addressing issues in the local Black community, and the exploitation of Black women in particular.

As promised, Matthews wasted no time telling the audience that they needed to support the urgent cause of helping southern newcomers to the city. She told the audience, "Oh, help us in this work. We cannot do it all. We need a bucket brigade all over this city; the colored women need some help on these lines."[84] She told the clergymen that she and the other volunteers at the White Rose Mission Home had accomplished a lot with few resources and they needed support from the federation. She reported that within a year the Home "had 482 meetings with an attendance of 6,901" while organizing "kitchen gardens, cooking classes, and neighborhood meetings" with "not a dollar behind them." She argued that they could no longer continue the important work if they did not receive financial assistance from more churches in the city. She concluded her speech, "My house, my colored house, if you will allow that expression, is on fire."[85] It is unknown whether or not Matthews received help from the federation after impressing on them the significance of the White Rose Mission Home. What is evident is that Matthews created a Home that withstood the ambivalence of public support for Black women's causes. Her mission of advocating for southern migrant women extended well beyond her death in 1907.[86] The Home continued its traveler's aid services, courses, and employment assistance until its doors closed in 1984.[87]

Matthews was not alone in her racial project of disrupting labor reform discourses that centered the exploitation of white workers. Her younger contemporary Anna Julia Cooper also inserted southern migrant women into labor reform discourses by demanding that the country turn its attention to transforming the working conditions of Black women in domestic service. Matthews worked with Cooper as the chairwoman of the Committee on Domestic Science as part of the Hampton Institute Negro Conference. Their committee made annual appeals to the conference to pool resources to provide basic necessities for southern Black women in northern cities. Writing on behalf of the committee, Matthews declared in the 1899–1900 annual report of the conference that migrants in tenement homes needed health services, nurseries to take care of their children while they worked, gymnasiums for recreation, reading circles, and public baths. She noted that members of the committee had already begun the work that she requested from the conference.[88]

While serving on the committee, Cooper also did the discursive work of disrupting the association of domestic service with slavery in her writings and speeches to insert domestic workers into the labor reform movement. She asserted that Black women were more deserving of labor reform than European immigrants because they were American citizens who had built the United States from its very inception. Cooper's writings on Black women household workers are another example of the robust and nuanced resistance of Black women in the late nineteenth century. [89]

Anna Julia Cooper

Anna Julia Cooper is less well known than Victoria Earle Matthews for her writings about Black women's labor issues in the late nineteenth and early twentieth centuries. As Beverly Guy-Sheftall noted, scholars have critiqued Anna Julia Cooper for what they perceive to be "her elitism with respect to ordinary Black women and her uncritical attachment to the conservative ideology of true womanhood because of her own middle-class status," and she is therefore linked with "her middle class sisters whose notions about racial uplift distanced them from the masses of working, less respectable women."[90] Vivian May has begun the work of adding more texture to this narrative about Cooper's class identity, theories, and activist work. May argues that there were many factors that complicated Cooper's middle-class status. Cooper did not have the same class privileges as some of her colleagues such as Mary Church Terrell and Ida Gibbs Hunt. Unlike her contemporaries whose parents paid for their college tuition, Cooper's mother labored as a domestic servant and Cooper had to work her way through college, although she had entered Oberlin with a tuition scholarship.[91] Cooper also did not have the protections of married life in a highly patriarchal society. She was subjected to the scrutiny of Booker T. Washington and her other Black male contemporaries throughout her career because she was outspoken and a widow who never remarried.[92] In the words of Vivian May, Cooper was also "constantly at economic risk" as she struggled to take care of two foster children and five adopted grandnieces and grandnephews with her low wage teaching salary, and without the safety net of a husband's income.[93]

While Cooper did not face the same struggles as Black women in domestic service, she was certainly no stranger to the ways in which racial, class, and gender inequalities shaped the materiality of Black women's lives. Like Victoria Earle Matthews, Cooper was committed to changing public discourse about wage-earning southern Black women through writing, public speaking, research, and teaching. Her analysis of domestic service was broader in scope than Matthews's perspectives because she lived longer than Matthews. Thus, she could further develop her views on race and domestic service over a period of time. She shared the belief that most Black clubwomen and white women social reformers articulated at the turn of the century that the home was critical to the well-being of the nation.[94] As Beverly Guy-Sheftall explained, "This desire to purify the home and society was seen by Cooper and other Black women to be a part of their definition of racial uplift, but it was also consistent with efforts on the parts of reform women in general to uplift the entire society."[95]

In this section and in the following chapter, I argue that what distinguished Cooper's perspectives about the home from most of her contemporaries was that she exposed it as a site of racial, class, and gender inequalities for Black women. In this section, I begin examining Cooper's late-nineteenth-century writings about the exploitation of Black women household workers, and I trace the development of her ideas and scholar activism on domestic service into the early twentieth century in Chapter 6, which is the next chapter in this book. I think that it is important, however, to begin the analysis of her classic book, *A Voice from the South*, in this chapter to situate it within the context of the late-nineteenth-century national labor reform movement because it is recognized as a defining text for what we now know as Black feminist thought, and is less known as a significant intervening text that challenged immigrant and native-born white reformers for excluding Black women household workers from the movement.

In the wake of late-nineteenth-century Irish immigrant women's labor activism to end white slavery, Cooper published *A Voice from the South by a Black Woman from the South* in 1892 in which she made bold declarations about the exploitation of Black women in domestic service and their invisibility in the national reform movement. Impatient with the glaring omission of Black household laborers from the agendas of white native-born and immigrant labor movements that had captured the attention of the country, Cooper declared, "But how many have ever given a thought to the pinched and down-trodden colored women bending over wash-tubs and ironing boards—with children to feed and house rent to pay, wood to buy, soap and starch to furnish—lugging home weekly great baskets of clothes for families who pay them for a month's laundry-ing barely enough to purchase a substantial pair of shoes!" Cooper implied that working-class white American and European immigrant workers had no idea what labor exploitation really was. It was southern Black women, Cooper argued, who endured slavery. She asserted, ". . . ah, come with me, I feel like saying, I can show you workingmen's wrong and workingmen's toil, which, could it speak, would send up a wail that might be heard from the Potomac to the Rio Grande; and should it unite and act, would shake this country from Carolina to California." [96]

She also targeted white social reformers who "went into pious agonies at the thought of the future mothers of Americans having to stand all day at shop counters" and European immigrant union organizers in the North who "still need an interpreter to communicate with their employer" and "will threaten to cut the nerve and paralyze the progress of an industry that gives work to an American [black] born-citizen." Consequently, she found it "impossible to catch the fire of sympathy and enthusiasm for most of these labor movements at the North" because there were Blacks in the South who "toiled year in and year out, from sunrise to dusk, for fifty cents per day, out of which they must feed and shelter and clothe themselves and their families!" [97]

Cooper argued that domestic workers were just as valuable to the nation's economy as European immigrant industrial workers who were rioting in the North and just as important as white women who worked in local stores. In a speech entitled "Woman versus the Indian," she put domestic service on an equal footing with white women's occupations by declaring that "shop girls and serving maids, cashiers, and accountant clerks" whether they were "laboring to instruct minds, to save souls, to delight fancies, or to win bread" were critical to the nation. She asserted that women who worked in all occupations gave "not only tone directly to her immediate world, but her tiniest pulsation ripples out and out, down and down, till the outermost circles and the deepest layers of society feel the vibrations."[98] She argued that Black women's concentration in domestic service during slavery and afterwards did not indicate that they were inherently subordinate to whites. On the contrary, she argued that Black women's domestic work was critical to the home, and therefore indispensable to the U.S. economy and the world's economy.

Cooper stressed the importance of Black women's household labors seven years later in her article in the magazine The *Southern Workman* entitled "Colored Women as Wage Earners." In the article, Cooper blurred the lines that divided the public and private spheres by arguing that the home was a paid and unpaid workplace for Black women. She used her own quantitative research to construct the argument that Black women were unrecognized for the value of the reproductive labors that they did in their own homes, and they were severely underpaid for the work that they did in their places of employment. Her research on Black women's household labors led her to conclude that Black women were greater contributors to the economy than white women. She explained, "a large percentage of the productive labor of the world is done by women . . . of 1,137 colored families 650, or 57.17 percent, are supported wholly or in part by female heads. So that in comparison with white, female heads of families and others contributing to family support, there is, by a house to house enumeration, quite a large excess on the part of colored women."[99] Cooper was just getting started in her scholar-activism for wage-earning Black women with her bold declarations in *A Voice from the South* and *The Southern Workman*. She continued asserting the significance of Black domestic workers and their labors well into the twentieth century as they came to dominate the ranks of domestic service in northern cities.

Conclusion

The late nineteenth century was a defining period of African American and Irish immigrant women's resistance to labor exploitation in domestic service. They put their hands on race by pulling from threads of labor and social reform discourses to assert the significance of their personhood and labors in the Progressive Era. Irish immigrant and African American women, however, situated themselves in these Progressive-Era discourses in distinct ways.

Wage-earning women of Irish descent employed several methods to insert themselves into white femininity by defining their labors within the context of slavery. The Irish agitators used slavery as a metaphor to describe their working conditions because it had become part of the national discourse in efforts to reform white male labor, and it reasserted their privileges as white women. White slavery also resonated with working-class Irish women because it was a mobilizing metaphor that Irish nationalists had used since the mid–1800s in Ireland's campaign for independence from British rule.[100] Irish women labor organizers and Irish domestic workers likened the exploitation of Irish women's labors in factories and private homes with Britain's colonial rule over Ireland. Irish women in domestic service worked in concert with labor organizers and unions that also rallied under the banner of white slavery. They joined the Knights of Labor and other labor organizations with prominent Irish leadership to rally for better wages and working conditions on behalf of white immigrant workers. While labor organizations rarely fought specifically to transform domestic service, Irish immigrant servants' ability to join these predominately white organizations made them whiter. Women leaders of Irish descent in the labor organizations integrated all Irish immigrant women into the national labor reform movement of protecting white "working girls" by campaigning for native-born and immigrant white wage-earning women and developing alliances with elite native-born white women.

Slavery was not just a metaphor for African American women. Late-nineteenth-century clubwomen and domestic workers were only a few decades out of slavery, an institution that continued impacting their lives long after its abolition. As formerly enslaved workers, they labored in a country and in an occupation that had yet to fully recognize them as wage earners and U.S. citizens. Hence, Black women labored at disassociating themselves and domestic service from the not-so-distant history of slavery. Southern migrant women insisted to domestic service employers that there be an end to their workday and that they receive living wages. Clubwomen, who had intimate experiences with domestic service through their mothers who worked as domestics or having worked as servants themselves, inserted migrant women into labor and social reform discourses of their time that had excluded Black women. Cooper and Matthews argued that Black women were native-born U.S. citizens who were entitled to protection from labor exploitation and sexual abuse. Cooper especially denounced national reform efforts that prioritized remedying the labor exploitation of working-class whites who had recently arrived in the United States over that of Black women from the South "bending over wash tubs" since slavery.

It took less time for Irish immigrant women to succeed in expanding the boundaries of whiteness for women of Irish descent than it took for African American women to dismantle the underpinnings of race. By the early twentieth century, Irish immigrant women had become whiter, and their female descendants could access a greater array of women's occupations by the early twentieth century. Irish American women could avoid domestic work altogether and pursue careers as secretaries, stenographers, schoolteachers, and nurses. Throughout the Northeast, Irish American women made an impressionable mark on the teaching profession. In 1908, the daughters and granddaughters of Irish immigrant women made up 26.2 percent of all teachers in Buffalo, New York; 26.4 percent in Fall River, Massachusetts; 49.6 percent in Worcester, Massachusetts; 29.9 percent in Lowell, Massachusetts; 24 percent in Providence, Rhode Island; and 38 percent in Scranton, Pennsylvania.[101]

The prevailing historical narrative is that Irish American women's entrance into native white women's occupations signaled that Irish immigrant women had successfully created a pathway for themselves and their daughters to enter the white middle class. I argue, however, that Irish immigrant women's transition into the white middle class cannot be fully explained by the social elevation of their female descendants. Although they were whiter and their numbers in household service had declined, they still represented over 50 percent of workers in domestic service. In 1900, for example, 54 per cent of Irish-born women were still in domestic service.[102] During 1912 and 1913 alone, nearly 87 percent of the Irish women who emigrated to America worked in some form of private or public domestic service.[103] Furthermore, second-generation Irish women, who did not become teachers, remained a generational step behind Italian and Jewish immigrant women who were leaving manufacturing jobs to become saleswomen, bookkeepers, and clerks.[104] As historian Stephen Steinberg put it, "Irish women started out on a lower occupational threshold than either Italians or Jews, and remained one generational step behind."[105]

While exiting domestic service was a gradual process for Irish immigrant women, they certainly transitioned out of domestic service much sooner than African American women. The percentage of immigrant white women in the occupation declined as southern Black women entered domestic service in greater numbers in the twentieth century. The number of white domestic workers fell by 40 percent while the number of Black domestic workers rose by 43 percent in northeastern cities between 1900–1930.[106] Unlike their Irish counterparts whose daughters did not have to work in domestic service, the majority of African American women and their daughters remained concentrated in domestic work until the 1970s.

In Chapter 6, the next chapter of this book, I trace the staggered transition of Irish immigrant women into the white middle class. I also examine the labor organizing, institution-building, and scholar-activism of twentieth-century African American domestic workers, clubwomen, and labor organizers who continued the enormously groundbreaking racial project of nineteenth-century Black women to dismantle the ties between domestic work and slavery, while asserting African American domestic workers' rights to safe working conditions and living wages.

6

Irish Immigrant Women Become Whiter, African American Women Dignify Domestic Service

—————————————————————◄O►—

By the 1920s, Irish immigrant women had become whiter and gained greater access to jobs outside of domestic service while Black women became the majority of workers employed in the once-Irish-dominated occupation in the U.S. northeast by the 1930s. In this chapter, I document the racialization of Irish immigrant women and the activism of Black women in the early twentieth century to initiate further research and discussion about how working-class white women experienced race and ethnicity in their occupations and how Black women developed a discursive foundation for addressing long-lasting labor struggles rooted in race and gender. Black and Irish immigrant women's divergent and overlapping histories show the endurance of labor struggles rooted in intersecting racial, class, and gender inequalities for African American women, and for white working-class women, even when they do not politically identify with African American women's labor movements.

As I argued in Chapter 5, there were a number of factors that led to Irish immigrant women becoming whiter, including their insistence that they were white working ladies who did not do "Black," or slavish, work; the exclusion of African American women from, and the integration of Irish immigrant women into, labor and social reform movements by labor and social reformers; the political and economic influence of the Catholic Church and its mission to aid Irish immigrant women; the political power of Irish male politicians, employers, and business owners; legal racial segregation; and the state and federal government's persistent exclusion of African Americans from the political, economic, and social rights of U.S. citizenship. Irish immigrant women's access to a wider array of early-twentieth-century occupations dominated by white women, in which Black women were still discriminated against, attested to Irish immigrant women's white privilege and the hardening of racial boundaries that relegated Black women to domestic service.

The prevailing historical narrative about Irish immigrant women, however, does not trace their working experiences after leaving domestic service in the early twentieth century. According to the narrative, Irish immigrant women's exit from domestic service was immediate, and they never returned to the occupation. They ascended into American middle-class life as housewives who adopted (white) middle-class customs that they learned from their employers to socialize their children into higher social classes. Historian Maureen Murphy noted that after working in private homes, Irish immigrant women "knew how to dress; they knew fine linen and the linens of good furniture; they could set a beautiful table . . . they realized that education, a good appearance, and social graces would carry their children a long way."[1] Their acculturation, as Kerby Miller and Patricia Mulholland Miller argued in their study of Irish immigration, "pushed their families up the long road of respectability and eventual prosperity . . ."[2]

I assert that what is missing from this neat American immigrant story is African American women and the revelations that their history brings to immigrant women's labor histories. African American women's labor histories require that we never lost sight of the impact of race, class, and gender on working women's lives. This comparative chapter of Irish immigrant and African American women's early twentieth century labor histories bares insight into how Irishness, as a racial construct, continued to impact Irish immigrant women's labor experiences. In the absence of literature on how race impacted Irish immigrant women's transition out of domestic service, I use Irish immigrant women's self-narrated stories as a starting point from which to probe further into the various ways whiteness materialized in their lives.[3] Their oral histories reveal that Irish immigrant women's exit from domestic service was not monolithic, linear, nor always finite.

As Irish immigrant women worked at attaining the full privileges of whiteness in the U.S. labor economy, Black women worked at transforming an occupation that they now dominated in both the North and South. Relegated to domestic service because of discriminatory hiring practices that were beneficial to Irish and other immigrant white women, Black women continued putting their hands on race through their everyday-putting-food-on-the-table-labor, intellectual work, resistance, activism, and labor organizing to demand labor reform in domestic service.

I argue that organized resistance to the labor exploitation of Black women in domestic service in northern cities expanded in the twentieth century. Domestic workers solidified their resistance to racial inequalities in household employment as union labor organizers in the 1930s to urge employers to hire domestic workers for living wages and demand that city, state, and the federal governments pass legislation to protect them from labor exploitation. Black clubwomen, clergymen, writers, journalists, and labor organizers joined domestic workers' struggle to transform the working conditions of domestic service by writing public letters, dissertations, newspaper articles, songs, speeches, and petitions to change the meaning of race and household employment.

This chapter documents how domestic workers and their allies collectively argued that Black women were independent, wage-earning, highly skilled workers whose domestic service labors were equally important to (if not more important than) all other forms of work deemed worthy of protection under labor laws. To make this argument, domestic workers and their allies exposed the institutionalization of intersecting racial, class, and gender inequalities in the labor economy that had persisted in the United States since slavery. I assert that their collectively produced discourse of labor rights for Black women became critical for domestic worker organizing throughout the twentieth century, and for immigrant women of color today.

Before preceding to the next section in this chapter, it is important for me to say that domestic service work had multiple meanings for Black women. It was portable labor. It had been contracted out to white households in a racialized and gendered convict leasing system in the South in the early twentieth century.[4] It was also labor that African American women asserted control over by using their domestic skills as tickets out of the South into other parts of the country where they asserted their right to better wages, living conditions, and educational opportunities for their children. Domestic work could also be a marker of status. Black women were who we now call excellent event planners and caterers who were highly sought after in both Black and white communities. In addition, as historian Sharon Harley explained, "For most Black women, opportunities for social status existed outside the labor market—in their family, neighborhood, and organizational and church lives."[5] Black women who did domestic work to put food on their own tables took pride in being competent and productive members of their communities and families. They used their cooking, cleaning, and planning skills not only in white households, but to build and sustain churches, benevolent associations, and mutual aid societies in their own communities. Hence, domestic labor was both exploited by white families and institutions, and owned by African American women themselves. Black women's labor activism in the early twentieth century was fueled by these overlapping historic, systemic, and deeply personal meanings for Black women and their communities.

Assimilation at the Margins of White Female Respectability

Frances Duffy Hoffman, 21 years old, applied for domestic service jobs at an employment agency in Brooklyn after leaving Ireland in 1923. After Hoffman told her uncle that she had applied for domestic service jobs, he told her that she should never apply for domestic service jobs again. As he put it, "That [domestic service] is for colored people." Hoffman's uncle advised her to stop looking for household work and inquire about openings for cleaning positions at the Brooklyn State Hospital. Hoffman followed her uncle's advice, and she secured a job at the hospital within a few days. Hoffman worked at the hospital three days a week with lodging and food provided and was paid a consistent wage. While Hoffman's uncle believed that domestic service work should be performed by African Americans, Hoffman's duties at the hospital were strikingly similar to those of Black women in domestic service. As a maid for the hospital, Hoffman cooked meals, cleaned linens and floors, and cared for the personal needs of patients. In a larger sense, however, Hoffman's uncle was right. By the 1920s, domestic service had become undeniably Black women's work.

In addition to increased Black women's migrations from the South, immigration laws created avenues for Irish immigrant women to access white women's occupations. In the 1920s, the courts sharpened the distinctions between African Americans, recent European immigrants, and European immigrants who had been living in the United States for at least one generation. The Immigration Act of 1921 mandated that no more than 3 percent of persons from a single nation could be admitted into the United States. This law reflected dominant nativist sentiments and fears among native born whites that millions of unassimilable southern and eastern European immigrants would flood into the United States after World War I.

United States lawmakers assumed that European immigrants who were already living in the United States or were part of the 3 percent who could enter the country could be assimilated into white American culture. As historian David Roediger explained, "The power of the national state was crucial in this context [the 1920s]. It gave new immigrants their firmest claim to whiteness and their strongest leverage for enforcing those claims . . . When much of the citizenry doubted the racial status of European migrants, the courts almost always automatically granted their full whiteness in naturalization cases . . ."[6] The legal solidification of white supremacy in immigration policies, racial segregation laws, and the federal government's refusal to grant African Americans citizenship rights certainly cemented racial inequalities among women in the labor economy.

Unlike married Black women who worked in domestic service for most of their lives, Irish immigrant women had the option of leaving domestic service after marriage. By 1900, second-generation Irish women could more easily enter the needle trades and other manufacturing jobs, whereas the majority of Black women remained concentrated in domestic service for several generations. In the early twentieth century, Irish immigrant women still most easily found employment in working-class service occupations, as reflected in Frances Hoffman's story. Irish immigrant women who were not deterred from working in domestic service worked in private homes until they got married or found other types of jobs. As Rose Kelly Laughlin, who emigrated from Ireland in 1925 put it, "As soon as I put my foot in the country, I knew what I'd be doing because I didn't have the education. I knew I'd be minding children or something like that."[7] Bridget Delia O'Neill, who emigrated from County Claire, Ireland, in 1921 to New York City at the age of 23, attributed her difficulty finding employment outside of domestic service to heightened nationalism after World War I. Her difficulty finding a nursing job in New York led her to regret her decision to migrate to America. According to O'Neill, "They thought we were pigs here in America. They didn't welcome us by no means in them days ... There were signs that said 'No Irish apply' ... And the reason was because we didn't help the English in the struggle ... The Irish stayed neutral. They didn't help in the conflict with Germany."[8]

Frustrated with her limited job prospects, O'Neill resigned to working for an elderly Jewish woman. While O'Neill's employer was nice to her, she did not like having to provide around-the-clock care, which kept her from participating in social activities planned by other Irish domestic workers in the neighborhood. Dissatisfied with her isolated existence, O'Neill left the position to work for her employer's daughter. The daughter owned a three-story home in Manhattan and O'Neill developed friendships with the six Irish servants who already worked there. O'Neill retired from her job and became a housewife when she married her husband, Patrick.

Meeting traditional expectations for housewives could be difficult for Irish immigrant women who were on the margins of the middle class. Irish immigrant men did not always earn enough to immediately purchase a home after marriage nor hire domestic servants and support the entire household on their own. O'Neill's life was unsettled for quite some time after her marriage. She and Patrick moved to six different tenement apartments until he found stable employment and could afford to purchase a house. Some Irish immigrant housewives operated small home businesses to supplement their husbands' incomes in financially unstable marriages. Ellen Bergheim remembered that her mother quit her job working for a Jewish family in Manhattan after marrying her first husband. She rented out rooms and started a candy store and delicatessen in their home to help meet the expenses of the household.[9] Bridget Jones, who left domestic service after meeting her husband at an Irish social dance in Brooklyn, worked for supplemental wages by operating a boarding-house inside their home. As she recalled, "I stayed home and took care of the house. The fellows that stayed with us were known as boarders. We had a lot of fun. They all played an instrument. They played the violin or the accordion and we sang and we danced."[10] Later in life, Jones expressed support for women's decisions to work outside of the home. She explained, "I thought my job was to stay home because ten months after I was married my daughter was born. So, that was it. Then, you're supposed to take care of your home and your children. I don't think there was anyone going to work after they got married like nowadays. It is very good to go to work and get a good start in life."[11]

Mary Ellen Ryan, who emigrated to New York City in 1920, quit her job cleaning hotel rooms after getting married and opened five boardinghouses for Irish immigrants. Reflecting on her life, Ryan boasted that she never worked as a domestic, although she had worked as a maid at a hotel. She explained, "I've been proud that I said I couldn't be a servant in somebody's house and I worked towards that. I took every opportunity. I had five small buildings and it was in the middle of the Depression."[12] Ryan's claim that she could avoid domestic work because she was a hard worker echoes the "pull yourself up by your boot straps" discourse that has been used to deny institutionalized racism and its impact on racial minority communities. Contrary to Ryan's narrative, opening a boardinghouse was not only destined for hardworking (read: white) women. Southern Black migrant women and Caribbean immigrant women also opened and operated boardinghouses for migrants from their hometowns. Institutionalized racism and sexism are what distinguished native born and immigrant Black women's circumstances from those of Irish immigrant women like Ryan. Married Black women had to continue working as domestics while earning supplemental income from their home businesses because their husbands were paid even lower wages than white immigrant working-class men. Black women were also barred from most occupations outside of domestic service.

Some Irish immigrant women, however, had no option but to return to domestic service after their husbands died or experienced job-related illnesses and injuries. Bridget Ryan McNulty and Catherine Concannon left their domestic service jobs after marrying mechanics for railroad companies. After their husbands died from lung and artery diseases contracted from working on the railroad, McNulty and Concannon returned to domestic service.[13] Some married Irish immigrant women returned to domestic work when their husbands' employment was unstable. Mary Condon left her waitressing job and returned to domestic service when she and her husband had difficulty making ends meet after their fourth child was born. Daytime work as a domestic had more flexible hours than waitressing, thereby allowing her to spend more time with her children while earning income to supplement her husband's low wages. Condon explained, "He had a job, but didn't get good pay. My philosophy on raising children was you spend as much time raising four as you do one . . . My husband was in a job in the city and there was no way in the world that we were going to get out of that area, at least until the children were raised . . . I was committed for a long time to getting a job like some did . . ."[14]

The Irish immigrant women who continued to work in domestic service in the early twentieth century had a greater chance of securing higher wage and status positions than Black women who were doing the same work. Irish women were often hired as governesses for upper-middle-class and wealthy white families shortly after arriving in the United States.[15] At times, state officials at Ellis Island intervened to help Irish immigrant women in the job market before they even applied for domestic service positions. Bridget McGeoghegan, who migrated from Clonmany, County Donegal, Ireland, in 1923 at the age of 22, remembered an official changing her name on her passport from Bridget McGeoghegan to Bertha McGaffighan to help her find respectable work. As he told her, "Your name is going to be Bertha McGaffighan from now on." While it is unclear why the port official changed Bertha's last name to another name that was distinctly Irish, he might have changed the spelling of the name to distance it further from its Gaelic origin and pronunciation. The port official might have assumed that "McGaffighan," the more Anglicized version of "McGeoghegan," would distance Bridget further from the Gaelic culture, which was not racialized as white, or respectable in a U.S. context. Bridget herself explained the official's motive for changing her first name. As she recalled, "Well, years ago people used to laugh about Irish girls that came out here. They called them Biddys sometimes. You worked for working families and so forth. So, anyway, they changed it to Bertha . . . I didn't want to be haggling with them."[16] Although port officials changed the names of many immigrants from all backgrounds, the intent behind changing Bridget's name was to disassociate her from the negative stigma associated with Irish servants who were often referred to as Biddy, which was a stereotypical nickname for Bridget. The port official might have believed that if her first name were Bertha she might have a better chance of making a favorable impression on a potential employer than if she had the name of the archetypal lazy and temperamental Irish servant Bridget, or "Biddy."

Some Irish newcomers could avoid the stigma of Black women's work (domestic service) by applying for cleaning and cooking jobs at Catholic hospitals as was the case with Frances Duffy Hoffman whom we met early in this chapter. Performing these care labors in a hospital, a racially segregated institution that enforced strict racial boundaries between whites and Blacks, and a white feminized space deemed a proper workplace for respectable white women workers, elevated the status of Irish immigrant women and their manual labors. The racial boundaries in hospital employment were so stark that not even formally trained African American nurses could secure employment in hospitals outside of Black communities. As Jane Edna Hunter, a surgical nurse trained at the Hampton Institute, was told in 1905 by a white doctor when she arrived in Cleveland, Ohio, in search of a nursing job: "white doctors did not employ nigger nurses."[17] After being turned away from hospitals, Hunter could only find jobs cleaning office buildings and working in private homes before becoming president of the Working Girls' Home Association (later known as the Phyllis Wheatley Association).

Irish immigrant women were able to secure employment in white hospitals in urban centers like New York City because of the political power of the Irish in state and religious institutions. The Irish-influenced Tammany Hall made executive decisions for hospitals in the city and allocated state funding to Catholic run hospitals.[18] The state-funded Catholic institutions since the nineteenth century to provide moral instruction and services to poor immigrant Irish mothers and children who were blamed for vices and disease epidemics in urban areas.[19] Nurses, nuns, and maids in Catholic hospitals were valued because they were viewed as women who promoted good morals and cleanliness among the "degenerate" poor and immigrant populations.[20] Irish immigrant women hospital workers did feminine caregiving labor in a capacity that was "naturally" suited for white women.

Irish immigrant women, however, were not always welcomed in occupations dominated by native-born white women. Despite the myriad accents heard in the multicultural hub of New York City, Kathren MaGennis Lamberti was refused a job at a telephone company in New York City in 1921 because of her Irish brogue. Lamberti recalled, "I wanted to get into the telephone company, but they wouldn't take me because of my Irish accent. They told me to come back. They wanted me to come back when I spoke 'New York.' I said, 'What is New York?' 'New York is English like the rest of us,' the manager said, 'We can't take you with that Irish accent."[21] As African American politician and civil rights leader Dr. Anna Arnold Hedgeman discovered while working at an employment agency, telephone companies made a concerted effort to hire applicants that fit the initials L-H-P (Long Haired Protestants). She documented this discriminatory practice out of concern for Black women who were barred from positions outside of domestic service.[22]

Lamberti's experience signals that Irish immigrant women were sometimes forbidden to work in jobs reserved for native-born white women. However, even though she returned to domestic service after the telephone company declined her application, her racial, ethnic, and religious identities afforded her the opportunity to find a job elsewhere before too long. A local order of the Knights of Columbus, the world's largest Catholic fraternal organization, helped her secure employment as a waitress at the Crescent Country Club.[23] Waitressing was also low-paying work, but it was preferable to domestic service. Irish immigrant women might have preferred the standardized tasks, wages, and working hours in waitressing. Irish immigrant women may also have viewed waitressing as a more suitable occupation for white women. Country clubs denied membership to Blacks, and restaurants were racially segregated.[24]

Although some single, widowed, and married Irish immigrant women continued working in domestic service and other types of service occupations throughout the 1920s, employment options continued to widen for them throughout the next decade, thereby leaving the occupation to primarily Black women who dominated nearly every rank of domestic service in the North by the 1930s.

Claiming the Dignity and Skills of Domestic Work: A Communal Racial Project

While Irish immigrant women gained greater access to occupations beyond domestic service, African American women remained restricted to domestic service for several generations. As Brenda Faye Clegg stated in her study of Black migrant women in the Depression era, ". . . the majority of working Black women—despite age, social position, education, background or locality worked in domestic service, mostly in private households."[25] The southern economy remained weak in comparison to the northern economy, and southern women continued migrating North for better wages. The South suffered from a boll weevil attack on cotton crops in 1915 driving down wages to seventy-five cents a day or less. In the same year, massive floods throughout the South left many homeless. Primarily Black women from Georgia, the Carolinas, Virginia, and Florida traveled by steamers and trains to seek better employment and housing for themselves and their families in New York, Philadelphia, Pittsburgh, Newark, Baltimore, and Washington, D.C.[26] In addition to their search for employment, Black women left the South to escape unrelenting institutionalized and violent racism. While some migrants managed to etch better lives in the North, low wages kept the majority of Black families in debt and relegated them to poor living conditions. Most working-poor Black families lived in cold water flats owned by white landlords who charged Black tenants exorbitant rents for living spaces that would have been shut down by the Department of Health today. The poorly lit, unventilated apartments had no hot water and inadequate bathing facilities. To stay warm in bitter cold temperatures, tenants had few options but to use kerosene. As an Urban League investigator reported, these conditions made living in cold water flats dangerous and a breeding ground for diseases such as tuberculosis."[27]

African American migration increased exponentially during and immediately following World War I. Seeking to escape racial violence and economic depression in the South, African Americans were in search of the higher-paying jobs in the war industry they heard about in the North.[28] Black women who had worked as domestics prior to the war found employment on assembly lines in factories. After the war, white men returned to the factory jobs, push-ing Black women back into domestic service. When women were hired for manufacturing jobs, employers favored European immigrants. Rose Schnei-derman, president of the Women's Trade Union League and a colleague of Irish labor organizer Leonora O'Reilly, explained the sentiments behind such discriminatory hiring practices: ". . . the colored girl is not acceptable for fac-tory work as the white girl (foreign or native born), since the colored girl comes from an agricultural environment and whites (foreign) come from sweat shops and trade . . . factory work requires too much grind for the colored girl who was not willing to endure hard work."[29] Some Black migrant women started their own businesses as hairstylists in commercial buildings and in their own homes. A smaller minority found jobs in clerical and sales positions in Black-owned businesses and on rare occasions in white-owned stores. But working in domestic service was the only employment option for the vast majority of Black women.

With no federal nor state laws to protect them from labor exploitation in domestic service, Black women expressed their resistance in song. In 1928, Texas native and blues singer Hallie Burleson recounted the hardships of low pay, disrespect, and lack of privacy in domestic service in "Sadie's Servant Room Blues." Burleson sang: "This here job don't pay me much. They give me just what they think I'm worth. I'm going to change my mind, yeah, change my mind. 'Cause I keep the servant room blues all the time. I receive my com-pany in the rear. Here these folks don't want to see them here . . . They have a party at noon. A party at night. The midnight parties don't ever break up right. I'm going to change my mind, yea, change my mind. 'Cause I keep the servant room blues all the time."[30] In the same year blues singer Bessie Smith, a native of Tennessee, recorded her own painful memories and those of the women she knew. "All day long I'm slavin', all day long I'm bustin' suds . . . Gee, my hands are tired, washin' out these dirty duds. Lord, I do more work than forty-'leven Gold Dust Twins . . . Got myself a achin' from my head down to my shins. Sorry I do my washin' just to make my livelihood . . . Oh, the washwoman's life, it ain't a bit of good." [31] The deeply emotional lyrics of blues singers during the time make it clear that the conditions for Black women domestic workers were in dire need of change.

Indeed, resistance had already been waged in northeastern cities by late-nineteenth-century clubwomen and African American domestic workers who were engaged in individual acts of resistance, scholar activism, and institution-building to demand better working conditions for Black women in domestic service. Resistance to the particular exploitation of Black women in domestic service expanded in the 1920s and 30s when Black women migrated to north-ern cities in record numbers. Black clubwomen, many who had migrated from the South, continued building settlement homes to provide critical resources to migrants concentrated in the poorest sections of cities and lowest wage occupations. As historian Deborah Gray White explained, "Helping rural Black women establish themselves in urban areas had special significance for Black women's clubs because so many members had made the lonely and dangerous migration themselves."[32] Some clubwomen also formed labor organizations to directly address the concerns and needs of domestic workers. Black women scholars, journalists, and civil rights activists produced quantitative and qualitative research to document the working conditions of Black domestic workers. Labor organizers, many of whom were members of the Communist Party USA, worked directly with domestic workers to advocate for higher wages. And, most importantly, Black women in domestic service established their own labor organizations to advocate for better working conditions in the occupation. In short, many segments of Black communities were actively working to transform the terms of domestic service for Black women in the early twentieth century. Their resistance laid a significant foundation for activism against exploitation in domestic service for decades afterwards.

African American Clubwomen

Clubwoman and scholar Anna Julia Cooper has been credited for being among the first to articulate what we now call Black feminist thought and womanist thought. Less attention has been paid to her writings, speeches, and community work regarding Black women's labor struggles in domestic service. As discussed in the previous chapter, Cooper's scholar-activism on the subject of domestic service began in the late nineteenth century with the publication of *A Voice from the South* and "Colored Women as Wage Earners." Her scholar-activism on racial, class, and gender inequalities in the labor economy and her advocacy for Black women in domestic service deepened in the early twentieth century. Cooper's approach to transforming the working conditions of Black women went beyond socializing and training them to become "efficient servants" through settlement work and vocational training, an approach most readily adopted by some of her colleagues who established settlement homes. Instead, Cooper held political, religious, and educational institutions accountable for the working conditions of African American women. She also remained particularly attuned to and outspoken in her activism about how the white privileges of European immigrant women impacted the working lives of Black women.[33]

Cooper believed that settlement homes were especially beneficial for Black women in domestic service because Black women were excluded from city social services that were often extended to wage-earning European immigrant women. She joined the board of trustees of the Colored Settlement House and supervised its programs beginning in 1906. As supervisor, she appealed to philanthropists to support the Colored Settlement House by citing an example of "a wealthy citizen of Baltimore" who established public laundries where "a poor washer-woman may, at reasonable cost for soap and starch, wash and iron under perfectly sanitary conditions and with the best approved appliances."[34] As Cooper declared, water provided by settlement homes was essential for Black women's work and overall quality of life. According to the North Carolina native, wage-earning Black women and their children were just as deserving of access to libraries, reading rooms, art exhibitions, kitchens, lectures on social and economic subjects, music and arts classes, and other resources that settlement homes provided to European immigrant women. In her 1913 essay entitled "The Social Settlement: What It Is, and What It Does," Cooper also exposed settlement homes that refused to assist Black women. After citing the discriminatory history of Hull House in Chicago, the "Gospel" Jewish settlement in New York City, and other white settlement homes, she noted, "Paradoxically enough, the very period of the world that witnesses the most widespread activity in uplift movements and intensest devotion to social service finds in America the hard wall of race prejudice against Negroes most emphatically bolted and barred."[35]

Cooper also advocated for domestic workers' inclusion in the Fair Labor Standards Act and Social Security by making the argument that domestic service was significant, respectable, and skilled labor. In her speech entitled "On Education," Cooper debunked the racial stigma associated with domestic service and Black southern migrants. She asserted, "We hear a great deal about Negroes leaving the rural districts and congregating in cities . . . You and I know what an agonizing wail there is throughout the country on the degeneration of the Negro servant . . . They tell you that the Negro is more degenerate under freedom than he was under slavery; they extol the virtues, the amiability and reliability of the old time servant class, whom they tell you they loved by reason of their excellencies of character as well as their faithfulness of service."[36] Cooper deconstructed this myth by asserting that wage-earning Black domestic workers were skilled workers who advanced U.S. capitalism. As she put it, Black household workers were the "cream" of "natural endowment" and represented the "thrift, the mechanical industry, the business intelligence, the professional skill, the well-ordered homes, and the carefully nurtured families that are to be found in every town and hamlet where the colored man is known."[37] She argued that Black women in domestic service were not only beneficial to the U.S. economy, but they were indispensable and valuable to racial uplift because they had access to intimate knowledge that could help the race. She asserted, "'The help' can by her silent, self-respecting dependableness preach unanswerable sermons before audiences that you and I can never reach . . . Is it not worthwhile for some school to undertake the work seriously, candidly, devotedly, or sending out a stream into these channels of usefulness so full of promise, so rich in opportunities for the race?"[38]

Rooted in her belief that the value of Black women's domestic labors was never recognized by their employers, Cooper insisted that African American women take domestic science courses for the purpose of demanding higher wages. She explained, "The conclusion is a corollary to this that the trained domestic, like the trained nurse, will demand the pay, and will deserve the treatment that are accorded intelligent and efficient services professionally rendered in whatever calling of life."[39] In this sense, she agreed with other Black clubwomen and white women who advocated for domestic science courses. Like them, she believed that women could demand higher wages and, as a result, have greater job stability if they were trained in domestic science.

What distinguished Cooper from white women leaders of the domestic science movement was that her support for domestic science courses was rooted in her concern about the materiality of Black women's lives, a commitment and belief she expressed several decades earlier in *A Voice from the South*. Cooper believed that domestic workers were entitled not only to fair wages, but also to a "general thorough" education that went beyond how to manage a home. She declared that domestic science courses should be considered on par with other forms of education, and those who chose to study domestic science should have access to the only "sane education" which gives "training of head, hand, and heart . . . or, more literally mind, body and spirit."[40]

Cooper was not alone in her mission to improve the working conditions of domestic workers. In the words of Beverly Guy Sheftall, the next generation of clubwomen continued and expanded the work that Cooper started.[41] Nannie Helen Burroughs, Cooper's former student at M Street High School in Washington, D.C., founded the National Training School for Women and Girls in Washington D.C., in 1909 "because she wanted to prepare Black women for employment in areas that were open to them."[42] Employment opportunities were curtailed for Black women leaving the South and seeking jobs in the North after the end of World War I in 1918. Particularly concerned about the struggles of domestic workers, Burroughs established the National Association of Wage Earners (NAWE) in 1920 with Mary McLeod Bethune, founder of the Daytona Educational and Industrial Training School for Negro Girls in 1904 in Florida, which later became Bethune-Cookman College.[43]

NAWE members declared that they were motivated to establish an organization for Black women because the American Federation of Labor protected male workers and the Women's Trade Union League of America demanded rights for white women workers in the industrial trades, yet "our women have no organization standing with them and for them in their struggle of economic and advancement and protection."[44] As historian Sharon Harley explained, "While reform-oriented, the association was no less radical than most of the trade unions of the period . . . this association was quite progressive in its publicly stated goals on behalf of women."[45] Burroughs and Bethune

FIG. 7 Photograph of students of Burroughs' National Training School for Women and Girls circa 1911–1920. Credit: Library of Congress Prints and Photographs Division.

led the association's drive to organize 10,000 southern Black migrant domestic workers.[46] In 1924, President Burroughs and Vice President Bethune declared that domestic workers could not "advance unless they become organized producers ... Working together we can advance to a place of influence and respect in the labor world."[47] Although the association was unable to incorporate a union of domestic workers, they purchased a "practice house" where they taught domestic science to southern migrant workers. The association believed that training in domestic science would allow domestic workers to demand living wages. Members of the association also operated a factory where they employed African American women to make work dresses, caps, and aprons for sale by mail order.

The White Rose Home for Colored Working Girls is another example of how African American clubwomen built institutions to address the working conditions of southern migrant Black women. As discussed in the previous chapter, clubwoman Victoria Earle Matthews established the Home in 1897 and it remained in full operation after her death in 1907. The clubwomen who operated the Home in the early twentieth century continued offering temporary lodging and traveler's aid and employment services to new arrivals in New York City. In 1923, they expanded the Home's traveler's aid service to assist Caribbean immigrant women who arrived at Ellis Island.[48] Migrants from the

South and the Caribbean sought assistance from the Home throughout the 1920s and 30s, and the Home continued providing services for Black women and their families until it closed in 1984.

Clubwomen's settlement homes were especially critical for Black women during the Depression era. While employment was scarce for most people during the financial crisis, it was even more scarce for Black women. They faced competition with white European immigrant women who re-entered domestic work after their husbands were laid off from their jobs, or after the women themselves had lost factory or retail work. The Employment Department of the Young Women's Christian Association in New York City reported in 1929 that some domestic service employers fired Black women to hire their white competitors or refused to hire Black women at all. Employers justified their decisions with claims that Black women were dirty, dishonest, and unreliable. Employers had also declared Black women difficult because of the terms that the wage-earning women set for their employment. Some of the job seekers did not want to work with children while others preferred cooking for families over cleaning homes. As one proud southern migrant noted, she was unwilling to take any kind of job because she was used to working for wealthy families and was "bewildered by the recent changes."[49]

Alice Brown Fairclough's 1929 study of southern Black women and Caribbean immigrant women in New York City revealed that sometimes African American women faced job competition with Caribbean immigrant women.[50] Some domestic service employers preferred to hire Caribbean immigrant women over African American women because they thought "foreign Blacks" would work for lower wages. Some employers also assumed that women from the British West Indies could emulate British housekeeping traditions.[51] When African American women were hired over European immigrant women, they were expected to perform the most arduous tasks for the lowest wages and preference was given to "light colored girls."[52] Black women found it hard to pay for rent and utilities, transportation to work, and occasional recreational activities with their low wages.

Unable to meet the costs of living, Black domestic workers took residence in homes established by Black clubwomen. As Frances Thornton noted in her 1936 master's thesis on southern migrant women in Harlem, the Young Women's Christian Association's Emma Ransom House was Harlem's only women's hotel and could house up to 236 women. The House helped its residents and women in the larger Harlem community find employment. It placed well over seven hundred women in jobs in 1935 alone.[53] In addition to receiving assistance from friends and family already settled in northern cities migrants sought lodging, occupational training classes, and childcare services from the New York Colored Mission (founded in 1870), the Lincoln Settlement in

Brooklyn (1908), Hope Day Nursery (1911), Utopia House (1928), and Club Caroline (1928).[54]

Beginning in the 1930s, Black women in domestic service started labor organizations to address their own working and living conditions. Establishing the unions was a bold declaration to lawmakers and employers that domestic workers were in fact skilled workers. Members of the Domestic Workers' Union (DWU) along with smaller domestic worker unions inspired by the DWU in Brooklyn, Westchester, Newark, and Washington, D.C., demanded legislation to standardize working conditions and wages in domestic service. These laws, domestic workers argued, would force employers to treat them as skilled workers, and, more to the point for DWU members, union workers.

The Domestic Workers' Union

In 1936, one of the largest meetings on the labor concerns of African American women took place at the Abyssinian Baptist Church in Harlem. Over three hundred African American domestic workers filled the sanctuary to hear Dora Lee Jones engage with representatives from the NAACP, the New York State Federation, the Women's Trade Union League, and the Negro Labor Committee in a discussion about the exploitation of Black women in domestic service. [55] In her speech, Jones insisted that changing the working conditions of African American women required a two-pronged approach that involved creating federal and state laws to protect domestic workers as a special class of laborers and working directly with domestic workers, employers, and clergymen on the ground.

While little information is known about Jones' personal background, she developed a public profile in New York City as the leader of the Domestic Workers' Union (DWU). The DWU initially began as several unions of Black and Finnish women who lived in Yorkville, Harlem, Portchester, and Sunnyside, Queens. Jones directed the Sunnyside location and became the public representative of the organization. The unions met at a headquarters building in a Finnish neighborhood in Harlem. The offices were destroyed during the 1935 Harlem riots, during which residents of Harlem broke windows of white-owned businesses in their neighborhoods after hearing a rumor that an African American teenage boy was beaten to death for stealing merchandise from the Kress Five and Ten Store at 256 West 125 Street. This forced the DWU to relocate its headquarters to the Upper East Side.[56]

After relocating, the DWU reached new heights in their organizing efforts. The union became a part of the American Federation of Labor's Building Services Employees International Union (BSEIU). They made history as the first labor union specifically for domestic workers and affiliated with a major federally recognized labor organization. In 1936, the AFL issued the union a charter establishing the DWU as Local 149 of the BSEIU. After the DWU was chartered other locals emerged in Westchester, Newark, and Brooklyn.[57] DWU members were inclusive in their approach as they recognized the strength in numbers and solidarity. As the DWU slogan declared, "every domestic worker" is a "union worker."[58]

With little support from state governments and no support from the federal government, domestic workers took matters into their own hands to advance their agenda to regulate domestic service. Dora Lee Jones and other DWU members, like their predecessors Matthews and Cooper, believed in working with local and national women's and labor organizations. Jones worked with the National Association for the Advancement of Colored People (NAACP), the Women's Trade Union League, the New York State Federation, the Women's Trade Union League, and the Negro Labor Committee from 1936 until 1940 to campaign for legislation to protect domestic workers. Improving the working lives of Black women was an enormous task especially during the Depression. As the Department of Labor's Women's Bureau reported in 1938, "Though women in general have been discriminated against and exploited through limitation of their opportunities for employment, through long hours, low wages, and harmful working conditions, such hardships have fallen upon Negro women with double harshness."[59] Unable to find employment in domestic service during the Depression, Black women in New York City stood on the street corners of the Bronx and waited for white employers to hire them for day work. African American women writers and activists Ella Baker and Marvel Cooke were the first to dub the street corners the Bronx slave markets.

Jones tried several strategies to overcome the obstacles that left Black women with few options, but to stand on street corners for work. She and a group of DWU members spent several weeks walking down the streets of the Bronx trying to convince Black domestic workers who participated in the slave markets to join the Domestic Workers' Union to no avail because most Black domestic workers were skeptical of unions. Jones therefore turned to religious institutions to set the moral tone for employing domestic workers who participated in the slave markets. She worked with Black ministers to encourage their church members to overcome their fears of unions and join the DWU. Jones also worked with local rabbis to convince employers to hire DWU members. In the 1930s, more Jewish families employed domestic workers than in previous decades and Jones thought that rabbis could change the minds of employers more quickly than she or other domestic workers could. As she explained to Vivian Morris in a personal interview, "We have sent out a suggestion to the rabbis in the various synagogues, and white clergymen, that they should stress to their congregations that they should stop hiring the girls from the slave marts at starvation wages."[60] The DWU hoped to create a class of employers who were sensitive to the needs and humanity of domestic workers by working directly with local churches and synagogues. Jones also envisioned synagogues and Black churches working together to set up centers in their respective neighborhoods where Black women and Jewish employers could negotiate the terms of employment beginning at a minimum wage in a safe place.

Jones' idea of creating a coalition between the DWU and religious institutions produced some results. Although they were not able to shut down the markets, the standard rates that employers offered to day laborers increased slightly. They also convinced some employers to hire union workers. Employers who hired workers from the union agreed to sign a contract guaranteeing a fifty-cent hourly rate and carfare for a sixty-hour week with one day off and two weeks of paid vacation. Employers also consented to paying the fifty-cent union fees on behalf of their employees. This was a bold standard set by the DWU, especially since the standard rate established by prospective employers during the Depression could be as low as fifteen or twenty cents an hour or four dollars for a forty-hour work week that demanded life-threatening tasks such as washing upper-story windows and onerous tasks such as childcare.[61]

While Jones and DWU members recognized the importance of developing new strategies, they also practiced forms of organizing similar to the settlement homes of the late nineteenth century. Since the earlier migrations of Black women, the overwhelming majority preferred to live outside of their employers' homes. This living arrangement presented opportunities for domestic workers and their allies to congregate. Like the White Rose Mission Home, the DWU headquarters was a place where Black women in domestic service got together to talk about their jobs or met for support when they were unemployed, cooked meals, planned social events, and discussed political matters. What made the DWU headquarters distinct from earlier settlement homes was that domestic workers themselves directed the activities. It was a busy place full of organizing energy and discussion. When Vivian Morris visited the DWU headquarters to interview Dora Lee Jones, she was greeted by a "sharp eyed, nimble white worker" who was preparing petitions. Afterwards, she heard a group of African American women drinking coffee and eating sandwiches discussing a scathing article by journalist Damon Runyon about housewives' treatment of domestic workers. Morris reported that a "smooth toned young girl" read the article to women who had either left their reading glasses at home or admitted that they could not read.[62]

Although Dora Lee Jones was the lead spokesperson for the union, she was not the only DWU member to confront lawmakers publicly about the concerns of Black domestic workers. DWU member Rosa Rayside testified at a House of Representatives' labor subcommittee meeting in 1935 to convince lawmakers to pass the Lundeen Unemployment and Social Insurance Bill. It was one of the first proposed bills to promise benefits to all unemployed workers "whether they be industrial, agricultural, domestic, office, or professional workers, and to farmers, without discrimination because of age, sex, race, color, religious, or political opinion or affiliation."[63] Rayside declared that the bill was especially vital to domestic workers, those who worked in private homes because they could not find jobs as stenographers and teachers, and housewives "forced into the domestic line" because their husbands could no longer support them. She testified, "It is essential that any bill designed honestly to give security to workers against unemployment should include domestic workers . . . The employers have taken advantage of the crisis to force wages of domestic help below a subsistence level . . . they contract for the full-time work of the house worker in exchange for a 'good' home. In many cases, the accommodations consist of a folding cot in the hallway, and the poorest sort of food." Rayside also cited stories of a woman who received only fifty cents for a full day's work, another woman who received $1.25 for working eight hours a week and had to pay seventy cents for carfare, and women whose employers brought them across state lines to work for less than what they paid domestic workers already living in New York City.[64] Roosevelt Administration officials shot down the bill with claims that it was a communist plot. While the Labor Committee voted in favor of the bill, the Rules Committee did not allow it to move to the House floor for debate.[65]

Black women continued demanding change despite legislative setbacks, and sometimes they were successful at thwarting policies that would have legalized labor exploitation in domestic service. The perception that Black women servants were dirty in habit and hygiene had shaped public discourse in northern cities since the latter half of the nineteenth century. Fears of diseased Black servants resurfaced in the 1930s and led to health ordinances requiring domestic workers to undergo medical inspections before working in private homes.[66] Domestic workers in New Rochelle, New York; and Englewood, Newark; and Tenafly, New Jersey; demanded that their city governments abolish the ordinances and create new laws that would protect them as workers by arguing that their own health was actually at risk because they came into contact with unsanitary substances and objects in their employers' homes.[67] Their protests forced many of their local city councils to vote down the measure.

DWU members, however, faced challenges that were so great that they could not possibly overcome them alone. The Depression made it nearly impossible for the Domestic Workers' Union to raise money for their campaigns and the BSEIU offered the Domestic Workers' Union limited financial assistance. It was difficult for domestic workers to garner support from larger labor unions that continued to focus their efforts on improving the wages of white workers in the industrial trades. In addition, circumstances during the financial crisis were dire for household workers and they were therefore less likely to go on strike.[68] While Black women remained on the periphery of trade union organization's agendas, they were significant to the civil rights and labor agendas in Black communities. As such, domestic workers were joined by writers, activists, and community organizers who amplified their cause and the urgency of transforming domestic service for Black women.

Journalists, Activists, and Community Organizers

Trying to transform the working conditions of Black women in domestic service was truly a communal project. Similar to late-nineteenth- and early-twentieth-century Black clubwomen who believed that their fates and agendas were intimately connected to the struggles of their Black working-class sisters, activists working to achieve political and economic rights for Blacks in the twentieth century knew that their civil rights agendas were integral to the struggles of Black domestic workers.

Writers for Black newspapers were influential in bringing city and statewide attention to the exploitation of Black women day laborers. Bell Taub, a writer for *The Liberator*, reported:

> In contrast with the civil war days, these wage slaves perform the obliging function of auctioning themselves off to their employers. Another obliging feature of their plight is that they are neither fed nor sheltered nor paid wages for the hundreds of hours which they stand and wait for employment! Propped up against, store-walls at street corners they stood. The women will occasionally rest weary bodies on old discarded grocery boxes. In their hands they hold a brown paper bag. In that bag is their promise of comfort for the day—a dry piece of bread for lunch, also a few torn bits of work clothes. The average wage they earn is three dollars a week with hourly wages ranging from 20 cents to 30 cents an hour. [69]

Tom O'Connor, a journalist for the *PM* newspaper, wrote a feature story about Rowina Douglas, a 26-year-old African American woman who migrated from Baltimore, Maryland, to New York City to work in domestic service in 1935. Faced with severely limited employment opportunities, Douglas was forced to stand for hours each day on the corner of 170th Street and Townsend Avenue until an employer came along to hire her for day work. Douglas and the other women who stood with her worked for slave wages since the women who hired them were unable (or unwilling) to pay minimum wages. O'Connor reported: "Many of them [the housewives] are poor themselves and couldn't afford any domestic help if they had to pay decent wages or keep a regular employee. Many others just don't like to plan their housework regularly and would rather walk to the corner and pick up a maid for a day when they feel like it just as they'd pick up a lamb chop or a head of cabbage at the store." [70]

Yet media coverage of what became known as the Bronx Slave Markets could be exploitative itself. Except for Douglas, the women in the photograph featured in O'Connor's article all faced the wall. The caption states that "When these women saw the cameraman, they turned their backs—all except Rowina Douglas, who knew her picture was going to be taken and didn't care. Some are camera shy because they're on relief."[71] Women who participated in the Bronx Slave Markets were also vulnerable to sexual assault. As Belle Taub noted six years before O'Connor's report, "Our beautiful girl, propped against the wall of Woolworth's five and ten, tells of one of her friends being lured to so-called 'bachelor's apartment' where she barely escaped an attack."[72] A photographer for O'Connor's article captured a scene of a white man who approached Rowina Douglas in the doorway of a Woolworth's store.

While Douglas refused his advances, there were other day workers who engaged in sex work to supplement their low wages from domestic work and meet the needs of their children.[73] A woman who referred to herself as "Miss P.G.A." attributed sexual arrangements in domestic service to the lack of social services to support domestic workers in a time of financial crisis. She wrote to the *Amsterdam News*:

> White grandfathers, fathers and sons stand and beckon at you for an hour at a time. One asked me whether I work at night. He said some of the girls refused night work. I asked if his wife was at home and he said she was on a vacation and asked me to be a nice baby, etc. These Negro women have been refused relief. The employment agencies do not have any day or part-time work. If they buy a job they are many times cheated of their fee and they are forced to pay the same high rents."[74]

Civil rights activist and labor organizer Ella Baker and investigative journalist Marvel Cooke were the first to dub the street corners in the Bronx, Brownsville, and Brighton Beach and other areas of the city "slave markets." Like working-class Irish immigrant women of the Progressive era, journalists and domestic workers themselves used slavery as a metaphor to describe the working conditions of domestic workers on these corners. African American domestic workers and their allies, however, operationalized the metaphor differently than white labor reformers. As historian Premilla Nadasen explained, "For them [African Americans], slavery was a trope that connected past and present, illuminated power relations, and spoke to kin, community, and a legacy of racism."[75] African American writers and labor activists made frequent comparisons between the street corners where Black women stood for day work and slavery to urge local government officials to pass legislation to protect Black women day workers from labor exploitation.

Ella Baker, who had worked briefly as a domestic worker herself, and Cooke, turned the city's attention to the markets in a five-part series published in *The*

Crisis that detailed their experiences talking to women who participated in the Bronx Slave Markets while posing as day laborers themselves.[76] As Cooke put it, the markets were where Black women waited in "rain, or shine, in bitter cold or under broiling sun, to be hired by local housewives looking for bargains in human labor."[77] Cooke and Baker documented the heart-wrenching stories of these women. Described by Cooke and Baker as a friendly and intelligent girl, Millie Jones told them that she had to wash fifteen windows every day in a six-room apartment and if the employer found a speck on one of the windows, she had to wash every single window again. She also had so much laundry to wash and iron that it took her two full working days to complete the job. And the laundry had to be folded in a particular way.[78] Baker also uncovered day workers' stories about white men who came to the street corners to elicit sex from them and the complicity of their wives in their plans to exploit the workers. As historian Barbara Ransby put it, "white female employers were just as eager to use them [Black women] for their muscle as their husbands were to use them for their sexual services."[79]

Vivian Morris, investigative journalist for the Federal Workers Project of the Works Progress Administration (WPA) picked up where Cooke and Baker left off probing further into the slave markets into the late 1930s. She was also among the first journalists to publicize the labor organizing of Dora Lee Jones and the Domestic Workers' Union to alter disparaging public perceptions about the day workers. Morris hoped that publishing more stories on the Bronx Slave Market would force the city to pay attention to the injustices that occurred and bring the exploitative hiring practices to an end. Day laborers were blamed for introducing sexual vices to local neighborhoods by engaging in prostitution. Black women who stood on the street corners for temporary housework jobs were also accused of swindling the system, or working while receiving subsidies from the federal government. This was an all-too-familiar tale for Morris. A she wrote, working-poor Black women had been the source of blame for political and economic problems in the city for decades.

Like Baker and Cooke, Morris went straight to the source to hear the women explain what happened and the circumstances that brought them there. She hopped on a subway headed to the Kingsbridge Road section of the Bronx when she knew most women would have completed their day's work and would be heading back to their own homes. While walking down Kingsbridge, Morris attempted to speak with two women who were in a hurry and refused to slow down and talk to her. One woman told Morris that she needed to go home and cook, whereas the other woman kept walking briskly past her. Morris' luck changed when she met a third woman named Rose Reed, a "kindly middle-aged woman of about forty." Reed did not suspect that Morris was a journalist and assumed that she was "new on the job."

She opened up to Morris fairly quickly and shared her opinion about the Bronx Slave Market as Morris walked back to the subway station with her. Reed expressed that there was a lot that needed to be done to improve the working conditions of domestic workers, but she "got a fair salary and the conditions under which she worked were not as bad as the majority of her fellow workers found them."

Reed worked eight hours a day and could only take a lunch break on one day. She was paid $3.50 a day and carfare.[80] Reed's story surprised Morris because it was a stark contrast to the "fifteen and twenty cents per hour scale of the women who frequented the slave marts." Although Reed thought her working conditions were fair, she remained disappointed that other Black women "worked like oxen." Reed admitted that other women's experiences hit close to home because she had once worked for slave wages and she credited God and her spirituality for guiding her to a better job. While her "back was almost breaking from the work" on the job, Reed sang "I Got to Get Rid of This Heavy Load" and "Go Down Moses" to help her think of a way to reach "salvation from that awful work." That following Sunday she met a woman at church who told her about the Domestic Workers Union. The woman said that her employers treated her nicely and recommended that she join the union. According to Morris, Reed told her that she joined the union "to keep the madam from asking her about it again" and that it "was one of the best things she ever did in her whole life."[81]

After joining the union Reed claimed that the "conditions and wages were so good" that she "could hardly believe it." A proud member of the DWU for six years, Rose showed Morris her union book and boldly inquired, "Are you in the union?" When Morris replied no, Reed advised, "You can't fight your battles alone." Then Reed offered to take Morris to the union hall the following day at noon. She warned Morris that she would want to join after seeing "the spirit and great work going on there."[82] Morris consented. The next day Reed led her to a building in the heart of Yorkville where Morris met the Executive Secretary Dora Lee Jones, "a plump, energetic, round-faced Negro woman with all-engulfing eyes."[83] Morris soon learned that Jones was the driving force behind a union that was changing the working conditions for Black women in significant ways.

African American male writers also joined efforts to transform working conditions for Black women in domestic service. Richard Wright, who had established working relationships with Communist Party members, documented domestic workers' accounts of sexual exploitation. To gather data for his novel *Black Hope*, Wright went undercover to investigate employment agencies that sent agents to the South to lure Black women into prostitution with false promises of employment in New York City.[84] He also collected confidential government records about the street corner markets and conducted interviews with one hundred and fifty-nine African American women in domestic service in New York City. The interviewees shared with him their experiences of sexual assault and harassment on the job. One woman recalled that a male employer asked her to fix her hair like Shirley Temple to satisfy his sexual fetish. Some women also mentioned during their interviews that male employers physically assaulted them. As one woman asserted, "I was in the kitchen and I had to stand on a chair to reach something in the top closet, as I reached up, the husband came in and put his hand up my dress." [85]

Playwright and branch manager of the New York State Employment Service Mary Frances Gunner also added to the body of research on the exploitation of Black women household workers. She documented the exploitation of rural Virginia migrants in her master's thesis about employment agencies in Brooklyn, New York. Gunner reported, "These girls are sent up in groups, and their baggage is checked to the employer who is supposed to meet the girls at the train. The girls work for a period of time without wages until the money advanced for their railroad fare and other expense is repaid. In some cases, the girls did not know what wage they were supposed to receive." [86] Gunner also noted that the southerners were often placed in homes with inadequate living facilities and employers who could not afford to pay domestic workers livable wages. In some cases, live-in domestics were not given a personal room and were expected to sleep on a cot. [87]

African American writers' investigative journalism and data collection forced city-wide newspapers to report on the exploitation of Black women in domestic service. The *New York Times* published similar stories about the sexual exploitation and labor trafficking of southern African American women. Mr. Moss, a New York license commissioner, told reporters for the newspaper that unlicensed agencies brought Black women to New York to work ostensibly as domestics. "In many cases," he said, "the girls are discharged for incompetence and then turned out on the streets and made dependent on public relief. The majority of girls brought here by these unlicensed agencies are Negro girls from the South and Polish and Bohemian girls from the mining towns . . ." [88] Florence Kravis was one of many white women arrested for running an employment agency without a license and for making false employment promises to southern Black women. Kathryn Kalish and Jennie P. McGee of the City License Department claimed that Kravis brought "thousands of girls, mostly from South Carolina, into Brooklyn." [89]

City-wide coverage of the slave markets pushed city government officials to address the problem to ward off the negative publicity. New York City mayor Fiorella LaGuardia and New York State labor commissioner Frieda Miller formed a committee to investigate the markets. The committee members, however, were more concerned with hiding the problem than solving it. Members insisted that Black women drove down business for the stores that they stood in front of and it was not altogether clear that they were victims of sexual abuse. They believed that Black women were prone to sexually lewd behavior. The committee opened employment offices on Simpson Street and on Elliott Place where domestic workers and employers could bargain for day work out of plain sight, but this effort merely shielded the problem without addressing Black workers' rights. Neither the committee nor the New York State Employment Service held employers to a minimum wage or to standard work hours so domestic workers could be just as easily exploited in the offices as on the streets.[90]

Black communal support for domestic workers was unrelenting despite legislative setbacks. Clergymen and Black-owned newspapers across the country supported the labor organizing of domestic workers by challenging negative portrayals of them in the media, and sometimes at the expense of Irish immigrant women. William Jacob Walls, 42nd Bishop of the African Methodist Episcopal Zion Church in New York, wrote a response to the 1937 film *Maid of Salem* that was published by the *Chicago Defender* and *Amsterdam News*. Bishop Walls expressed his anger about the film's portrayal of an enslaved Black household servant, a voodoo practitioner, as the cause for the late-seventeenth-century witch trials in Salem, Massachusetts. Walls argued that the writers of the film got it wrong. The servant accused of witchcraft was not Black. She was an Irish immigrant woman named Goody. He insisted that the negative depiction of Black domestic servants was part of a larger agenda to disparage the Black race. He explained, "The picture entitled 'The Maid of Salem' showing at the Chicago theatre is another instance of the habit of producers to defame the Race by sinister implications on the screen. History is distorted to make it appear that a slave called Tituba started the witchcraft . . ." Walls did not deny that a Black servant was arrested during the trials, yet he contended that the Irish servant was the one to blame for the hysteria that plagued the town. As he proclaimed, "Mark you, the picture makes the mobbish officers arrest only the colored slave and connects her with the 1688 Boston incident, in place of the Irish woman servant." [91] While it is debatable whether an Irish immigrant or Black servant was the primary target of the trials, what is significant about Wells' response is that it reflected the ways in which African American respectability politics involved upholding images of Black household workers above their Irish counterparts.

A year after Bishop Walls's response was published, Alfred A. Duckett, civil rights advocate and journalist for the *New York Age*, exposed an Irish housewife for exploiting a Black household worker. Duckett reported, "Not in the deep heart of the South, nor in some barbaric or untamed country, but right in the heart of civilized Brooklyn, today there is a forty-nine-year-old Negro woman being kept virtually a slave by an Irish housewife, forced to do heavy housework, make beds, shovel coal, and sweep floors . . . Elisa Denny, has been the victim of robbery and exploitation on the part of several families in the vicinity." Duckett pleaded with readers to "get together under a common cause and fight for this helpless Negro woman."[92] This was not an unfamiliar tale. The housewife that Duckett discussed in the article was one of hundreds of white employers who exploited Black women during the 1930s. What is striking about the story is that Duckett made a point of highlighting her ethnicity, which he might have done to point to the irony of an Irish woman exploiting an African American woman, considering the history of Irish oppression.

African American women members of the Communist Party USA (CPUSA) also supported the agenda of domestic workers through "on-the-ground" labor organizing. Black left feminists, as historian Erik McDuffie coined this radical group of labor activists, urged the Communist Party to take an intersectional approach to combating labor exploitation. More specifically, they insisted on the significance of addressing how the intersectionality of racial, gender, and class inequalities endemic to capitalism most negatively impacted Black women in domestic service. They argued that African American domestic workers' struggles in white homes "were part of the larger, worldwide struggle against capitalism, imperialism, and white supremacy . . ."[93] Through their writings and actual work with domestic workers, Black left feminists foregrounded domestic workers' intellect while arguing that their labor experiences reflected the triple oppression of race, class, and gender in the United States. They presented domestic workers "as social commentators and agitators who spotlight and rail against race, class, and gender discrepancies that are played out in and outside the household domestic front."[94]

The Party's initial efforts to organize domestic workers began in the 1920s when CPUSA member Fanny Austin, a Communist and domestic worker herself, lead the Harlem Women Day Workers League. According to McDuffie, The American Negro Labor Congress's newspaper, the *Negro Champion*, referred to the league as a domestic workers union. While the relationship between the league and the Workers Party was unclear, McDuffie explained, the "group [the Harlem Women Day Workers League] signaled Harlem Communists' belief that unionization, not bourgeois respectability, offered exploited Black domestic workers the best protection."[95] During the 1930s, Black left feminists expressed solidarity with Jones and the Domestic Workers Union.[96] CPUSA member Louise Thompson Patterson publicly denounced the Bronx Slave Markets and commended the efforts of the Domestic Workers' Union to eliminate exploitation in domestic service. She also insisted that the American Federation of Labor should make a concerted effort to unionize African American domestic workers.[97]

Domestic workers also collaborated with leftist teachers in adult education classes as well as with journalists and other middle-class professionals.[98] As historian Barbara Ransby noted, the Domestic Workers Union and the Harlem

FIG. 8 Photograph of an unidentified domestic worker posing for an article about domestic workers' labor struggles to appear in the *Daily Worker*, a newspaper published by the Communist Party USA. The brooch on her coat signals that she might have been a member of the party. Credit: *Daily Worker* and *Daily World* Collection held at the Tamiment Library and Robert F. Wagner Archives, New York University, by permission of the Communist Party USA.

Housewives League "represented collective action around the common interests of women."[99] Both organizations waged campaigns to combat the high cost of living and demand more effective federal and state relief programs for women and their families. One of the largest gatherings of domestic workers, housewives, leftist activists, and clubwomen took place in Chicago, Illinois, in February 1936 at the National Negro Congress. The National Council of Negro Women sponsored the meeting to foster discussions about the working and living conditions of Black women across labor niches. Congress passed a resolution at the end of the three-day meeting stating that participants would work to organize more domestic workers into trade unions under an umbrella organization that would be known as the Domestic Workers' Association. The association would be sponsored by the Congress, which would work to integrate it into the American Federation of Labor.[100] Thompson attended and left the meeting optimistic about bringing to fruition the goals outlined in the resolution. She predicted that the next time the Congress was scheduled to meet participants would have "a different story to tell, of accomplishment, of a struggle nearer the goal of the liberation of Negro women from bitter exploitation and oppression."[101]

Thompson was on target with her prediction that the conference would lead to more localized organizing to address the labor struggles of domestic workers. The Brooklyn delegates of the Congress formed an executive committee of eight people to form a Brooklyn Local of the Domestic Workers' Association immediately after leaving the conference. As the brief history of the Brooklyn Local reads, Mr. Malcolm Martin, legal adviser and Brooklyn attorney, was the lead organizer of the committee. The co-founders included Mrs. Bussy (organizer), Mrs. Carrie Johnson; Emily Knowles (treasurer); Victoria Martin (secretary); Mrs. Allabrooke, Miss Helen Washington, and Miss Nettie Joseph. They launched the Brooklyn Local in February 1937, and by May 1 of the same year they secured a location at 14 Troy Avenue in Brooklyn.

The Brooklyn Local's primary goal was to "secure higher wages and better working conditions" and to become affiliated with the American Federation of Labor, as the Manhattan Local had already achieved.[102] The Brooklyn Local, however, declared that what made them distinct from other the other locals was that they integrated a wage scale into their employer-employee agreement. The wage scale was as follows: Cooks (female, $18.00 per week); Cooks (male, $25.00 per week); Chamber Maids ($12.00 per week); General House Worker ($10.00 per week); Day's Worker ($.50 per hour); Part Time Worker (5 hours, $8.00 per week); Laundress ($.50 per hour); Mother's Helper (summer time, $9.00 per week); Cleaners ($.60 per hour); and Couples ($125.00 per month). The agreement also outlined additional terms for better working conditions, including not requiring employees to report to work before 7 a.m. nor leave after 7 p.m. While there was a glaring and unjustifiable wage gap between women and men cooks in their wage scale, the association's agreement communicated to prospective employers that domestic workers were highly skilled laborers.[103]

While it is unknown how long the Brooklyn Local was in existence, a picture of member Mabel Thompson from circa 1950 (shown in Figure 9) suggests that it was active for over a decade.[104] The original lines on her photograph indicate that she was going to be featured in a story about the association in the *Daily Worker,* thereby signaling that she might have had a leadership role in the association.[105] The local expanded during its existence and became the United Building Service and Domestic Workers Association of Brooklyn. The organization included domestic workers, handymen, porters, and general building service workers who created an alliance because domestic workers and building service workers were not protected under labor laws. The association produced a pamphlet appealing to housewives to support their members by agreeing to pay them standard wages with Social Security and Workmen's

FIG. 9 Photograph of Mabel Thompson, member of the Domestic Workers Association of Brooklyn, New York, circa 1950s. Credit: *Daily Worker* and *Daily World* Collection held at the Tamiment Library, New York University, by permission of the Communist Party USA.

Compensation. Making a special appeal for African American women on the basis of their citizenship, the association declared:

> We ask the public to accept these elementary standards. We appeal for a new understanding of what a domestic worker should be required to do. These are American standards. They are standards of fair play. They are aimed at ending the second-class citizenship of domestic workers, especially Negro domestic workers, who, more than any other category of labor, face hardships and discrimination that no decent American should tolerate.[106]

The National Urban League and the Harlem branch of the Young Women's Christian Association also worked directly with domestic workers to address labor exploitation in household employment. The National Urban League in Brooklyn and New York developed The Visiting Housekeeper Project, later adapted by Urban League branches across the country, to create "WPA jobs for women with only domestic work experience."[107] Through the project the League arranged for household workers to care for the needs of people who were most detrimentally impacted by the Depression. They took care of the immediate personal needs of the disabled and instructed families on how to make nutritious meals with limited means. The League argued that domestic workers were best suited for the project because of their "native intelligence and sympathy, and by their own experience in meeting adversity."[108] The League also imitated earlier projects of Black clubwomen and collaborated with women's organizations to establish training programs for domestic workers. This approach, they argued, especially helped women coming from the South who needed to get their foot in the door in the economically depressed northern labor markets in which they faced job competition with domestic workers already settled in New York and women with college degrees and industrial training who worked in household employment because they could not find work in their fields.

Ultimately, domestic workers and their allies faced a similar task to that faced by late-nineteenth-century domestic workers and clubwomen. In a country that had yet to recognize Black women as U.S. citizens, they had to convince domestic service employers, lawmakers, and labor organizations, which focused primarily on working-class white worker struggles, that the home was a public, wage-earning, workspace for Black women that should be regulated. This argument required white lawmakers, employers, and labor organizations to radically shift their political, economic, and personal beliefs about race, capitalism, and household work. Consequently, except for progressive white employers, most employers chose not to hire domestic workers who were union members.

In addition, no major labor organization was committed to tackling institutionalized racism and sexism and the specific issues that domestic workers confronted in the intimate confines of their workspaces. Although the DWU was an AFL-affiliated union, the AFL focused primarily on the issues confronting manufacturing employees. With very limited support from the AFL, domestic workers were left out of three critical New Deal legislative decisions—the 1935 Social Security Act, the 1936 National Labor Relations Act, and the 1938 Fair Labor Standards Act.[109] The Social Security Act provided a system of old-age benefits that would have been especially critical for African American domestics who worked past retirement age. The National Labor Relations Act guaranteed employees the right to bargain, which would have given domestic workers more power to demand fair wages and working conditions. The Fair Labor Standards Act could have protected domestic workers from labor exploitation since it established a minimum wage, a 44-hour work week, and time-and-a-half compensation for overtime.

It was challenging to maintain a cohesive united front against exploitation in domestic service among domestic workers into the 1940s to challenge these legislative setbacks. As Dora Lee Jones explained, increasing union membership was difficult because some women worked only part-time, while others worked only one hour a day. This fine line between the employed and unemployed made it hard for some part-time workers to see themselves as viable members of a labor movement. In addition, some potential members could not afford the union dues, although the DWU tried to keep its union fees at an affordable price. Other women chose not to join unions because they were willing to work for low wages to survive in what was the most economically depressed era in U.S. history. Although domestic workers and their allies were unable to transform domestic service, what is most significant about their activism and labor organizing is that they laid a critical foundation for labor organizers to lead a nationwide labor movement for minimum wage and standard work hours in domestic work several decades afterwards.

Black left feminists maintained their solidarity with domestic workers throughout the 1940s and 50s. It was domestic worker organizing that sparked Esther V. Cooper's interest in leftist politics, and she sought to bring visibility to the labor organizing efforts of domestic workers in her writing and research to argue for the inclusion of domestic workers in federal and state employee laws. What is known today about the resistance of domestic workers to labor exploitation in the 1930s is largely due to her detailed study of African American domestic worker union organizing in Washington, D.C.; Chicago; Newark; and New York City.[110] In addition, Marvel Cooke kept a watchful eye on the Bronx Slave Markets—although the New York City government had abandoned efforts to shut down the markets—and wrote a five-part series in the leftist newspaper the *Daily Compass* when it resurfaced in the 1950s. As she reported, women "still stand in all sorts of weather in order to get a chance to work. They are still forced to do an unspecific amount of work under unspecified conditions, with no guarantee that, at the end of the day, they will receive even the pittance agreed upon."[111] CPUSA member Claudia Jones also continued producing literature about the exploitation of wage earning Black women. According to the labor organizer in her 1949 article, "An End to the Neglect of the Problems of the Negro Woman!", "Negro women—as workers, as Negroes, and as women—are the most oppressed stratum of the whole population."[112]

The *Daily Worker* remained committed to covering domestic worker organizing. While the exact year and date of when Dora Lee Jones's Domestic Workers Union dissolved, reporting by the leftist newspaper and journalists Vivian Morris and Marvel Cooke reveal that the union was still active into the 1950s.[113] Nina Evans, president of the union in 1949 and described by her friends as an accomplished pianist, told a writer for the newspaper that one of the union's goals was to "stamp out the spreading slave markets, rising again since their wartime disappearance." She also declared that it was up to the union to "combat that evil," and that domestic workers deserved better working conditions because the "intelligence, experience, and tact of the domestic worker demand dignity and decent compensation for her profession."[114]

FIG. 10 Photograph of Nina
Evans, president of the Domes-
tic Workers' Union, July 7, 1949.
Credit: *Daily Worker* and *Daily
World* Collection held at the
Tamiment Library, New York
University, by permission of the
Communist Party USA.

The DWU was instrumental in securing jobs for domestic workers under the
terms that it set for employers. The contract required employers to guarantee
a sixty-hour week with one day off a week and two weeks of paid vacation
after one year of employment."[115] While leading the DWU, Evans was also an
active member of the Non-Partisan Citizens Committee for the Election of
W.E.B. Du Bois as U.S. Senator of New York. Bishop William J. Walls was
the honorary chair of the committee, and Paul Robeson was its prime fund-
raiser. Evans' membership on the leftist committee reveals that her approach
to leading the DWU was nuanced and comprehensive.[116] The original lines
on her photograph (see Figure 10) indicate that she was also going to be featured in a story about domestic worker organizing in the *Daily Worker*. Her
inclusion in the *Daily Worker* and involvement in Du Bois's campaign for the
U.S. Senate signals that she had significant roles in the overall African American labor movement of the 1950s.[117]

Social Security benefits were eventually extended to domestic workers in
1950 because African American women continued pushing the federal government to recognize domestic workers as skilled laborers. African American
domestic workers continued organizing throughout the 1950s, 60s, and 70s

because they knew that there was still more work to do to change their working conditions after this legislative win. The Montgomery Bus Boycott of 1955, for example, would not have gained as much traction and public attention had it not been for their participation in the planning of the boycotts. As Ella Baker put it, domestic workers who "walked long distances to work to support the protest, had been indispensable" to the boycotts.[118] Domestic workers were major consumers of public transportation, and when they refused to ride the bus to work the system lost a significant source of patronage, and their employers were forced to take note of the anger Black women felt about racial inequalities and their working conditions.[119]

Literary works by African American writers continued expressing the perspectives of domestic workers on race and labor. In 1956, playwright Alice Childress published "Like One of the Family . . . conversations from a domestic's life," which had originally appeared in the Marxist newspaper *Freedom* and later in *The Baltimore Afro-American*. Each of the sixty-two chapters featured Mildred's conversations with her close friend Marge about her daily experiences as a domestic worker. While describing her inspiration for writing the book, Childress noted, "Mildred is based upon my aunt Lorraine who was a domestic worker all of her life, a wonderful woman who refused to exchange dignity for pay."[120]

Nationwide alliances between domestic workers, middle-class African American women, and larger African American organizations continued throughout the 1960s and 70s. Title VII of the Civil Rights Act of 1964 barred employment discrimination on the basis of race, color, religion, sex, or national origin for employers with fifteen or more employees. Domestic worker Dorothy Bolden worked with the Urban League chapter in Atlanta, Georgia, to establish and spearhead the National Domestic Workers Union of America (NDWUA) in 1968. Although it was never officially recognized as a union and most of its members were residents of Atlanta, neither the NDWUA members nor President Bolden altered the organization's name during its twenty-eight-year existence. Their decision indicated how strongly the members thought of themselves as professional workers and the importance of amplifying Black household workers' struggles across the country.

The National Committee on Household Employment (NCHE) organized a national convention in 1969 to address racial issues in domestic service. During the convention domestic workers banded together to form the Household Technicians of America (HTA). The name of the organization reflected the members' pride in their skilled work and their ownership of it. As Geraldine Miller, co-founder of HTA, explained, "I like the idea of being able to know that I could go into someone else's home and make it look good to me—you know. I was the judge of what it should look like." After completing her work,

Miller recalled that she would say to herself, "Gee, that looks good to me."[121] The title Household Technicians of America must have resonated with wage-earning women who did not attend the National Committee on Household Employment Conference. After the meeting, the HTA expanded to include over thirty local branches and twenty-five thousand members throughout the South, Southwest, and West Coast.[122] Throughout the 1970s, the NCHE and HTA worked together to push for legislation to increase the minimum wage and expand its coverage to include domestic workers.

Shirley Chisolm, the first Black congresswoman and first major party Black candidate to run for president of the United States, stood in solidarity with domestic workers at the congressional hearings on the bill. She delivered a testimony to Congress about her mother's experiences working in domestic service to make the argument that domestic workers deserved a minimum wage. She also attended the national convention of domestic workers and urged them to continue fighting for labor protections.[123] Southern migrant Black women continued pushing local governments for labor rights. Ruby Duncan, a domestic worker and southern migrant resident of Las Vegas, Nevada, lead other Black women in service work in a state and national campaign for welfare rights.[124]

Domestic workers and their allies saw some of the fruits of their labors in the 1970s. The Fair Labor Standards Act, which granted workers a federal minimum wage, was amended in 1974 to include domestic workers.[125] Domestic workers were also granted unemployment insurance in 1976.[126] These were monumental accomplishments considering that domestic workers had been excluded from the protection of state and federal laws for over a century. While these were historic decisions, domestic workers still had a long way to go to reach full coverage under labor laws. Babysitters and companions to elderly persons remained excluded from the Fair Labor Standards Act. All household workers were excluded from the National Labor Relations Act, which granted employees the right to organize; the Occupational Safety and Health Act, which guaranteed safe working conditions; and civil rights laws that protected workers from employment discrimination.[127] The struggle to pass legislation to fully protect domestic workers in their workplaces continues to this very day.

Conclusion

Working-class Irish immigrant women were whiter by the 1920s. They could more easily exit domestic service and choose from a wider array of occupations than what was available to them in the late nineteenth century. Irish immigrant women's transition out of domestic service, however, was not always immediate. Anti-Irish discriminatory hiring practices forced some Irish immigrant women to seek employment in private homes after seeking employment in native born white women's occupations. Irish immigrant women who worked outside of domestic service remained concentrated in service occupations cleaning hospitals and hotels, caring for the personal needs of hospital patients, and waitressing in restaurants. While these labors resembled those of domestic service, Irish immigrant women in those occupations could say that they were not doing "colored work," although they were not fully protected from labor exploitation. Some Irish immigrant women who left domestic service after marriage had to work for supplemental income to survive on the margins of the white middle class, while some returned to domestic service after their husbands became injured on the job or died from job-related illnesses.

While Irish immigrant women worked to position themselves securely in the white middle class, African American women continued working at dismantling the underpinnings of institutionalized racial, class, and gender inequalities that made the labor exploitation of Black women in domestic service possible. The early-to-latter half of the twentieth century was a critical period of labor organizing for African American women across social classes to transform domestic service. Domestic workers and their allies demanded that employers and lawmakers see domestic workers the way that Black communities knew them to be. They were highly skilled, independent, wage-earning women who deserved legal protection in their workplaces. Domestic workers and their allies pushed for federal and state legislation to protect domestic workers from labor and sexual exploitation in their workplaces. More specifically, they insisted that domestic workers deserved access to unemployment insurance, livable wages, safe working conditions, paid sick leave, regulated work hours, and protection from dehumanizing work requirements.

Their efforts created a public discourse and established cross-class alliances that became the foundation of a national domestic worker movement that emerged in the proceeding decades. The Civil Rights Movement and the persistent exclusion of domestic workers from labor laws sparked a fire under African American women across the country to create more branches of domestic worker organizations and women's committees that collaborated across state lines to address the exploitation of African American women in domestic service. Although their approaches varied, like their predecessors, they asserted that domestic workers were highly skilled and respected members of their communities who should be protected in private homes. The activism and labor organizing of domestic workers and their allies since the late nineteenth century produced some historic legislative advances for domestic workers in the 1970s.

When the majority of African American women transitioned out of domestic service in the 1980s, they fought for labor rights in other professions, leaving the occupation primarily to immigrant women of color, primarily from the Caribbean, Latin America, and Asia, and some working-class African American women. African American women of the nineteenth and twentieth centuries, however, left behind a legacy of work and ideas that created a foundation upon which women of color in domestic service fight for labor rights today. Like the African American women who preceded them, they assert that they are highly skilled workers who deserve the same protection as all other workers covered under labor laws.

Conclusion

—◄○►—

Putting Hands on
Race Continues

When I began researching the histories of Irish immigrant women in domestic service, I hoped that I would come across a photograph or minutes from a women's labor organization meeting showing evidence of Irish immigrant and African American women protesting labor exploitation in domestic service together. As I continued my research, I realized that their histories spoke to each other in ways that revealed more illuminating truths about race and possibilities for cross-racial women labor organizing than I was initially seeking. African American and Irish immigrant women's overlapping histories of labor exploitation and white male supremacy in the U.S. South and Ireland, and the similar ways in which they were racialized, allow us to see common ground from which women can challenge labor exploitation and white male supremacy across their racial differences. Black and Irish immigrant women's different racial projects and trajectories in the labor economy, however, reveal critical dialogues about race, gender, and labor that need to occur across and within white, black, and immigrant communities of color.

The relationality of African American and Irish immigrant domestic workers' histories bare important lessons for these communities, especially in this political era of heightened white nativism and misogyny; anti-worker legislation; and anti-immigrant and anti-Black violence and legislation. Since the 2016 election of an overtly white supremacist president in the United States, there have been significant rollbacks on workers' rights, women's rights, voting rights, and immigration policies after nearly two centuries of civil rights

activism for the political rights of racial minorities, women, and wage earners. Although the white working class voted overwhelmingly for President
Trump, he has introduced and signed trade and anti-worker rights' legislation that has in turn curtailed the power of majority white labor unions; shut
down factories that employ primarily white workers; and plummeted agricultural sales for white farmers.[1] The emergence of a national labor movement
of primarily white teachers in predominately Republican states shows that
Congressional attacks on workers' benefits and Obamacare have impacted
white women in low-wage occupations.[2] The teachers' strikes also reflect the
enduring class struggles of the white working class in women-dominated service occupations.

Regaining the rights for women workers that have been dismantled and
gaining rights that were never extended to women workers require difficult
and uncomfortable discussions about race. Irish immigrant women's racial
labor histories should provoke much-needed conversations within white
communities about the pitfalls of white male supremacy for the white working class. The white working class has a long history of voting for political
candidates who evoke racism towards African Americans and immigrants
of color, although doing so has rarely improved their lives in any substantial way. The white working class remains vulnerable to massive layoffs from
manufacturing jobs; inadequate healthcare services; and lack of access to
vital natural resources such as clean air, soil, and water in rural communities. Irish immigrant women's racial history serves as a poignant reminder
to them that their own ancestors were not always viewed as fit for U.S.
citizenship.[3]

The Irish Bridget, or the trope of the racially inferior, lazy immigrant
woman who did not deserve living wages and safe working conditions is now
often associated with Latin American immigrant women. There have been
many racial tropes of European immigrant women in the nineteenth century from which white women can draw to critically analyze how racism has
impacted their communities. For example, white women who claim Italian
ancestries can look at the ways in which Italian women were racialized as too
bossy and unattractive to ever serve white American families. White women
who claim German ancestries can look to the trope of the German woman
who was too grotesque to serve white families because she could not speak
English and cooked with too much garlic. All of these stereotypes served as
white nativist justifications to deny working-class white immigrant women living wages and political rights.

The transition of Irish immigrant women into white women's jobs, however, changed the ways in which these women were viewed publicly. The
daughters of Erin went from being domineering and uncivilized Irish Bridgets
to model immigrant women. Historian Margaret Brennan captured this

sentiment when she noted: "Credit is due to the Irish Bridget for pioneering the way for the Irish to become accepted by native-born Americans and for helping the Irish, as a group, move into the American middle class."[4] This narrative renders invisible the labor struggles of working-class Irish immigrant women that continued throughout the early twentieth century and that arguably still exist for Irish American women. Revisiting Irish immigrant women's struggle for labor rights and their experiences of ethnic and gender discrimination in the labor economy in the early twentieth century should provoke conversations among working-class white women about the pitfalls of white supremacy for their own economic interests. Distancing themselves from African Americans did not result in uniform upward mobility for all descendants of the famine-era Irish as indicated in the colloquial sayings "shanty Irish" and "lace curtain Irish." Although Irish immigrants were recipients and ardent supporters of white privilege, their racialized gender histories make clear that white supremacy as practice and ideology has not fully benefited them economically, nor politically.

As with whiteness studies, public discussions about the struggles of the white working class often subsume women's experiences under those of men. There is much to unpack about race, gender, and the Irish experience that could lead to broader discussions about class and gender inequalities across white communities. Irish immigrant women's gradual transition outside of domestic service can serve as a useful starting point to interrogate the hegemonic narrative that white immigrants "made it" in America because of hard work and determination that other groups lack, such as African Americans and Latin American immigrants. Tracing Irish immigrant women's class struggles past the late nineteenth century can provoke conversations about persistent class divisions in Irish American communities, and white communities more broadly. Irish immigrant women's history could serve as a blueprint for asking pressing questions about white working-class women such as: How do white working-class women experience poverty? What are the ways in which they uphold white supremacy to express their own class anxieties and racial hatred? And why do they consistently vote for misogynist white men who will never advocate for them? Asking these sorts of questions can initiate discussions about race that have been pushed under the rug for far too long in white communities. When discussions about racism are avoided or dismissed, white supremacy rears an ugly head that threatens to take the country back several centuries not only for African Americans, but also for whites and immigrants of color.

Putting African American and Irish immigrant women's labor and migration histories into conversation with one another also makes the stories of African American women visible in whiteness studies where they have been invisible. David Roediger's *Wages of Whiteness* and Noel Ignatiev's *How the Irish Became White* could not account for the labor histories of Irish immigrant men without the histories of Black men and the scholarship of Black male thinkers such as Frederick Douglass, W.E.B. Du Bois, and Frantz Fanon.[5] African American women intellectuals must also be inserted into Irish immigrant women's histories. Late-nineteenth-century satirical images of the Irish Bridget alone signal that African American women were integral to Irish immigrant women's labor histories. The intellectual work of African American domestic workers and clubwomen is a significant touchstone for deepening understandings about the racial underpinnings of Irish women's experiences in the United States, and those of white and immigrant women's experiences more broadly. A history of whiteness without African American women's intersectional theories and activism will always stop short of fully interrogating the foundation of inequalities and injustices embedded in labor and immigration.

Analyzing Irish immigrant women's history through the lens of African American women's labor history and theories reveals that Irish immigrant women settled into a country where slavery shaped their own labor experiences. They encountered race in their workplaces even when they did not labor alongside African American women because the work they did had already been racialized prior to their arrival in the United States. The racial and labor history of Irish immigrant women in the United States, however, was different from that of their male counterparts because of their gender and concentration in a labor niche that could not be redefined as white women's work in the way that manual work could be redefined by Irish immigrant men as working-class white men's work. In addition, Irish immigrant women labored in a country where not even native-born white women had been granted full American citizenship. Because of this, it took much longer for Irish immigrant women to fully whiten themselves than it did for Irish immigrant men.

Revisiting African American domestic workers' history reintroduces discussions about how racial inequalities in the labor economy impact Black women. In the twenty-first century, African American women's labor struggles have become subsumed in larger political discussions about the disenfranchisement of African American communities. While African American women have remained the most ardent grassroots political organizers in our communities, we have left behind discussions about our own labor struggles in our contemporary activism and scholarship. Discussions about the particular labor struggles of Black women have declined since the 1970s and 80s, or shortly after the majority of working-class African American women transitioned out of household employment. On average, Black women are still paid less than white men and women and Black men across occupation. We should revisit Black women's labor history to trace and address persistent inequalities in the labor economy that continue to impact Black women today.

Rereading African American women's labor histories through a comparative lens also exposes the expansive implications of African American women's theories and activism. Because of the long history of marginalization of Black women in academic scholarship, scholars have mostly produced individual case studies about Black women. Scholars have only recently begun to explore Black women's labor and migration histories in comparison with those of immigrant women. My work asserts that African American women developed nuanced theories about race, migration, and labor because they had to address how migration, immigration, and white supremacy impacted the working lives of Black women to fight against labor exploitation in domestic service.

So often, the histories of African American women have also been divided along class lines in academic study. An integrated history of domestic workers' activism and the community work of clubwomen against the labor exploitation of Black women in domestic service opens new avenues for exploring the complexities of class for clubwomen and how they were significant thinkers and doers of their time on the subjects of race, migration, and labor. Outside of Black feminist circles, W.E.B. Du Bois and Booker T. Washington's debates and theories have become the standard through which Black intellectual thought on race and labor have been analyzed for several decades, although African American women were foundational to Du Bois and Washington's influential theories and scholarship, and social movements within Black communities. It was through African American women's labor organizing, community work, and institution-building to address labor exploitation in domestic service that clubwomen and domestic workers developed what we now call an intersectional approach to dismantling systemic inequalities in the U.S. labor economy.

Black women's intersectional approach was relevant to an array of issues that impacted most women's lives historically and today. As Beverly Guy-Sheftall argued, the history of Black women's activism forces a reconceptualization of "women's issues to include poverty, racism, imperialism, lynching, welfare, economic exploitation, sterilization abuse, decent housing, and a host of other concerns that generations of black women foregrounded."[6] African American domestic workers today are continuing the political organizing legacy of their nineteenth- and twentieth-century predecessors by demanding the Unseen in their campaign for labor rights, which include voting rights, economic empowerment, criminal justice reform, decent housing, living wages, and healthcare coverage for low-wage workers.

African American domestic workers were an instrumental organizing force in Georgia Democratic gubernatorial candidate Stacey Abrams's 2018 campaign. As members of Care in Action, the political organizing arm of the National Domestic Workers Alliance, domestic workers in Georgia mobilized more than 250,000 voters for the historic midterm election. If it were not for the illegal voter suppression of gubernatorial Republican candidate Brian Kemp, who oversaw his own election as the acting Georgia secretary of state, Abrams could have become the first Black woman governor in the history of the United States. After Abrams conceded a hard-fought challenge to the election results, members of Care in Action insisted in an open letter that they wrote to Abrams that they would continue fighting for all of the rights that she made central to her campaign. Quoting the great civil rights historian Vincent Harding, they proclaimed, "I am a citizen of a nation that has yet to come into being."[7]

Within the past few years, labor organizations across the United States have begun using African American domestic workers' political organizing history as a guide for addressing a wide range of labor issues that impact both women and men workers across race. The website for the American Postal Workers Union, for example, features an article about the washerwomen's strike that African American women organized in Atlanta, Georgia, in 1881. As the article reads, "A little known yet largely successful job action waged in 1881 by black women in Atlanta is credited with helping to set the stage for a century of labor and civil rights struggles."[8]

What remains promising for disrupting racial injustices in domestic service is that today's largest labor organizations now include the concerns of domestic workers. Since the founding of the Building Service Employees Union (BSEIU) in 1921 by a group of Irish, Turkish, African, Spanish, and Eastern European janitors in Chicago, it has grown into the Service Employees International Union (SEIU) representing over two million workers, 25 percent of whom identify as immigrants. The enormous growth of the organization is partly due to the way in which they have expanded the definition of service work to include the traditional forms of domestic service and corporatized service work that includes cleaning, cooking, and taking care of others. This wide definition transformed SEIU into a broad-based coalition of domestic workers, food service workers, janitors, healthcare workers, and security guards.

This cross-labor and cross-racial organizing has been significant for working-class African American women. While immigrants from the Philippines, Latin America, and the Caribbean have largely taken their places in domestic service, working-class African American women continue to labor in some of the lowest paying and least respected service occupations that offer the poorest medical and dental coverage. Some working-class African American women work part-time and full-time in private homes; others clean office buildings and schools; prepare meals at schools, fast-food restaurants, and hospitals; and dominate nursing assistant positions that require the most backbreaking tasks in the medical field. African American women, who are members of the SEIU, have support from a large coalition of service workers with powerful political influence. The SEIU organized fast-food workers into a national movement demanding a $15-an-hour minimum wage, registered over eight million low-wage workers for health-care coverage through the Affordable Care Act, and helped home care workers negotiate contracts for livable wages. While organizing campaigns to increase the wages of service workers, the union has amassed political power. It has become a union that Democratic presidential candidates actively court for their endorsement. The labor organizing of the SEIU, therefore, has the potential to transform how service occupations are viewed in the United States. It is important to note that it is difficult for working-class African American women to assert their labor concerns in right-to-work states, even when they are union members. And twenty-seven out of fifty states in the United States are right-to-work states. Thus, there is much work to be done to address the enduring labor struggles of African American women.

Labor organizations that focus specifically on the employment conditions of domestic workers have strengthened in number since the founding of the Domestic Workers' Union of Harlem in 1934. Historian Premilla Nadasen has uncovered the significant activist histories of African American domestic workers who built a national movement from the 1950s until the 1970s to end labor exploitation in domestic service. As working-class African American women transitioned out of domestic service in the latter half of the twentieth century, immigrant women of color took their places. After the Hart-Cellar Immigration Act of 1965 lifted immigration restrictions that were legalized in the 1920s, the percentage of undocumented immigrants increased.[9] Like the newly arrived southern Black migrant women and Irish immigrant women from previous decades, employers sought to hire the "greenest" women in the country. Immigrant workers built multiracial labor organizations that remain active in the struggle to transform the slave-like conditions of the occupation. Taking cues from their predecessors, leaders of Domestic Workers United (DWU) took courses that included lessons on the history of African Americans, Mexican Americans, and Irish immigrants in domestic service to deepen their understandings of the racial politics of household work in the United States.

The trainings, protests, meetings, and petitions in domestic worker organizations have produced historic results. After several years of organizing, domestic worker organizations in New York State persuaded lawmakers to sign into law the Domestic Worker Bill of Rights in November 2010. The bill pronounced that domestic workers have the right to overtime pay at time-and-a-half, a day of rest every seven days, three paid days of rest each year after one year of work for the same employer, and legal recourse for sexual or racial harassment.[10] The California Bill of Rights, signed into law in 2014, extended overtime protection to caregivers and childcare providers. Other states and a city followed suit: by 2017, Nevada became the eighth state to pass the bill, and Seattle, Washington, passed the bill in 2018.[11] Similar to their African American predecessors of the nineteenth and twentieth centuries, domestic workers and their allies continue producing and circulating their own research data about the labor exploitation of women of color in domestic service employment. In 2018, the National Domestic Workers Alliance published the very first quantitative study about the labor struggles of Latina domestic workers in South Texas.[12]

While this was a significant step toward ending labor exploitation in domestic service, domestic worker organizations continue pushing for more legal protections. In November 2018, the National Domestic Workers Alliance announced that they are working with Representative Pramila Jayapal and U.S. Senator Kamala Harris to introduce the first National Domestic Workers Bill of Rights to Congress in 2019. If passed by Congress, employers will be required to provide domestic workers with meal and rest breaks and adhere to the Civil Rights and Occupational Health and Safety Act protections. The bill also requires contractual agreements between employers and domestic workers and more paid sick leave, health care, training programs, and retirement benefits for domestic workers.[13]

In this recent broad-based movement to end labor exploitation in domestic service, however, discussions about race are sometimes marginalized because it is considered a topic that might create divisions between members of the organizations. What I remember most vividly about attending the "Justice in the Home: Domestic Work, Past, Present, and Future" Conference at Barnard College in 2014 was a Caribbean immigrant domestic worker who articulated her frustrations about labor organizing across race and ethnicity during the question-and-answer segment of a panel discussion. She told the panelists that addressing the working conditions in domestic service required open and honest conversations about racial divisions between domestic workers themselves. She noted that it was difficult convincing Latina household workers to work with her and other Caribbean women on domestic worker rights projects because they feared that working with Black women would hinder their efforts to achieve better working conditions. The sensitivity of her comment was evidenced by the hesitance among conference participants to engage her concern.

The histories of Irish immigrant and African American women reminds us that race is foundational to labor rights. Research and dialogue about the similarities and distinctions between women's labor experiences has the potential to strengthen working relationships in labor organizations, as well as the development of cross-racial organizing for workers' rights that does not obfuscate racial differences. In a country that insists on making race matter in all things, and where women are most susceptible to labor exploitation, women will always have to put their hands on it to fully access what they need and want.

Acknowledgments

I had a harmonious support system while completing this book. I am indebted to the persistent nudging and questioning of my mother, Mona Taylor Phillips. She has traveled with me intellectually, emotionally, and sometimes physically along this journey of tracing the histories of domestic workers. She also never let me forget the audaciousness and keen racial insights of the middle-class women in our family. Her memories of those whom our family affectionately calls "The Alford Sisters" (our aunts and grandmothers from Chattanooga, Tennessee, by way of LaGrange, Georgia) pushed me to take seriously the groundbreaking work of southern African American clubwomen.

My aunt Tara Harrison and my late father, Derrick "8 Ball" Phillips, supplemented my mother's support with comforting meals and sage advice. My father also taught me the importance of imagination and creativity in constructing histories. He lovingly told stories, made memories, and treasured connections with family that sometimes traced back centuries. He would often "travel" from nineteenth-century Georgia to twentieth-century Michigan to share with me richly detailed stories about his working-class and southern-migrant aunts and grandmothers who raised him in Detroit. They, like the women in my mother's family, inspired the title of this book. I could not have asked for a more supportive partner. My husband, Dennis Cunningham, attended programs where I presented my research; traveled to some of the archives with me; read drafts of my chapters; learned how to cook; and helped clear away any weeds that got in the way of me writing.

My family network was buttressed by those I call "no-nonsense" scholars at women's colleges and universities. I am forever grateful to Beverly Guy-Sheftall and Mary Hawkesworth. The transformative influence of Beverly Guy-Sheftall's scholarship is interwoven throughout all of the chapters. Mary Hawkesworth's staunch support of my work and deep engagement with my ideas helped fuel my research from its nascent stages until the publication of this book. I also greatly appreciate Nancy Hewitt for supporting my work, and Gloria Wade Gayles for giving me the first opportunity to interview Black women who labored as domestic workers through her Spelman Independent Scholars Oral History (SIS) Project.

I am very thankful to have worked with Kimberly Guinta, Editorial Director at Rutgers University Press. Her guidance, ideas, and expertise were invaluable throughout the publishing process. The difficult questions and comments of Cecelia Cancellaro, anonymous reviewers, and the late historian Leslie Brown were also immensely helpful for my work.

Many thanks are also owed to Claire Sahlin, Ann Staton, and Abigail Tilton, who are the Associate Dean, former Dean, and Dean of the College of Arts and Sciences at Texas Woman's University (TWU), respectively. The Dean's Office and the Office of Research and Sponsored Programs at TWU provided resources that were necessary for my travels to various archives throughout the United States and Ireland. I am also fortunate to teach a diverse community of students at a women's institution where the politics of race and migration is both its past and present.

Lastly, this book would not have been possible without those whom I affectionately call "old-school black women" and intensely Irish archivists. In their own stern ways, they directed me to archival sources that have been instrumental in constructing this comparative history of domestic workers. Their protection of and pride in primary sources constantly reminded me of the significance of the women whom I researched.

Notes

Introduction

1. I borrow this phrase from James Baldwin's *The Evidence of Things Not Seen* (New York: Henry and Holt, 1985). The title refers to the Bible, Hebrews chapter 11:1.
2. Unlike their Irish Protestant predecessors who migrated to America during the first three decades of the nineteenth century as skilled workers who established businesses and purchased land, the poor Catholic Irish women who largely hailed from small family farms during the famine era and afterwards were initially despised by native-born whites; see Noel Ignatiev, *How the Irish Became White* (Routledge: New York, 1995), 38–40.
3. Lawrence Glasco, "Ethnicity and Social Structure: Irish, Germans and Native-Born of Buffalo, New York, 1850–1860" (PhD diss., State University of New York at Buffalo, 1973), 201, 205, 208, 224–225; Susan J. Kleinberg, "Technology's Stepdaughter: The Impact of Industrialization Upon Working Women, Pittsburgh, 1865–1890" (PhD diss., University of Pittsburgh, 1973), 207–211; David Katzman, *Seven Days a Week: Women and Domestic Service in Industrializing America* (New York: Oxford University Press, 1978), 80.
4. Scholars have begun to examine the physical and cultural work Native American and White women settlers did to mold ideologies of domesticity during the late nineteenth and early twentieth centuries; see Jane E. Simonsen's *Making Home Work: Domesticity and Native American Assimilation in the American West, 1860–1919* (Chapel Hill: The University of North Carolina Press, 2006).
5. I use Black and African American interchangeably for stylistic variety.
6. Thomas F. Gossett, *Race: The History of an Idea in America* (Dallas: Southern Methodist University Press, 1963), 58–59, 73; Melissa N. Stein, *Measuring Manhood: Race and the Science of Masculinity, 1830–1934* (Minneapolis: University of Minneapolis Press, 2015), 35–42.
7. Evelyn Nakano Glenn, *Unequal Freedom: How Race and Gender Shaped American Citizenship and Labor* (Cambridge: Harvard University Press, 2002), 18.
8. Howard Winant. *The World Is a Ghetto: Race and Democracy since World War II* (New York: Basic Books, 2001), 369.

9. Michael Omi and Howard Winant, *Racial Formation in the United States: From the 1960s to the 1990s,* 2nd ed. (Routledge: New York, 1994), 56.

10. Quoted from Simonsen, *Making Home Work,* 2.

11. Tonya Hart, *Race, Poverty, and the Negotiation of Women's Health in New York City* (New York University Press, 2015), 18.

12. See Deirdre Cooper Owens, *Medical Bondage: Race, Gender, and the Origins of American Gynecology* (Athens: University of Georgia Press, 2018); Andrew T. Urban, *Brokering Servitude: Migration and the Politics of Domestic Labor During the Long Nineteenth Century* (New York: New York University Press, 2018); Bronwen Walter, *Outsiders Inside: Whiteness, Place, and Irish Women* (New York: Routledge, 2001), 60–71.

13. Coretta Scott King, "Statement of Coretta Scott King on the Nomination of Jefferson Beauregard Sessions, III for the United States District Court Southern District of Alabama, Senate Judiciary Committee," 13 Mar 1986: 4.

14. Katie Rogers, "White Women Helped Elect Donald Trump," *New York Times,* 9 Nov 2016; Claudia Sandoval, "Choosing the Velvet Glove: Women Voters, Ambivalent Sexism, and Vote Choice in 2016," *The Journal of Race, Ethnicity, and Politics* 3, no. 1 (2018): 26–28, doi:10.1017/rep.2018.6.

15. Groundbreaking comparative studies about Irish immigrant and Black men include Noel Ignatiev, *How the Irish Became White* (Routledge, New York, 1995); David Roediger, *Wages of Whiteness: Race and the Making of the American Working Class* (Verso: New York, 1991); and Matthew Frye Jacobson, *Whiteness of a Different Color: European Immigration and the Alchemy of Race* (Cambridge: Harvard University Press, 1998).

16. Quoted from Beverly Guy-Sheftall's critique of the lack of gender analysis in scholarship on African American literature before the 1990s; see Beverly Guy-Sheftall, *Daughters of Sorrow: Attitudes toward Black Women, 1880–1920.* (Brooklyn: Carlson, 1990), 2.

17. Mary Condon, New Yorkers at Work Oral History Collection OH.001, New York University Wagner Labor Archives, 2 Nov 1980.

18. Mary Church Terrell, *A Colored Woman in a White World* (Amherst, NY: Ransdell Inc., 1940); Anna Julia Cooper, "L'attitude de la France à l'égard de l'esclavage pendant la revolution." (PhD diss., University of Paris, 1925); Anna Julia Cooper. "The Negro Problem in America," Pan African Conference in London, England, 1900; Ida B. Wells et al., *The Reasons Why The Colored American Is Not in the World's Columbian Exposition: The Afro American's Contribution to Columbian Literature* (Chicago: Clark Street, 1893).

19. Charles Lemert and Esme Bhan, *The Voice of Anna Julia Cooper: Including a Voice from the South and Other Important Essays, Papers, and Letters* (New York: Rowman & Littlefield Publishers, 1998), 180.

20. Tera Hunter, *To 'Joy My Freedom: Southern Black Women's Lives and Labors after the Civil War* (Cambridge: Harvard University Press, 1998), 78.

21. Sarah Haley, *No Mercy Here: Gender, Punishment, and the Making of Jim Crow Modernity* (Chapel Hill: University of North Carolina Press, 2016), 4.

22. Ashley Cleek, "The Route of Division," *Alzazeera America,* 31 May 2015, http://projects.aljazeera.com/2015/05/birmingham-bus

23. Faye Dudden, *Serving Women: Household Service in Nineteenth-Century America* (Middletown: Wesleyan University Press, 1983), 32.

24. Leslie Harris, *In the Shadow of Slavery: African Americans in New York City, 1626–1863* (Chicago: University of Chicago Press, 2004), 98.

25. Dudden, *Serving Women*.
26. Minutes of the National Association of Colored Women, August 1908: 15–16, Library of Congress NACW Collection.
27. Minutes of the National Association of Colored Women, August 1908, 53.
28. Letter to Nannie Helen Burroughs, August 1937, Nannie Helen Burroughs Collection, Library of Congress.
29. Judith Rollins, *Between Women: Domestics and Their Employers* (Philadelphia: Temple University Press, 1985); Gerda Lerner, *Black Women in White America: A Documentary History* (New York: Vintage Books, 1972); Jacqueline Jones, *Labor of Love, Labor of Sorrow: Black Women, Work, and the Family from Slavery to the Present* (New York: Vintage Books, 1985). Elizabeth Clark-Lewis, *Living In, Living Out: African American Domestics in Washington D.C., 1910–1940* (Washington D.C.: Smithsonian Institute Press, 1994); Bonnie Thornton Dill, *Across the Boundaries of Race and Class: An Exploration of Work and Family among Black Female Domestic Servants* (New York: Garland Publishing, 1993); Hasia Diner, *Erin's Daughters in America: Irish Immigrant Women in the Nineteenth Century* (Baltimore: Johns Hopkins University Press, 1983); Vanessa May, *Unprotected Labor: Household Workers, Politics, and Middle-Class Reform in New York* (Chapel Hill: University of North Carolina Press, 2011); Faye Dudden, *Serving Women: Household Service in Nineteenth Century America* (Middletown: Wesleyan University Press, 1985); and Margaret Lynch-Brennan, *The Irish Bridget: Irish Immigrant Women in Domestic Service in America, 1840–1930* (New York: Syracuse University Press, 2009).
30. Descriptions of Chinese servants quoted from David E. Sutherland, *Americans and Their Servants: Domestic Service in the United States from 1800–1920* (Baton Rouge and London: Louisiana State University Press, 1981), 41.
31. Isabel Wilkerson, *The Warmth of Other Suns: The Epic Story of America's Great Migration* (New York: Vintage Books, 2010), 538.
32. Jennifer Morgan, "Some Could Suckle Over Their Shoulder: Male Travelers, Female Bodies, and the Gendering of Racial Ideology, 1500–1770," *The William and Mary Quarterly* 54 (Jan 1997): 189, 191; Deborah Gray White, *Ain't I a Woman: Female Slaves in the Plantation South* (New York: W.W. Norton and Company, 1999), 29.
33. The definition of the servant problem was quoted from David E. Sutherland's *Americans and Their Servants: Domestic Service in the United States from 1800–1920* (Baton Rouge: Louisiana State University Press, 1981), xi. I argue that the framing of the servant problem was racialized.
34. Edward E. Baptist, *The Half Has Never Been Told: Slavery and the Making of American Capitalism* (New York: Basic Books, 2014), xxi–xxii.

Chapter 1 Putting Racial Formation Theory to Work

1. Lawrence O'Donnell, "Lawrence: 'Stunned' by John Kelly's attack on Rep. Wilson," *The Last Word*, by MSNBC, Aired 9 Oct 2017. Visit this link to view the video clip of O'Donnell's segment: http://www.msnbc.com/the-last-word/watch/lawrence-stunned-by-john-kelly-s-attack-on-rep-wilson-1077490243772
2. Frederica Wilson represents the 24th Congressional District in Florida, which includes parts of Miami-Dade and southern Broward counties.
3. The other soldiers were sergeants Bryan Black, Jeremiah Johnson, and Dustin Wright.

4. Jonathan Capehart, "'Trump's Benghazi': Frederica Wilson wants the truth about what happened to La David Johnson in Niger," *Washington Post*, 19 Dec 2017. Also, see video of Frederica Wilson's interview on MSNBC recounting details of Trump's phone call to the Johnson family: "'He died as a hero': Congresswoman Wilson remembers Sgt. La David T. Johnson," *Morning Joe*, by MSNBC, Aired 18 Oct 2017, https://www.msnbc.com/morning-joe/watch/-he-died-as-a-hero-congresswoman -on-sgt-johnson-1075895363756

5. Florida-based journalists challenged the accuracy of Kelly's memory of Wilson's speech at the ceremony. See Alex Daugherty, Anita Kumar, Douglas Hanks, "Video of Frederica Wilson's 2015 speech shows John Kelly was wrong," *Miami Herald*, 18 Oct 2017, http://www.miamiherald.com/news/politics-government /article179952536.html

6. O'Donnell, "Lawrence: 'Stunned.'"

7. O'Donnell, "Lawrence: 'Stunned.'"

8. O'Donnell, "Lawrence: 'Stunned.'"

9. O'Donnell, "Lawrence: 'Stunned.'"

10. Grace Hale, *Making Whiteness: The Culture of Segregation in the South, 1890–1940* (New York: Vintage, 1998), xi.

11. I borrowed this phrase from my *Signs* article about archival research methods for examining racialization and women's migration histories; see Danielle Phillips, "Moving with the Women: Tracing Racialization, Migration, and Domestic Workers in the Archive," *Signs: Journal of Women and Culture in Society* 38 (Winter 2013): 379–404.

12. Jennifer Morgan, "'Some Could Suckle Over Their Shoulder': Male Travelers, Female Bodies, and the Gendering of Racial Ideology," *The William and Mary Quarterly* 54 (1997): 169.

13. Morgan, "Some Could Suckle Over Their Shoulder,'"184.

14. Londa Schiebinger, *Nature's Body: Gender in the Making of Modern Science* (Boston: Beacon Press, 1993), 116–117; Thomas F. Gossett, *Race: The History of an Idea in America* (Dallas: Southern Methodist University Press, 1963), 48.

15. Schiebinger, *Nature's Body*; Deirdre Cooper Owens, *Medical Bondage: Race, Gender, and the Origins of American Gynecology* (Athens: University of Georgia Press, 2017), 158.

16. Thomas F. Gossett, *Race: The History of an Idea in America* (Dallas: Southern Methodist University Press, 1963), 48.

17. Melissa N. Stein, *Measuring Manhood: Race and the Science of Masculinity, 1830–1934* (Minneapolis: Minnesota, 2015), 16.

18. Gossett, *Race*, 58.

19. Stein, *Measuring Manhood*, 38.

20. Rana A. Hogarth, *Medicalizing Blackness: Making Racial Difference in the Atlantic World, 1780–1840* (Chapel Hill: The University of North Carolina Press, 2017), 3.

21. Schiebinger, *Nature's Body*; Cooper Owens, *Medical Bondage*; Stein, *Measuring Manhood*; Barbara Ehrenreich and Deirdre English, *For Her Own Good: 150 Years of the Experts' Advice to Women* (New York: Anchor, 1989).

22. Deborah Gray White, *Arn't I a Woman?: Female Slaves in the Plantation South* (New York: W.W. Norton and Company, 1999), 27.

23. Deborah Gray White, *Arn't I a Woman?*, 30.

24. Cooper Owens, "Perfecting the Degraded Body: Slavery, Irish-Immigration, and American Gynecology," in *Power in History From Medieval Ireland to the*

Post-Modern World, eds. Anthony McElligott et al (Dublin: Irish Academic Press, 2011), 169.

25. Cooper Owens, "Perfecting the Degraded Body," 175–176.

26. Michael Omi and Howard Winant, *Racial Formation in the United States from the 1960s–1990s,* 1st ed. (New York: Routledge, 1986).

27. Michael Omi and Howard Winant, *Racial Formation in the United States,* 3rd ed. (New York: Routledge, 2015), 107.

28. Omi and Winant, *Racial Formation,* 109.

29. Omi and Winant, *Racial Formation,* 111.

30. Rob Haskell, "Serena Williams on Pregnancy, Power, and Coming Back to Center Court," *Vogue,* 15 Aug 2017, https://www.vogue.com/article/serena-williams -pregnancy-vogue-september-issue-2017

31. To view image, see Michael Cavna, "An Australian artist's racist Serena Williams car- toon receives swift and international blowback," *Washington Post,* 12 Sep 2018, https:// www.washingtonpost.com/news/comic-riffs/wp/2018/09/10/an-australian-artists -racist-serena-williams-cartoon-receives-swift-and-international-blowback

32. David R. Roediger, *The Wages of Whiteness: Race and the Making of the American Working Class* (New York: Verso, 1991), 173–178.

33. Evelyn Nakano Glenn, *Unequal Freedom: How Race and Gender Shaped American Citizenship and Labor* (Cambridge: Harvard University Press, 2002), 12–13.

34. Nakano Glenn, *Unequal Freedom,* 14.

35. Beverly Guy-Sheftall, ed. *Words of Fire: An Anthology of African-American Feminist Thought* (New York: The New Press, 1995), 2.

36. Mary Church Terrell, "The Progress of Colored Women," *Voice of the Negro* 1, no. 7 (July 1904): 292.

37. Guy-Sheftall, *Words of Fire,* 1–2.

38. Some of the seminal publications that examined the impact of intersecting social categories on women's lives, histories, and representations include: Beverly Guy- Sheftall's *Words of Fire: An Anthology of African-American Feminist Thought* (New York: The New Press, 1995); Paula Giddings' *When and Where I Enter: The Impact of Black Women on Race and Sex in America* (New York: W. Morrow, 1984); Patricia Hill Collins's *Black Feminist Thought: Knowledge, Consciousness, and the Politics of Empowerment* (Boston: Unwin Hyman, 1990); Akasha (Gloria T. Hull), Patricia Bell-Scott, Barbara Smith, eds., *But Some of Us Are Brave: All the Women Are White, All the Blacks Are Men: Black Women's Studies* (New York: The Feminist Press, 1993); Deborah King, "Multiple Jeopardy, Multiple Consciousness: The Context of a Black Feminist Ideology," *Signs: Journal of Women and Culture in Society* 14, no. 1 (Autumn 1988), 42–72; Bonnie Thornton Dill, "The Dialectics of Black Womanhood," *Signs: Journal of Women and Culture in Society* 4, no. 3 (Spring 1979): 543–555; Gloria Anzaldúa and Cherrie Moraga, eds., *This Bridge Called My Back: Writings by Radical Women of Color* (Watertown: Persephone Press, 1981); Lisa Lowe's *Immigrant Acts: On Asian American Cultural Politics* (Durham: Duke University Press, 1996).

39. Nakano Glenn, *Unequal Freedom,* 7.

40. Kimberlé Crenshaw, "Demarginalizing the Intersection of Race and Sex: A Black Feminist Critique of Antidiscrimination Doctrine, Feminist Theory, and Antiracist Politics," *The University of Chicago Legal Forum* issue 1, article 8 (1989): 139. The article may be downloaded at: http://chicagounbound.uchicago.edu/uclf/vol1989 /iss1/8

41. Evelyn Brooks Higginbotham, "African-American History and The Metalanguage of Race," *Signs: Journal of Women and Culture in Society* 17 (1992): 253.
42. Higginbotham, "African-American History," 255.
43. Dorothy Roberts, *Killing the Black Body: Race, Reproduction, and the Meaning of Liberty* (New York: Pantheon Books, 1997), 111–112.
44. Kimberlé Crenshaw, Leslie McCall, Sumi Cho, eds., "Toward a Field of Intersectionality Studies: Theory, Applications and Praxis," *Signs: Journal of Women and Culture in Society* 38, no. 4 (2013): 788.
45. Katherine Cusumano, "The Women of the Women's March: Meet the Activists Who Are Planning One of the Largest Demonstrations in American History," *W* magazine, 19 Jan 2017, https://www.wmagazine.com/story/womens-march-on -washington-activists-organizers
46. Dana Frank, "White Working-Class Women and the Race Question," *International Labor and Working-Class History*, no. 54 (Fall 1998): 80–81.
47. Dana Frank, "White Working-Class Women and the Race Question," 97.
48. Priya Kandaswamy, "Gendering Racial Formation Theory," in *Racial Formation in the Twenty-First Century*, eds. Daniel Martinez HoSang, Oneka LaBennett, and Laura Polido (Berkeley: University of California Press, 2012), 23–24.
49. Kandaswamy, "Gendering Racial Formation Theory," 26.
50. For a history of Irish indentured servants in the United States, see Don Jordan and Michael Walsh's *White Cargo: The Forgotten History of Britain's White Slaves in America* (New York: New York University Press, 2007).
51. Nakano Glenn, *Unequal Freedom*, 61; Bernard Bailyn, *Voyagers to the West: A Passage in the Peopling of America on the Eve of the Revolution* (New York: Vintage, 1988) 296–353
52. Eric Foner, *Reconstruction: America's Unfinished Revolution, 1863–1877* (New York: Harper & Row Publishers, 1988), 530.
53. Nakano Glenn, *Unequal Freedom*, 24; Ian Haney Lopez, *White By Law 10th Anniversary Edition: The Legal Construction of Race* (New York: New York University Press, 2006), 31.
54. Foner, *Reconstruction: America's Unfinished Revolution*, 496.
55. Lopez, *White By Law*, 83.
56. Nakano Glenn, *Unequal Freedom*, 61.
57. Nakano Glenn, *Unequal Freedom*, 20.
58. Roediger, *The Wages of Whiteness*, 20.
59. Phyllis Palmer, *Domesticity and Dirt: Housewives and Domestic Servants in the United States, 1920–1945* (Philadelphia: Temple University Press, 1989), 6.
60. Nakano Glenn, *Unequal Freedom*; 70, 74.
61. Andrew Urban, *Brokering Servitude: Migration and the Politics of Domestic Labor During the Long Nineteenth Century* (New York: New York University Press, 2018), 8.
62. Nakano Glenn, *Unequal Freedom*, 82.
63. Roediger, *The Wages of Whiteness*, 25.
64. Noel Ignatiev, *How the Irish Became White* (New York: Routledge, 1995), 41.
65. Quoted from Matthew Frye Jacobson's *Whiteness of a Different Color: European Immigrants and the Alchemy of Race* (Cambridge: Harvard University Press, 1998), 48.
66. April Schultz, "The Black Mammy and the Irish Bridget: Domestic Service and the Representation of Race, 1830–1930," *Éire-Ireland Journal* 48, nos. 3, 4 (Fall/Winter

2013): 176–212; Andrew Urban, "Irish Domestic Servants, 'Biddy' and Rebellion in the American Home, 1850–1900, *Gender and History* 21 (August 2009): 263–286.

67. Roediger, *The Wages of Whiteness*; Ignatiev, *How the Irish Became White*; Matthew Frye Jacobson, *Whiteness of a Different Color: European Immigrants and the Alchemy of Race* (Cambridge: Harvard University Press, 1998).

68. Janet Nolan, *Ourselves Alone: Women's Emigration from Ireland, 1885–1920* (Lexington: University of Kentucky Press, 1989); Hasia Diner, *Erin's Daughters in America: Irish Immigrant Women in the Nineteenth Century* (Baltimore: Johns Hopkins University Press, 1983); Maureen Murphy, "Charlotte Grace O'Brien and the Mission of Our Lady of the Rosary for the Protection of Irish Immigrant Girls, *Mid-America: An Historical Review* 74 (October 1992): 253–270; Faye Dudden, *Serving Women: Household Service in Nineteenth Century America* (Middletown: Wesleyan University Press, 1985); Margaret Lynch-Brennan, *The Irish Bridget: Irish Immigrant Women in Domestic Service in America, 1840–1930* (New York: Syracuse University Press, 2009); eds. Marion Casey and J.J. Lee, *Making the Irish American: History and Heritage of the Irish in the United States* (New York: New York University Press, 2006).

69. Hasia Diner, *Erin's Daughters in America: Irish Immigrant Women in the Nineteenth Century* (Baltimore: Johns Hopkins University Press, 1983), xiv.

70. Some of these publications include Deirdre Cooper Owens, *Medical Bondage: Race, Gender, and the Origins of American Gynecology* (University of Georgia Press, 2017); Andrew T. Urban, *Brokering Servitude: Migration and the Politics of Domestic Labor During the Long Nineteenth Century* (New York University Press, 2018); Bronwen Walter, *Outsiders Inside: Whiteness, Place, and Irish Women* (New York: Routledge, 2001); April Schultz, "The Black Mammy and the Irish Bridget: Domestic Service and the Representation of Race, 1830–1930," *Éire-Ireland Journal* (Fall/Winter 2013) 48:3&4: 176–212; Stephen Steinberg, *The Ethnic Myth: Race, Ethnicity, and Class in America* (Boston: Beacon Press, 1981), 151–168.

71. Judith Rollins, *Between Women: Domestics and Their Employers* (Philadelphia: Temple University Press,1985), 51.

72. By no means an exhaustive list, these groundbreaking publications include: Gerda Lerner, *Black Women in White America: A Documentary History* (New York: Vintage Books, 1972); Jacqueline Jones, *Labor of Love, Labor of Sorrow: Black Women, Work, and the Family from Slavery to the Present* (New York: Vintage Books, 1985); Elizabeth Clark-Lewis, *Living In, Living Out: African American Domestics in Washington D.C., 1910–1940* (Washington D.C.: Smithsonian Institute Press, 1994); Bonnie Thornton Dill, *Across the Boundaries of Race and Class: An Exploration of Work and Family among Black Female Domestic Servants* (New York: Garland Publishing, 1993); Elizabeth Hafkin Pleck, *Black Migration and Poverty: Boston, 1865–1900* (New York: Academic Press, 1979); Jacqueline Jones, *Labor of Love, Labor of Sorrow: Black Women, Work, and the Family from Slavery to the Present* (New York: Vintage, 1986).

73. Brittany C. Cooper, *Beyond Respectability: The Intellectual Thought of Race Women* (Urbana: University of Illinois Press, 2017), 9.

74. Katt Williams, "Great America" Comedy Tour, Jacksonville, Florida, Netflix Original, 2018.

75. Erica Werner and Ed O'Keefe, "White House Chief of Staff: Trump not expected to extend DACA Deadline," *Washinton Post*, 6 Feb. 2018, http://wapo.st/2BHPjgK ?tid=ss_mail&utm_term=.438080b0fb2d

76. Anne McClintock, *Imperial Leather: Race, Gender and Sexuality in the Colonial Conquest* (New York: Routledge, 1995), 108.
77. McClintock, *Imperial Leather*, 99.
78. McClintock, *Imperial Leather*, 99.
79. Deborah Valenze, *The First Industrial Woman* (New York: Oxford University Press, 1995), 174.
80. Palmer, *Domesticity and Dirt*, 139.
81. James Baldwin and Raoul Peck, *I Am Not Your Negro: A Companion Edition to the Documentary Film Directed by Raoul Peck* (New York: Vintage Books, 2017) 103.

Chapter 2   The Lost Files of Irish Immigration History

1. David Lloyd, "Black Irish, Irish Whiteness and Atlantic State Formation," *The Black and Green Atlantic: Crosscurrents of the African and Irish Diaspora,* eds. Peter D. O'Neill and David Lloyd (New York: Palgrave McMillan, 2009), 13.
2. Jennifer Nugent Duffy, *Who's Your Paddy? Racial Expectations and the Struggle for Irish American Identity* (New York: New York University Press, 2014), 52.
3. Brian Borohme the Younger, *Ireland: A Kingdom and a Colony* (London: C. Dolman, 61, New Bond Street, 1843) 232–234.
4. Terence McDonough, ed., *Was Ireland a Colony?: Economy, Politics, Ideology and Culture in Nineteenth Century Ireland* (Dublin: Irish Academic Press, 2005), 4.
5. It is important to note that not all Anglo-Irishmen supported British rule. Some Anglo-Irish politicians, activists, writers, and clergymen including Jonathan Swift, Henry Grattan, and Charles Stewart Parnell were outspoken leaders who denounced Britain's policies and supported Irish nationalism; see Kerby Miller, *Emigrants and Exiles: Ireland and the Irish Exodus to North America* (New York: Oxford University Press, 1985), 42, 270, 389.
6. L. P. Curtis Jr., *Anglo Saxons and Celts: A Study of Anti-Irish Prejudice in Victorian England* (Bridgeport: University of Bridgeport, Connecticut, 1968), 61.
7. Frederick Douglass, *My Bondage and My Freedom* (New York and Auburn: Miller, Orton, and Mulligan, 1855), 98. Douglass's book was reprinted with an introduction by historian David W. Blight, see F. Douglass, *My Bondage and My Freedom, Introduction and Notes by David W. Blight* (New Haven: Yale University Press, 2014).
8. Curtis Jr., *Anglo-Saxons and Celts*, 57.
9. David Lloyd, "Black Irish, Irish Whiteness and Atlantic State Formation," in *The Black and Green Atlantic: Crosscurrents of the African and Irish Diaspora,* eds. Peter D. O'Neill and David Lloyd (New York: Palgrave McMillan, 2009), 17.
10. Richard S. Dunn, *A Tale of Two Plantations: Slave Life and Labor in Jamaica and Virginia* (Cambridge: Harvard University Press, 2014) 368–412.
11. Curtis Jr., *Anglo-Saxons and Celts*, 4.
12. Theresa McBride, *The Domestic Revolution: The Modernisation of Household Service in England and France 1820–1920* (New York: Holmes and Meier Publishers, 1976), 19, 82. Women led emigration to Australia beginning in the early twentieth century; see Hasia Diner, *Erin's Daughters in America: Irish Immigrant Women in the Nineteenth Century* (Baltimore: The Johns Hopkins University Press, 1983), 33.
13. Mona Hearn, *Below Stairs: Domestic Service Remembered in Dublin and Beyond, 1880–1922* (Dublin: The Lilliput Press, 1993), 77.
14. Joseph J. Lee, *Ireland: Politics and Society, 1912–1985* (Cambridge: Cambridge University Press, 1989), 3–4.

15. Lee, *Ireland: Politics and Society*, 3–4.

16. Hearn, *Below the Stairs*, 67.

17. Eve Walsh Stoddard, *Positioning Gender and Race in (Post)Colonial Plantation Space: Connecting Ireland and the Caribbean* (New York: Palgrave MacMillan, 2012), 196.

18. Margaret Lynch-Brennan, *The Irish Bridget: Irish Immigrant Women in Domestic Service in America, 1840–1930* (Syracuse: Syracuse University Press, 2014), 28.

19. Lynch-Brennan, *The Irish Bridget*, 13.

20. Anne McClintock, *Imperial Leather: Race, Gender, and Sexuality in the Colonial Contest* (New York: Routledge Press, 1995), 56.

21. See Bronwen Walter, *Outsiders Inside: Whiteness, Place, and Irish Women* (New York: Routledge Press, 2001), 90–91; and Bronwen Walter "Irish Domestic Servants and English National Identity," in *Domestic Service and the Formation of European Identity*, A. Fauve-Chamoux, ed. (London: Oxford, 2004), 482.

22. Walter, *Outsiders Inside*, 99.

23. Deborah Valenze, *The First Industrial Woman* (New York: Oxford University Press, 1995), 174.

24. Walter, *Outsiders Inside*, 23.

25. Curtis Jr., *Anglo Saxons and Celts*, 57.

26. Raymond Scupin, *Race and Ethnicity: An Anthropological Focus on the United States and the World* (Prentice Hall: New Jersey, 2002), 109.

27. John Kelly, *The Graves Are Walking: The Great Famine and the Saga of the Irish People* (New York: Henry Holt & Company, 2012), 4.

28. Kelly, *The Graves Are Walking*, 4.

29. Christine Kinealy, "Was Ireland a Colony? The Evidence of the Great Famine," in Terence McDonough, ed., *Was Ireland a Colony?: Economy, Politics, Ideology and Culture in Nineteenth Century Ireland* (Dublin: Irish Academic Press, 2005), 49.

30. Kelly, *The Graves Are Walking*, 51–55.

31. Diner, *Erin's Daughters in America*, 4.

32. The societies were part of a history of England transporting Irish Catholic labor to its colonies and the United States since the seventeenth and eighteenth centuries; see Don Jordan and Michael Walsh, *White Cargo: The Forgotten History of Britain's Whites Slaves in America* (New York: New York University Press, 2008); Hilary McDonald Beckles, "A 'riotous and unruly lot': Irish Indentured Servants and Freemen in the English West Indies, 1644–1713," *The William and Mary Quarterly Journal* (Oct. 1990).

33. Foster assisted in the emigration of approximately 1,250 Irish women to the United States from 1850–1857; see Andrew T. Urban, *Brokering Servitude* (New York: New York University Press, 2018), 29–30.

34. James Olson and Robert Shadle, eds., *Historical Dictionary of the British Empire, A–J* (Westport: Greenwood Press, 1996), 189; Stanley Currie Johnson, *Emigration from the United Kingdom to North America, 1763–1912* (New York: Routledge, 2013), 255; Louisa Agnes Money, *History of The Girls' Friendly Society* (London: Wells Gardner & Company, 1911), 11.

35. "New Phase of Immigrant Swindling," *New York Times*, 19 Oct 1860, 4.

36. Deirdre Cooper Owens, *Medical Bondage: Race, Gender, and the Origins of American Gynecology* (Athens: University of Georgia Press, 2017), 93–96.

37. Trevor McClaughlin, "Lost Children? Irish Famine Orphans in Australia," *History Ireland* 8 (2000): 31.

38. Lynch-Brennan, *The Irish Bridget*, xix.
39. Leslie Harris, *In the Shadow of Slavery: African Americans in New York City* (Chicago: The University of Chicago Press, 2003), 183.
40. Harris, *In the Shadow of Slavery*, 183.
41. Walter, *Outsiders Inside*, 69.
42. Faye E. Dudden, *Serving Women: Household Service in Nineteenth-Century America* (Hanover: University Press of New England, 1983), 32.
43. Dudden, *Serving Women*, 47.
44. Phyllis Palmer, *Dirt and Domesticity: Housewives and Domestic Servants, 1920–1945* (Philadelphia: Temple University Press, 1989), 5.
45. Dudden, *Serving Women*, 62.
46. Dudden, *Serving Women*, 60.
47. See Lynch-Brennan, "Ubiquitous Bridget, 41–49; and Frances Cavanah, ed., *We Came to America* (Philadelphia: Macrae Smith Company, 1954), 136–137.
48. Diner, *Erin's Daughters in America*, 70.
49. Lynch-Brennan, "Ubiquitous Bridget, xix.
50. See Roediger, *Wages of Whiteness*, 145; and Diner, *Erin's Daughters in America*, 89.
51. David E. Sutherland, *Americans and Their Servants: Domestic Service in the United States from 1800–1920* (Baton Rouge and London: Louisiana State University Press, 1981), 48–49.
52. Curtis Jr., *Anglo Saxons and Celts*, 90.
53. Curtis Jr., *Anglo Saxons and Celts*, 91.
54. Urban, *Brokering Servitude*, 49.
55. Edgar J. McManus, *Black Bondage in the North* (Syracuse: Syracuse University Press, 1973), 161.
56. McManus, *Black Bondage in the North* (Syracuse: Syracuse University Press, 1973), 166; A. Leon Higginbothem Jr., *In the Matter of Color: Race and the American Legal Process, The Colonial Period* (New York: Oxford University Press, 1978), 90.
57. Leslie Harris, *In the Shadow of Slavery: African Americans in New York City* (Chicago: The University of Chicago Press, 2003), 12.
58. Harris, *In the Shadow of Slavery*, 58.
59. Harris, *In the Shadow of Slavery*, 56.
60. Harris, *In the Shadow of Slavery*, 73.
61. Harris, *In the Shadow of Slavery*, 94.
62. Harris, *In the Shadow of Slavery*, 80, 264.
63. Eric Foner, Gateway to Freedom: The Hidden History of the Underground Railroad (New York: W.W. Norton & Company, 2015), 45.
64. Curtis Jr., *Anglo Saxons and Celts*, 96.
65. Kelly, *The Graves Are Walking*, 301.
66. Kelly, *The Graves Are Walking*, 301.
67. Morton based his theory about racial differences on measurements of African and Anglo-Saxon skulls; see Samuel Morton, *Crania Americana: or, A Comparative View of the Skulls of Various Aboriginal Nations of North and South America* (Philadelphia: John Penington, Chestnut Street, 1839), 15. Also, see Thomas F. Gossett's discussion of scientific racism, *Race: The History of an Idea in America* (Dallas: Southern Methodist University Press, 1963), 59–63.
68. Kelly, *The Graves Are Walking*, 301.

69. Noel Ignatiev, *How the Irish Became White* (Routledge: New York, 1995), 42; Leslie Harris, *In the Shadow of Slavery: African Americans in New York City* (Chicago: The University of Chicago Press, 2003), 247.

70. Deirdre Cooper Owens, "Perfecting the Degraded Body: Slavery, Irish-Immigration, and American Gynecology," in *Power in History: From Medieval Ireland to the Post-Modern World*, eds. Anthony McElligott et al (Dublin: Irish Academic Press, 2011),174, 182.

71. Deirdre Cooper Owens, "'Courageous Negro Servitors' and Laboring Irish Bodies: An Examination of Antebellum Era Modern American Gynecology." (Doctoral diss., University of California-Los Angeles, 2008), 186–191.

72. For a historical account of how the transportation of particularly Irish children to the West incited political and religious debates about race and immigration, see L. Gordon, *The Great Arizona Orphan Abduction* (Boston: Harvard University Press, 2001), 307–313.

73. The Cottage Place School was sponsored and established by the Children's Aid Society. It provided education for all poor white immigrant children and black children; see "Appeal for the Children's Aid Society," *New York Times*, 23 Jan 1861.

74. "Incidents in Cottage Place Industrial School," *Twenty Fifth Annual Report of Children's Aid Society* (New York: Wynkoop and Hallenbeck, 1877), 72.

75. Diner, *Erin's Daughters in America*, 62.

76. Quoted from Nakano Glenn, *Unequal Freedom*, 56.

77. Harris, *In the Shadow of Slavery*, 6.

78. Nakano Glenn, *Unequal Freedom*, 56.

79. Judith Rollins, *Between Women: Domestics and their Employers* (Philadelphia: Temple University Press, 1985), 51.

80. Dudden, *Serving Women*, 33.

81. Marjorie Howes, "How Irish Maids Are Made: Domestic Servants, Atlantic Culture, and Modernist Aesthetics," in *The Black and Green Atlantic: Crosscurrents of the African and Irish Diaspora*, eds. Peter D. O'Neill and David Lloyd (New York: Palgrave McMillan, 2009), 100.

82. Miss Leslie, *The Behavior Book: A Manual for Ladies* (Philadelphia: Willis P. Hazard, 1855), 104–105.

83. Harriet Beecher Stowe, *Uncle Tom's Cabin: A Tale about Life Among the Lowly* (London: George Routledge & Company, 1852), 226.

84. "Housekeeping, English and American: By an American," *Every Saturday: A Journal of Choice Reading*, 23 Jan 1869: 108.

85. Lynch-Brennan, "Ubiquitous Bridget, 332–335.

86. Dudden, *Serving Women*, 60.

87. Rollins, *Between Women*, 51–52.

88. Throughout the book, I sometimes refer to the stereotypes associated with both Irish immigrant and southern Black women with italicized pronouns "she," "her," "Mammy," "Bridget," and "Aunt Jemima" to emphasize the influence and power of the images.

89. Peter Flynn, "How Bridget Was Framed: The Irish Domestic in Early American Cinema, 1895–1917," *Cinema Journal* 50 (Winter 2011): 2.

90. Diner, *Erin's Daughters in America*, 80.

91. Palmer, *Dirt and Domesticity*, 146.

92. Palmer, *Dirt and Domesticity*, 5.

93. Palmer, *Dirt and Domesticity*, 139.
94. Nell Irvin Painter, *The History of White People* (New York: W.W. Norton & Company, 2010), 183.
95. Thomas F. Gassett, *Race: The History of an Idea* (New York: Oxford University Press, 1997), 287.
96. Roediger, *Wages of Whiteness*, 143–145.
97. Quoted from Jennifer Guglielmo, *Living the Revolution: Italian Women's Resistance and Radicalism in New York City, 1880–1945* (Chapel Hill: University of North Carolina Press, 2010), 6.
98. Elizabeth Hafkin Pleck, *Black Migration and Poverty: Boston 1865–1900* (New York: Academic Press, 1979), 24.
99. Harris, *In the Shadow of Slavery*, 280.
100. James Barrett, *The Irish Way: Becoming American in the Multiethnic City* (New York: The Penguin Press, 2012), 19.
101. Eric Foner, *Reconstruction: America's Unfinished Revolution, 1863–1877* (New York: Harper & Row, 1988), 479.
102. Foner, *Reconstruction: America's Unfinished Revolution*, 480.

Chapter 3   Southern Mammy and African American "Immigrant" Women

1. Elizabeth Clark-Lewis, *Living In, Living Out: African American Domestics and the Great Migration* (Washington D.C: Smithsonian Institution Press, 1994), 10.
2. Northern white employers often referred to northern-born black women domestic servants as "Dinah."
3. Trudier Harris, *From Mammies to Militants: Domestics in Black American Literature* (Philadelphia: Temple University Press, 1982), 24.
4. Kimberly Wallace Sanders, *Mammy: A Century of Race, Gender, and Southern Memory* (Ann Arbor: University of Michigan Press, 2008), 13.
5. Deborah Gray White, *Arn't I a Woman: Female Slaves in the Plantation South* (New York: W.W. Norton & Company, 1999), 55.
6. Deborah Gray White, *Arn't I a Woman*, 55.
7. Quoted from David Blight, *Race and Reunion: The Civil War in American Memory* (Cambridge: Harvard University Press, 2001), 41.
8. Quoted from Deborah Gray White, *Arn't I a Woman*, 58.
9. Deborah Gray White, *Arn't I a Woman*, 47.
10. Grace Elizabeth Hale, *Making Whiteness: The Culture of Segregation in the South* (New York: Vintage Books, 1998), 107; Wallace-Sanders, *Mammy*, 2008), 127; Deborah Gray White, *Arn't I a Woman*, 58.
11. Hale, *Making Whiteness*, 115.
12. Wallace-Sanders, *Mammy*, 3–6.
13. Quoted from Walter Johnson, *Soul by Soul: Life Inside the Antebellum Slave Market* (Cambridge: Harvard University Press, 1999), 90.
14. David E. Sutherland, *Americans and Their Servants: Domestic Service in the United States from 1800–1920* (Baton Rouge and London: Louisiana State University Press, 1981), 40.
15. Hale, *Making Whiteness*, 86.
16. Mary Johnson's novels remain accessible today and can be found easily on popular book sites, including Amazon and Google Books. See her novels: *Prisoners of Hope:*

A Tale of Colonial Virginia (1898), *Cease Firing* (1912), and *To Have and to Hold: A Tale of Colonial Virginia* (1900).

17. Leslie Harris and Daina Ramey Berry, eds., *Slavery and Freedom in Savannah* (Athens: University of Georgia Press, 2014), xix.

18. Karen L. Cox, *Dixie's Daughters: The United Daughters of the Confederacy and the Preservation of Confederate Culture* (Gainesville: University Press of Florida, 2003), 166.

19. See Mary M. Solari, *Confederate Veteran* 13 (Mar 1905), 123–124; Hale, *Making Whiteness*, 98.

20. Richard Follett, "Legacies of Enslavement: Plantation Identities and the Problem of Freedom," *Slavery's Ghost: The Problem of Freedom in the Age of Emancipation,* eds. Richard Follett, Eric Foner, and Walter Johnson (Baltimore: Johns Hopkins University Press, 2011), 52.

21. Trudier Harris, *From Mammies to Militants*, 25.

22. See Grace Elizabeth Hale's discussion of Black women domestics who worked in the homes of white mill workers and small farm owners in Hale, *Making Whiteness*, 102–103.

23. Hale, *Making Whiteness*, 103.

24. Blight, *Race and Reunion*, 286.

25. For studies of how gender and class impacted Black migrations from rural towns to cities in the South, see Tera Hunter's *To 'Joy My Freedom: Southern Black Women's Lives and Labors after the Civil War* (Cambridge: Harvard University Press, 1998); and Leslie Brown, *Upbuilding Black Durham: Gender, Class, and Black Community Development in the Jim Crow South* (Chapel Hill: The University of North Carolina Press, 2008).

26. Robin D. G. Kelley, *Race Rebels: Culture, Politics, and the Black Working Class* (New York: The Free Press, 1996).

27. Jacqueline Jones, *Labor of Love, Labor of Sorrow: Black Women, Work, and Family from Slavery to the Present* (New York: Vintage Books, 1986), 78.

28. Blight, *Race and Reunion*, 45.

29. Johnson, Follett, and Foner, eds., *Slavery's Ghost*, 3; Blight, *Race and Reunion*, 45–46.

30. Blight, *Race and Reunion*, 47.

31. Follett, "Legacies of Enslavement: Plantation Identities and the Problem of Freedom," *Slavery's Ghost*, 62–63.

32. Blight, *Race and Reunion*, 49.

33. Follett, "Legacies of Enslavement," *Slavery's Ghost*, 53.

34. Elizabeth Clark–Lewis, *Living In, Living Out: African American Domestics and the Great Migration* (Washington D.C: Smithsonian Institution Press, 1994), 10.

35. Evelyn Nakano Glenn, *Unequal Freedom: How Race and Gender Shaped American Citizenship and Labor* (Cambridge: Harvard University Press, 2002), 94–97.

36. Johnson, Follett, and Foner, eds., *Slavery's Ghost*, 4.

37. For a history of Black women's experiences in the Jim Crow South, see Anne Valk and Leslie Brown, *Living with Jim Crow: African American Women and Memories of the Segregated South* (New York: Palgrave MacMillan, 2010).

38. Black cities established shortly after emancipation in the South include Eatonville, Florida; and Mound Bayou, Mississippi.

39. Hunter, *To 'Joy My Freedom*, 26.

40. Quoted from Elizabeth Clark-Lewis, *Living In, Living Out*, 25.
41. Elizabeth Clark-Lewis, *Living In, Living Out*, 13.
42. Elizabeth Clark-Lewis, *Living In, Living Out*, 12, 20.
43. Eric Foner, *Reconstruction: America's Unfinished Revolution* (New York: Harper & Row, 2011), 140; Clark-Lewis, *Living In, Living Out*, 9-13.
44. Follett, "Legacies of Enslavement," *Slavery's Ghost*, 54, 60.
45. Hunter, *To 'Joy My Freedom*, 74-98.
46. Kelley, *Race Rebels*.
47. Tera Hunter, *To 'Joy My Freedom*, 89.
48. Foner, *Reconstruction*, 136.
49. For an historical account of the political and economic decline of the South, see C. Vann Woodward, *The Burden of Southern History* (Baton Rouge: Louisiana State University Press, 1960), 17, 105-106.
50. Quoted from Foner, *Reconstruction*, 136.
51. Lucy Maynard Salmon, *Domestic Service* (New York: The MacMillan Company, 1901), 175.
52. "Domestic Service in the South," *New-Orleans Times*, 30 Nov 1889.
53. "More Slavery at the South," by a Negro Nurse, *Independent*, 25 Jan 1912, 196-200.
54. Clark-Lewis, *Living In, Living Out*, 48.
55. Hunter, *To 'Joy My Freedom*, 29.
56. See testimony of Alfred Richardson, 7 July 1871, KKK Hearings, vol. 1, , 12, 18.
57. Sarah Haley, *No Mercy Here: Gender, Punishment, and the Making of Jim Crow Modernity* (Chapel Hill: The University of North Carolina Press, 2016) 30-31. According to Haley, between 1893 and 1900, Black girls and young women were arrested more than white men and women in their same age group combined.
58. Sarah Haley, *No Mercy Here: Gender, Punishment, and the Making of Jim Crow Modernity* (Chapel Hill: The University of North Carolina Press, 2016), 10.
59. Haley, *No Mercy Here*, 4-5.
60. Hunter, *To 'Joy My Freedom*, 187, 189-190.
61. Nakano Glenn, *Unequal Freedom*, 94-97.
62. Elsa Barkley Brown, "Negotiating and Transforming the Public Sphere: African American Political Life in the Transition from Slavery to Freedom," *Public Culture* 7, no. 1 (Fall 1994): 108.
63. Carol Anderson, *White Rage: The Unspoken Truth of Our Racial Divide* (New York: Bloomsbury, 2016), 46.
64. Joe Trotter, ed., *The Great Migration in Historical Perspective: New Dimensions of Race, Class, and Gender* (Bloomington: Indiana University Press, 1991), 17.
65. Evelyn Brooks Higginbotham, *Righteous Discontent: The Women's Movement in the Black Church, 1800-1920* (Cambridge: Harvard University Press, 1993).
66. Elizabeth Clark-Lewis, *Living In, Living Out*, 54.
67. Robert Coles, *The South Goes North: Volume III of Children of Crisis* (Boston: Little, Brown, and Company, 1967), 267.
68. James R. Barrett, *The Irish Way: Becoming American in the Multiethnic City* (New York: The Penguin Press, 2012), 1.
69. Barrett, *The Irish Way*, 1.
70. James M. Bergquist, *Daily Life in Immigrant America: How the First Great Wave of Immigrants Made Their Way in America* (Chicago: Ivan R. Dee, 2008), 170.
71. Quoted from Barrett, *The Irish Way*, 1.

72. Roediger, *Wages of Whiteness*, 150.
73. Roediger, *Wages of Whiteness*, 154.
74. Elizabeth Pleck, *Black Migration and Poverty: Boston, 1865–1900* (New York: Academic Press, 1979), 29.
75. David Yentis, "The Negro in Old Brooklyn: An Experiment in Sociological Reconstruction of the Life of a Racial Minority in a Northern City" (master's thesis: Columbia University, 1937), 54.
76. W.E.B. Du Bois, *The Philadelphia Negro: A Social Study* (Philadelphia: University of Pennsylvania Press, 1996 [1899]), 323.
77. Quoted from Follet, Foner, and Johnson's *Slavery's Ghost* to describe the "ideological, conceptual, and practical obstacles to freedom" for Blacks after emancipation that were rooted in the history of slavery; see Follet, Foner, and Johnson, eds., *Slavery's Ghost*, 2–3.
78. Tanya Hart argues in her comparative study of the health care agencies that targeted African American, Italian immigrant, and British West Indian women in New York City that the women's migrations occurred in overlapping time periods between 1880–1920 and informed each other; see Tanya Hart, *Health in the City: Race, Poverty, and the Negotiation of Women's Health in New York City, 1915–1930* (New York: New York University Press, 2015), 9.
79. I sometimes refer to southern Black migrant women in this chapter as African American women to distinguish them from Black Caribbean immigrant women.
80. "The Colored Refugees," *New York Times*, 11 Jul 1879.
81. "The Colored Refugees," *New York Times*, 1 Apr 1880.
82. Eric Foner, *Gateway to Freedom: The Hidden History of the Underground Railroad* (New York: W. W. Norton & Company, 2015), 29.
83. Hunter, *To 'Joy My Freedom*, 202.
84. Hunter, *To 'Joy My Freedom*, 202
85. Edward E. Baptist, *The Half Has Never Been Told: Slavery and the Making of American Capitalism* (New York: Basic Books, 2014), xv.
86. Pleck, *Black Migration and Poverty*, 27.
87. David M. Katzman, *Seven Days a Week: Women and Domestic Service in Industrializing America* (New York: Oxford University Press, 1979), 204.
88. Jennifer Morgan, "'Some Could Suckle over Their Shoulder': Male Travelers, Female Bodies, and the Gendering of Racial Ideology, 1500–1770," *The William and Mary Quarterly* 54 (January 1997): 178.
89. Pleck, *Black Migration and Poverty*, 27.
90. Katzman, *Seven Days a Week*, 205.
91. Katzman, *Seven Days a Week*, 206.
92. Pleck, *Black Migration and Poverty*, 28.
93. Katzman, *Seven Days a Week*, 207.
94. Wilmer Walton, "Colored Servants," *The Daily Register-Call* (Colorado), 4 Aug 1879.
95. *Daily Evening Bulletin* (San Francisco), 28 July 1879.
96. "Negro House Servants," *The Daily Inter Ocean* (Chicago), 1 Oct 1892.
97. See chapter 1 of this book for discussion of British labor schemes created during the famine era.
98. Katzman, *Seven Days a Week*, 213–214.
99. Mary White Ovington, *Walls Came Tumbling Down* (Harcourt, Brace and Company: New York, 1947).

100. "Pickney vs. Halligan," *Brooklyn Eagle*, 12 Dec 1877.

101. Edward Pickney, "Miss Pickney's Brother Says a Word," *Brooklyn Eagle*, 20 Jul 1877, 4.

102. Quoted from Clark-Lewis, *Living In, Living Out*, 92.

103. Pleck, *Black Migration and Poverty*, 76.

104. Pleck, *Black Migration and Poverty*, 76–77.

105. Pleck, *Black Migration and Poverty*, 90; Irma Watkins-Owens, *Blood Relations: Caribbean Immigrants and the Harlem Community, 1900–1930* (Bloomington: Indiana University Press, 1996), 65.

106. Watkins-Owens, *Blood Relations*, 65.

107. Watkins-Owens, *Blood Relations*, 66–67.

108. Watkins-Owens, *Blood Relations*.

109. Pleck, *Black Migration and Poverty*, 7.

110. Watkins-Owens, *Blood Relations*, 181; Yentis, "The Negro in Old Brooklyn," 46.

111. Janet Nolan, *Ourselves Alone: Women's Emigration from Ireland, 1885–1920* (Lexington: University of Kentucky Press, 1989), 78.

112. Leslie Harris, *In the Shadow of Slavery: African Americans in New York City* (Chicago: The University of Chicago Press, 2003), 241.

113. Yentis, "The Negro in Old Brooklyn," 48.

114. Yentis, "The Negro in Old Brooklyn," 48.

115. Yentis, "The Negro in Old Brooklyn," 54.

116. Yentis, "The Negro in Old Brooklyn," 49.

117. Vanessa May, *Unprotected Labor: Household Workers, Politics, and Middle-Class Reform in New York, 1870–1940* (Chapel Hill: The University of North Carolina Press, 2011), 113.

118. Yentis, "The Negro in Old Brooklyn," 49.

119. James R. Barrett, *The Irish Way: Becoming American in the Multiethnic City* (New York: Penguin Press, 2012), 110.

120. David E. Sutherland, *Americans and Their Servants: Domestic Service in the United States from 1800–1920* (Baton Rouge and London: Louisiana State University Press, 1981), 50.

121. Vanessa May, *Unprotected Labor*, 8.

122. See Chapter 4 of this book for illustrations and discussion of dark, animalistic Irish servants amidst southern Black women's migrations in the late nineteenth century.

123. Elizabeth Clark-Lewis, *Living In, Living Out*, 113.

124. Quoted from Vanessa May, *Unprotected Labor*, 11.

125. Nell Irvin Painter, *Standing at Armageddon: The United States 1877–1919* (New York: W.W. Norton & Company, 1987), 93.

126. See Chapter 4 of this book for a discussion of Irish immigrant and African American women's activism during the Progressive Era.

127. Painter, *Standing at Armageddon*, xlii–xliii.

128. Pleck, *Black Migration and Poverty*, 79.

129. Hart, *Health in the City*, 19.

130. Vanessa May, *Unprotected Labor*, 74.

131. Vanessa May, *Unprotected Labor*, 99.

132. Vanessa May, *Unprotected Labor*, 99.

133. Andrew T. Urban, *Brokering Servitude* (New York: New York University Press, 2018), 180.

134. May, *Unprotected Labor*, 99.

135. "Our New Congested Districts—the City Hospitals," *Charities* 13 (Mar 1905): 581–584; and "The Anti-Tuberculosis Movement in Another Small City," *Charities* 13 (Mar 1905): 586–587.
136. See Chapter 5 of this book for a more detailed discussion of Victoria Earle Matthews and the White Rose Mission Home.
137. To read more about Kellor's hierarchical categorization of European immigrant women, see Urban, *Brokering Servitude*, 185–186.
138. Frances A. Kellor, "Southern Colored Girls in the North: The Problem of Their Protection," 13 *Charities* (18 Mar 1905): 584.
139. Quoted from Hazel Carby, "Policing the Black Woman's Body in an Urban Context," *Critical Inquiry* 18 (Summer 1992): 740. It is important to note that middle-class Black women also participated in the surveillance of southern migrant women. This chapter (Chapter 3) of this book focuses on how white women social reformers' portrayal of the southern women as "immigrants" reinforced white supremacy amid increased Black women's migrations to northern cities.
140. Deirdre Cooper Owens, "Perfecting the Degraded Body: Slavery, Irish-Immigration, and American Gynecology," *Power in History: From Medieval Ireland to the Post-Modern World*, eds. Anthony McElligott et al. (Dublin: Irish Academic Press, 2011),169.
141. Deborah Gray White, *Arn't I a Woman?*, 31.
142. See Hazel Carby, "Policing the Black Woman's Body in an Urban Context," *Critical Inquiry* 18 (Summer 1992): 749.
143. Kellor, "Southern Colored Girls in the North," 585.
144. From 1906–1910, branches of the NLPCW were established in New York, Philadelphia, New Orleans, Savannah, Richmond, Charleston, and Jacksonville to aid southern Black women traveling North; see Susan D. Carle, *Defining the Struggle: National Organizing for Racial Justice, 1880–1915* (New York: Oxford University Press, 2013), 238.
145. Sarah Willie Layten, "The Servant Problem," *Colored American Magazine*, Jan 1907, 13–15.
146. May, *Unprotected Labor*, 100.
147. May, *Unprotected Labor*, 104.
148. Quoted from the official directory of the New York City Federation of Women's Clubs, see Ina Brevoort Roberts, ed. *Club Women of New York* (New York: Club Women of New York Company, 1913–1914), 161.
149. "Work to Domestic Service," *New York Times*, 20 Oct 1907.
150. Marcy Sacks, *Before Harlem: The Black Experience in New York City Before World War I* (Philadelphia: University of Pennsylvania Press, 2006), 135.

Chapter 4   Too Irish, Too Rural, Too Black

1. "Our Goddess of Liberty," *Frank Leslie's Illustrated Newspaper*, 16 Jul 1870.
2. Laura Shapiro, *Perfection Salad: Women and Cooking at the Turn of the Century* (Berkeley: University of California Press, 2009), 4.
3. Quoted from Shapiro, *Perfection Salad*, 4.
4. David M. Katzman, *Seven Days a Week: Women and Domestic Service in Industrializing America* (New York: Oxford University Press, 1978), 46–48, 62–63.
5. Katzman, *Seven Days a Week*, 27.

6. Janet Nolan, *Ourselves Alone: Women's Emigration from Ireland, 1885–1920* (Lexington: The University Press of Kentucky, 1989), 3; 78.

7. Stephen Steinberg, *The Ethnic Myth: Race, Ethnicity, and Class in America* (Boston: Beacon Press, 2001), 161.

8. Steinberg, *The Ethnic Myth*, 154; Katzman, *Seven Days a Week*, 67.

9. Historians have also argued that particularly Italian immigrant women were prohibited by their traditionally patriarchal husbands from working in domestic service. The idea that Italian immigrant women were submissive has been challenged by Jennifer Guglielmo in her study of Italian immigrant women activists in New York City; see Jennifer Guglielmo, *Living the Revolution: Italian Women's Resistance and Radicalism in New York City, 1880–1945* (Chapel Hill: University of North Carolina Press, 2010), 3.

10. See Jennifer Guglielmo and Salvatore Salerno, eds. *Are Italians White: How Race Is Made in America* (New York: Routledge Press, 2003), 11; Michael W. Grunberger and Hasia R. Diner, eds., *From Haven to Home: 350 Years of Jewish Life in America* (New York: George Braziller Press, 2004), 75–76; Nancy Cott and Elizabeth Pleck, eds., *A Heritage of Her Own: Toward a New Social History of American Woman* (New York: Simon and Schuster Press, 1979), 367–392.

11. Katzman, *Seven Days a Week*, 66.

12. Faye E. Dudden, *Serving Women: Household Service in Nineteenth-Century America* (Hanover: University Press of New England, 1983), 65.

13. Kimberly Phillips, *AlabamaNorth: African-American Migrants, Community, and Working-Class Activism in Cleveland, 1915–1945* (Urbana: University of Illinois Press, 1999), 40.

14. Bonnie Thornton Dill, *Across the Boundaries of Race and Class: An Exploration of Work and Family Among Black Female Domestic Servants* (New York: Garland Publishing, 1994), 16; Steinberg, *The Ethnic Myth*, 161.

15. "Kitchen versus Slop Shop," *New York Times*, 5 Mar 1893.

16. "Southern Servant Girls," *Brooklyn Eagle*, 23 Apr 1900, 7.

17. "Colored Servants," *New York Globe*, 29 Mar 1884.

18. "The Servant Girl Question," *Brooklyn Eagle*, 18 Mar 1888, 8.

19. Katzman, *Seven Days a Week*, 204.

20. Robert Tomes, "Your Humble Servant," *Harper's New Monthly Magazine*, Jul 1864.

21. Tomes, "Your Humble Servant."

22. "The 'Kitchen-Garden,'" *New York Times*, 24 Mar 1878.

23. "The 'Kitchen-Garden.'"

24. Quoted from caption to the Eureka mop advertisement; see "The Great 'Scrub' Race," 1870. Library of Congress Prints and Photographs Division.

25. Katzman, *Seven Days a Week*, 242.

26. "Housekeeping, English and American: By an American, *Every Saturday: A Journal of Choice Reading*, 23 Jan 1869, 108.

27. Housekeeping, English and American, 109.

28. Quoted from Janet Nolan, *Ourselves Alone: Women's Emigration from Ireland, 1885–1920* (Lexington: University of Kentucky Press, 1989), 93.

29. Charles Loring Brace, *The Dangerous Classes of New York and Twenty Years' Work among Them.* (New York: Wynkoop & Hallenbeck Publishers, 1872), 36.

30. Hasia Diner, *Erin's Daughters in America: Irish Immigrant Women in the Nineteenth Century* (Baltimore: The Johns Hopkins University Press, 1983), 113–114.

31. Brace, *The Dangerous Classes of New York*, 42.

32. Linda Gordon, *The Great Arizona Orphan Abduction* (Cambridge: Harvard University Press, 2011), 8–9.
33. "Effect of the Fifteenth Amendment," *Harper's Bazaar* magazine (New York), 4 Mar 1871. Accessed through the Miriam and Ira D. Wallach Division of Art, Prints and Photographs: Picture Collection, The New York Public Library, *The New York Public Library Digital Collections.* 1871-03-04. http://digitalcollections.nypl.org /items/510d47e0-fba6-a3d9-e040-e00a18064a99
34. James R. Barrett, *The Irish Way: Becoming American in the Multiethnic City* (New York: Penguin Books, 2013), 4.
35. "Domestic Servants," *New York Times*, 7 Jul 1872.
36. "Domestic Servants." *New York Times.*
37. M.E.P., "Those Servant Girls: Wishes they had one neck so that she could wring it," *Brooklyn Eagle*, 11 Mar 1897.
38. See Tera Hunter's historical note on Eaton in the 1996 University of Pennsylvania edition of W.E.B. Du Bois and Isabel Eaton, *The Philadelphia Negro: A Social Study* (Philadelphia: University of Pennsylvania, 1899), 425–426.
39. Isabel Eaton, "Special Report on Negro Domestic Service," *The Philadelphia Negro: A Social Study* (Philadelphia: University of Pennsylvania, 1899) 487.
40. Isabel Eaton, "Special Report on Negro Domestic Service," 487.
41. In cities like New York where the Irish far outnumbered Blacks, the majority of Black women were employed for the lowest-status and lowest-paying position of general house worker; see "Colored Servants," *New York Globe*, 29 March 1884.
42. "Ex-Lady," *New York Times*, 17 Feb 1895.
43. "Ex-Lady," *New York Times*, 17 Feb 1895.
44. "Letters of the Subject," *New York Times*, 10 Feb 1895.
45. Anonymous, *Our Jemimas: Addressed to the Middle Class by a Victim* (London: Houlston, 1880).
46. Anonymous, *Our Jemimas*, 56.
47. Anonymous, *Our Jemimas*, 60.
48. April Schultz, "The Black Mammy and the Irish Bridget: Domestic Service and the Representation of Race, 1830–1930," *Éire-Ireland Journal* 48, nos. 3 & 4 (Fall/Winter 2013): 179.
49. Annie Besant, *Annie Besant: An Autobiography* (London: T. Fisher Unwin, 1893), 335.
50. Diner, *Erin's Daughters in America*, xiv.
51. "The Irish Declaration of Independence," *Puck*, 9 May 1883. To view the image, see https://www.loc.gov/pictures/item/2012645471/
52. For a history of the Irish rebellions in the early twentieth century, see J. J. Lee, *Ireland 1912–1985: Politics and Society* (Cambridge: Cambridge University Press, 1989).
53. Andrew T. Urban, "Irish Domestic Servants, 'Biddy' and Rebellion in the American Home, 1850–1900," *Gender and History Journal* 21, no. 2 (2009): 264.
54. Andrew T. Urban, *Brokering Servitude* 57.
55. "The Goose that Lays the Golden Egg," *Puck*, 22 Aug 1883.
56. Sinéad McCoole, *No Ordinary Women: Irish Female Activists in the Revolutionary Years, 1900–1923* (Dublin: The O'Brien Press, 2004), 11–12.
57. Maria Luddy, *Women in Ireland: A Documentary History* 1800–1918 (Cork: Cork University Press, 1995), 241–242.
58. Kerby Miller, *Emigrants and Exiles: Ireland and the Irish Exodus to North America* (New York: Oxford University Press, 1985), 389.

59. See Chapter 5 of this book for fuller discussion about Leonora Barry and Leonora O'Reilly.

60. Samuel Morton, *Crania Americana: or a Comparative view of the Skulls of Various Aboriginal Nations of North and South America* (Philadelphia: J. Dobson Press, 1839), 3.

61. See Henry Strickland Constable's drawing of Irish Iberian, Anglo-Teutonic, and Negro heads in Henry Strickland Constable, *Ireland from One or Two Neglected Points of View* (New York: Liberty Review Publishing Company, 1899). Image was reprinted in George Bornstein's *Material Modernism: The Politics of the Page* (Cambridge: Cambridge University Press, 2001) 146 as well as several other academic books. The image is also referenced on several popular websites including Pinterest and Wikimedia Commons, and blog sites that detail the history of scientific racism.

62. George Bornstein's *Material Modernism: The Politics of the Page* (Cambridge: Cambridge University Press, 2001), 146.

63. Lucy Maynard Salmon, *Domestic Service* (New York: The MacMillan Company, 1901), 68.

64. Shapiro, *Perfection Salad*, 35.

65. Shapiro, *Perfection Salad*, 4.

66. Shapiro, *Perfection Salad*, 8.

67. Glenda Matthews, *Just a Housewife: The Rise and Fall of Domesticity in America* (New York: Oxford University Press, 1987), 102.

68. Maynard Salmon, *Domestic Service*, 300–301.

69. May, *Unprotected Labor*, 107–108.

70. Hazel Carby, "Policing the black woman's body in an urban context" *Critical Inquiry* 18, no. 4 (1992): 741.

71. See W.E.B. Du Bois and Isabel Eaton, *The Philadelphia Negro: A Social Study* (Philadelphia: University of Pennsylvania, 1899), 140–142; and Tera Hunter, *To 'Joy My Freedom: Southern Black Women's Lives and Labors after the Civil War* (Cambridge: Harvard University Press, 1998), 195–196.

72. Du Bois and Eaton, *The Philadelphia Negro*, 292–293.

73. Judith Walzer Leavitt, *Typhoid Mary: Captive to the Public's Health* (Boston: Beacon Press, 1996), 163.

74. Leavitt, *Typhoid Mary*, 14, 17.

75. Leavitt, *Typhoid Mary*, 19.

76. "Typhoid Mary asks for $50,000 from the City," *New York Times*, 3 Dec 1911.

77. Leavitt, *Typhoid Mary*, 54; Janet Brooks, "The Sad and Tragic Life of Typhoid Mary," *Canadian Medical Association Journal*: 154, no. 6 (15 Mar 1996): 915–916.

78. "Typhoid Carrier Tied to Epidemic: Poor Sanitation on Liner Is Also Blamed for Illness," *New York Times*, 26 Oct 1970.

79. Leavitt, *Typhoid Mary*, 100–101.

80. "Typhoid Carrier Tied to Epidemic: Poor Sanitation on Liner Is Also Blamed for Illness," *New York Times*, 26 Oct 1970.

81. Vanessa May, *Unprotected Labor*, 127.

Chapter 5   Irish Immigrant Women Whiten Themselves, African American Women Demand the Unseen

1. Evelyn Brooks Higginbotham, "African-American Women's History and the Metalanguage of Race," *Signs* 17, no. 2 (Winter 1992): 252.

2. I borrow the term "working ladyhood" from Nan Enstad's *Ladies of Labor, Girls of Adventure: Working Women, Popular Culture, and Labor Politics at the Turn of the Twentieth Century* (New York: Columbia University Press, 1999), 51.
3. I borrow the term "Unseen" from James Baldwin's *Evidence of Things Not Seen*. The title of this book refers to the biblical chapter Hebrews 11:1, which describes the definition of faith in making possible what seems impossible because it requires overcoming nearly insurmountable obstacles. What Irish immigrants fought for had been seen because they saw the privileges of whiteness. However, Black women had to demand the unseen because there had been no such thing as racial and gender equality for Black women.
4. Raymond Scupin, *Race and Ethnicity: An Anthropological Focus on the United States and the World* (Prentice Hall: New Jersey, 2002), 111–112.
5. Ed O'Donnell, "United Front: The Irish and Organized Labor," *Irish in America*, eds. Michael Coffey and Terry Golway (New York: Hyperion, 1997), 154.
6. "Hopes 'C.O.P.'s' Girl Did Not Eat the Soap," *Brooklyn Eagle*, 12 March 1897.
7. See discussion of the "help" in Chapter 2 of this book.
8. "C.O.P. Justifies Her Position," *Brooklyn Eagle*, 11 Mar 1897.
9. "C.O.P. Justifies Her Position," *Brooklyn Eagle*.
10. "C.O.P. Justifies Her Position," *Brooklyn Eagle*.
11. Working-class women also participated in feminine consumer culture, including purchasing dime novels and "nice" clothing to mark themselves as respectable ladies; see Nan Enstand, *Ladies of Labor, Girls of Adventure: Working Women, Popular Culture, and Labor Politics at the Turn of the Twentieth Century* (New York: Columbia University Press, 1999), 50.
12. "Sell the Bloomers and Work, Says One Servant," *Brooklyn Daily Eagle*, 10 Mar 1897.
13. The servants who wrote responses to J.S.G.'s letter questioned whether or not he was really Irish. Considering that the editors of the newspaper might not have verified his nationality, J.S.G. could have been a native-born white man who assumed an Irish identity to make his complaints about Irish serving women seem credible. On the other hand, if he were truly Irish, his complaints present an interesting case of the class divisions and politics between working-class and "lace curtain" Irish immigrants.
14. "Sharp Words for 'J.S.G.'," *Brooklyn Daily Eagle*, 10 Mar 1897.
15. "'Irish Rambler' Suggests a Servant Girl Trust," *Brooklyn Eagle*, 11 Mar 1897.
16. "Servant Girl Question," *Brooklyn Daily Eagle*, 10 Mar 1897.
17. Quoted from Andrew T. Urban, *Brokering Servitude*, 53.
18. *An Gaodhal: A Monthly Journal Devoted To The Preservation and Cultivation of the Irish Language and the Autonomy of the Irish Nation* (Brooklyn: Nolan Brothers, Steam Print, 515 and 517 Fulton Street, 1881), 13.
19. Irish laundresses and cooks, for example, made up the majority of the domestic worker assembly in the Knights of Labor; see Susan Levine, "Labor's True Woman: Domesticity and Equal Rights in the Knights of Labor," *The Journal of American History* 70 (1983): 328.
20. Laura Schwartz, "'What we think is needed is a union of domestics such as the miners have': The Domestic Workers' Union of Great Britain and Ireland 1908–1914," *Twentieth Century British History* 25 (June 2014): 173–198.
21. Theresa Moriarty, "'Who Will Look After the Kiddies?' Households and Collective Action during the Dublin Lockout, 1913," in Jan Kok, ed., *Rebellious Families: Household Strategies and Collective Action in the Nineteenth and Twentieth Centuries* (New York: Berghan Books, 2002), 112.

22. Robert E. Weir, *Knights Unhorsed: Internal Conflict in a Gilded Age Social Movement* (Detroit: Wayne State University Press, 2000), 11.

23. Alex Gourevitch, *From Slavery to the Cooperative Commonwealth: Labor and Republican Liberty in the Nineteenth Century* (New York: Cambridge University Press, 2015), 20.

24. Nell Nelson, "City Slave Girls," *Chicago Times*, 30 Jul 1888.

25. Lara Vapnek, *Breadwinners: Working Women and Economic Independence, 1865–1920* (Urbana: University of Illinois Press, 2009), 58.

26. See Lara Vapnek's discussion of Carroll D. Wright's report in Vapnek, *Breadwinners*, 36–38.

27. Annelise Orleck, *Common Sense and a Little Fire: Women and Working-Class Politics in the United States, 1900–1965* (Chapel Hill: University of North Carolina Press, 1995), 90.

28. Vapnek, *Breadwinners*, 44.

29. Alex Gourevitch, *From Slavery to the Cooperative Commonwealth: Labor and Republican Liberty in the Nineteenth Century* (New York: Cambridge University Press, 2015), 10.

30. Weir, *Knights Unhorsed*, 144–145.

31. Leonora Barry "Report to the Knights of Labor 1887," *Tenth Annual Report of the Bureau of Statistics of Labor and Industries of New Jersey* (Somerville, 1888), 202–203.

32. Leonora Barry, *General Proceedings of the Knights of Labor*, 1887: 1840–1841.

33. Leonora Barry, *General Proceedings of the Knights of Labor*, 1888: 1580–1581.

34. Susan Levine, *Labor's True Woman: Carpet Weavers, Industrialization, and Labor Reform in the Gilded Age* (Philadelphia: Temple University Press, 1984), 132.

35. See Nancy Dye Schrom, *As Equals and as Sisters: Feminism, Unionism, and the Women's Trade Union League of New York* (Columbia: University of Missouri Press, 1980), 60, 120.

36. "Working Women of Today as Viewed by Miss O'Reilly," *Women's Trade Union League Papers*, 20 Mar 1899.

37. Herbert A. Applebaum, *The American Work Ethic and the Changing Work Force: An Historical Perspective* (Westport: Greenwood Press, 1998), 120.

38. Carole Turbin, *Working Women of Collar City: Gender, Class, and Community in Troy, New York, 1864–1886* (Urbana: University of Illinois Press, 1992), 174.

39. Turbin, *Working Women of Collar City*, 174.

40. Leonora O'Reilly, "Has Sewing a Right to Learned Manual Training?" (master's thesis, Pratt Institute, 1900), 1.

41. Leonora O'Reilly, "Has Sewing a Right to Learned Manual Training?", 6.

42. Leonora O'Reilly, "A Few Thoughts Suggested on Reading," *Women's Trade Union League Papers*, 18 Jun 1907.

43. Gloria Wade Gayles, "Black Women Journalists in the South, 1880–1905: A Study of Black Woman's History," *Caliloo* 11/13 (Feb–Oct 1981), 138.

44. Clifford Griffith Roe and B. S. Steadwell, *The Great War on White Slavery, Or, Fighting for the Protection of Our Girls: Ignorance Is No Longer Innocence* (New York: Roe and Steadwell Publishing, 1911), 5.

45. Christopher Diffee, "Sex and the City: The White Slavery Scare and Social Governance in the Progressive Era," *American Quarterly* 57 (June 2005): 416.

46. Roe and Steadwell, *The Great War on White Slavery*, 5.

47. Charlotte O'Brien, an Irish activist and daughter of Irish patriot William Smith O'Brien, inspired efforts that lead to the establishment of the mission in 1883. For a full history of the mission, see Reverend Michael Henry, "A Century of Irish Emigration: Its Causes and Its Results," in *Mission of Our Lady of the Rosary for the Protection of Irish Immigrant Girls* (New York City: Barge Office and 7 State Street, 1900), 7–23.

48. Margaret Lynch-Brennan, *The Irish Bridget: Irish Immigrant Women in Domestic Service in America, 1840–1930* (New York: Syracuse University Press, 2009), 96.

49. Reverend Michael Henry, "A Century of Irish Emigration: Its Causes and Its Results," in *Mission of Our Lady of the Rosary for the Protection of Irish Immigrant Girls* (New York City: Barge Office and 7 State Street, 1900), 23.

50. Urban, *Brokering Servitude*, 95.

51. The Mann Act was cited as necessary evidence to arrest African American heavyweight champion Jack Johnson in 1912 for crossing state lines with a white woman named Belle Schreiber, although they had a consensual relationship; see Theresa Runstedtler, *Jack Johnson, Rebel Sojourner: Boxing in the Shadow of the Global Color Line* (Berkeley, CA: University of California Press, 2012), 134.

52. Deborah Gray White, *Too Heavy a Load: Black Women in Defense of Themselves, 1894–1994* (New York: W.W. Norton & Company, 1999), 24. White cites an excerpt from Cooper's *A Voice from the South* in her description of nation-making; see Anna J. Cooper, *A Voice from the South: By a Black Woman of the South* (New York: Oxford University Press, 1988 [1892]), 122.

53. Charles Lemert and Esme Bhan, *The Voice of Anna Julia Cooper: Including a Voice from the South and Other Important Essays, Papers, and Letters* (New York: Rowman & Littlefield Publishers, 1998), 170.

54. Tera Hunter, *To 'Joy My Freedom: Southern Black Women's Lives and Labors After the Civil War* (Cambridge: Harvard University Press, 1997), 94.

55. Edward Pinckney, "Miss Pinckney's Brother Says a Word," *Brooklyn Eagle*, 20 July 1877, 4.

56. "Pinckney vs. Halligan," *Brooklyn Eagle*, 12 Dec 1877. Interestingly, the employers' surname was of Irish origin.

57. Valerie M. Babb, *Whiteness Visible: The Meaning of Whiteness in American Literature and Culture* (New York: New York University Press, 1998), 140.

58. Hudsy Smith, "Partial History of White Rose Mission Industrial Association," 1899, Schomburg Center for Research in Black Culture, Manuscripts, Archives and Rare Books Division, The New York Public Library.

59. Shirley Wilson Logan, ed., *With Pen and Voice: A Critical Anthology of Nineteenth-Century African-American Women* (Carbondale: Southern Illinois University Press, 1995), xiv.

60. *New York Evening Telegram*, 20 Sept 1897.

61. Bruce Grit, "A Representative Club Woman," *The Colored American*, 20 Apr 1901.

62. Grit, "A Representative Club Woman."

63. Mary Kendal, "White Rose Home: Its Work and Need," date unknown. Schomburg Center for Research in Black Culture, Manuscripts, Archives and Rare Books Division, The New York Public Library.

64. Frances R. Keyser, "Report of the White Rose Home for the Summer of 1906," Schomburg Center for Research in Black Culture, Manuscripts, Archives and Rare Books Division, The New York Public Library.

65. "White Rose Industrial Association," date unknown. Schomburg Center for Research in Black Culture, Manuscripts, Archives and Rare Books Division, The New York Public Library.

66. A native of New Orleans, Alice Ruth Moore's first husband was the poet and playwright Paul Laurence Dunbar. She later married Henry A. Callis, a physician; and Robert Nelson, a poet and civil rights activist. Moore was an educator who wrote about African American women's labor experiences and their roles in the anti-lynching movement. Some of her works were controversial, and she had difficulty publishing them; see *The Works of Alice Dunbar-Nelson*, ed. Gloria T. Hull, vol. 1 (New York: Oxford University Press, 1988), xxxvi.

67. "White Rose Mission Settlement: Girls from Southern Ports Protected, Social Life for Servants, Mothers' Sewing Clubs Help Support Work, Race History Classes, and a Unique Library," *New York Evening Post*, date unknown. Schomburg Center for Research in Black Culture, Manuscripts, Archives and Rare Books Division, The New York Public Library.

68. *Black-Belt Diamonds: Gems from the Speeches, Addresses and Talks to Students of Booker T. Washington*, ed. Victoria Earle Matthews (New York: Fortune and Scott, 1898); Victoria Earle Matthews, "Aunt Lindy: A Story Founded on Real Life," *A.M.E. Church Review*, 1891.

69. St. Croix native-Hubert Harrison was a lead organizer of the Socialist Party in New York and the editor of the UNIA (United Negro Improvement Association) publication *Negro World*. For the first full-length biography of Harrison, see Jeffrey B. Perry, *Hubert Harrison: The Voice of Harlem Radicalism, 1882–1913* (New York: Columbia University Press, 2008).

70. *New York Evening Telegram*, 20 Sep 1897.

71. Victoria Earle Matthews, "Dangers Encountered by Southern Girls in Northern Cities," *Hampton Negro Conference Proceedings, Number IL* (July 1898), 68.

72. William Patrick Burrell and D.E. Johnson, *Twenty-Five Years History of the Grand Fountain of the United Order of True Reformers* (Richmond, VA: Grand Fountain, United Order of True Reformers, 1909), 502.

73. Beverly Guy-Sheftall, "*Daughters of Sorrow: Attitudes toward Black Women, 1880–1920* (Brooklyn: Carlson, 1990), 19.

74. Victoria Earle Matthews, "Dangers Encountered by Southern Girls in Northern Cities," 62.

75. Victoria Earle Matthews, "Dangers Encountered by Southern Girls in Northern Cities," 65.

76. Victoria Earle Matthews, "Dangers Encountered by Southern Girls in Northern Cities," 66.

77. Victoria Earle Matthews, "Dangers Encountered by Southern Girls in Northern Cities," 67.

78. Victoria Earle Matthews, "Dangers Encountered by Southern Girls in Northern Cities," 63.

79. Victoria Earle Matthews, "Dangers Encountered by Southern Girls in Northern Cities," 64.

80. Victoria Earle Matthews, "Dangers Encountered by Southern Girls in Northern Cities," 63.

81. Victoria Earle Matthews, "Dangers Encountered by Southern Girls in Northern Cities," 63.

82. Victoria Earle Matthews, "Dangers Encountered by Southern Girls in Northern Cities," 67.

83. Cheryl Hicks, *Talk with You Like a Woman: African American Women, Justice, and Reform in New York, 1890–1935* (Chapel Hill: North Carolina University Press, 2010), 111.

84. Victoria Earle Matthews, *Federation* (New York City: Federation of Churches and Christian Organizations in New York City, June 1902), 57–58.

85. Victoria Earle Matthews, *Federation*, 57–58.

86. Frances Reynolds Keyser, Matthews's longtime assistant, became superintendent of the Home after Matthews passed in 1907. During her tenure, Keyser continued the domestic science and literature courses and fundraising events at the Home while serving as a board member of the Young Women's Christian Association; see Judith Weisenfeld, *African American Women and Christian Activism: New York's Black YWCA, 1905–1945* (Cambridge: Harvard University Press, 1997), 85.

87. See "White Rose Mission and Industrial Association, Inc." memo written by President Mattie K. Daniels. Schomburg Center for Research in Black Culture, Manuscripts, Archives and Rare Books Division, The New York Public Library.

88. Victoria Earle Matthews, "Suggestions of the Committee on Domestic Science," *Hampton Negro Conference Number III* (Hampton: Hampton Institute Press, 1899), 36.

89. I analyze Anna Julia Cooper's twentieth-century writings about domestic service in Chapter 6, the next chapter in this book.

90. Beverly Guy-Sheftall, "Black Feminist Studies: The Case of Anna Julia Cooper," *African American Review* 43 (Spring 2009), 13.

91. Vivian May, *Anna Julia Cooper, Visionary Black Feminist* (New York: Routledge, 2007), 17.

92. Vivian May, *Anna Julia Cooper, Visionary Black Feminist*, 16.

93. Vivian May, *Anna Julia Cooper, Visionary Black Feminist*, 16.

94. Anna Julia Cooper's perspectives on child-rearing were distinct from some club-women and social reformers because she proposed a gender-balanced approach to child-rearing. She argued that "masculine" and "feminine" sides of truth should be "worked into the training of children"; see Anna Julia Cooper, *A Voice of the South*, 61.

95. Beverly Guy-Sheftall, *Daughters of Sorrow: Attitudes toward Black Women, 1880–1920.* (Brooklyn: Carlson, 1990), 42.

96. Anna Julia Cooper, *A Voice from the South*, 255.

97. Anna Julia Cooper, *A Voice from the South*, 254–256.

98. Anna Julia Cooper, *A Voice from the South*, 85–86.

99. Anna Julia Cooper, "Colored Women as Wage Earners," *The Southern Workman* 28 (August 1899): 295.

100. Irish activist Daniel O'Connell, for example, supported the abolition movement in the United States because he believed there were similarities between slavery and Britain's exertion of political and economic control over Ireland; see Angela Murphy, *American Slavery, Irish Freedom: Abolition, Immigrant Citizenship and the Transatlantic Movement for Irish Repeal* (Baton Rouge: Louisiana State University, 2010), 210.

101. Hasia Diner, *Erin's Daughters in America: Irish Immigrant Women in the Nineteenth Century* (Baltimore: The Johns Hopkins University Press, 1983), 97–98.

102. Kevin Kenny, *The American Irish: A History* (New York: Routledge, 2014), 187–188.
103. Margaret Lynch-Brennan, *The Irish Bridget*, 42.
104. Stephen Steinberg, *The Ethnic Myth: Race, Ethnicity, and Class in America* (Boston: Beacon Press, 2001), 164.
105. Stephen Steinberg, *The Ethnic Myth*, 164–166.
106. Jennifer Scanlon, *Inarticulate Longings: The Ladies' Home Journal, Gender, and the Promises of Consumer Culture* (New York: Routledge, 1995), 35.

Chapter 6   Irish Immigrant Women Become Whiter, African American Women Dignify Domestic Service

1. Maureen Murphy, "Birdie, We Hardly Knew Ye: The Irish Domestics," *The Irish in America,* eds. Michael Coffey and Terry Golway (Hyperion, New York, 1997), 145.
2. Kerby Miller and Patricia Mulholland Miller, "From 'Bridget' to 'Mother Machree,'" *Journey of Hope: The Story of Irish Immigration to America* (San Francisco: Chronicle Books, 2001), 17.
3. The oral histories that I am referring to are approximately 59 interviews with Irish immigrant women housed by the Ellis Island Immigration Museum's Bob Hope Memorial Library. While working as a researcher at the library, I created a research index from the interviews that tracks their labor experiences and perspectives about race in Ireland and the United States. I will draw from the index and the interviews in this chapter.
4. Sarah Haley, *No Mercy Here: Gender, Punishment, and the Making of Jim Crow Modernity* (Chapel Hill: The University of North Carolina Press, 2016), 4.
5. Sharon Harley, "When Your Work Is Not Who You Are: The Development of a Working-Class Consciousness among Afro-American Women," in *Gender, Class, Race and Reform in the Progressive Era,* eds. Noralee Frankel and Nancy S. Dye. (Lexington: University of Kentucky Press, 1991), 42. See also Bonnie Thornton Dill, "'Making Your Job Good Yourself': Domestic Service and the Construction of Personal Dignity," in eds. Ann Bookman and Sandra Morgen, *Women and the Politics of Empowerment* (Philadelphia: Temple University Press, 1998): 33–52.
6. David Roediger, *Working Toward Whiteness: How America's Immigrants Became White* (New York: Persus Books, 2005), 59, 61.
7. Rose Kelley Laughlin, interview by Janet Levine, Ellis Island Immigration Museum's Oral History Collection, April 30, 1995.
8. Bridget Delia O'Neill, Ellis Island Oral History Project Interview, 7 Nov 1999.
9. Ellen Bergheim, Ellis Island Oral History Project Interview, 10 Mar 1999.
10. Bridget Lacknee Jones, Ellis Island Oral History Project Interview, 16 Nov 1974.
11. Bridget Lacknee Jones, Ellis Island Immigration Museum's Oral History Project Interview, 16 Nov 1974.
12. Mary Ellen Ryan, Ellis Island Oral History Project Interview, 6 Nov 1995.
13. Bridget Ryan McNulty, Ellis Island Oral History Project Interview, 24 Nov 1998; Catherine Concannon, Ellis Island Oral History Project Interview, 15 Oct 1996.
14. Mary Condon, New Yorkers at Work Oral History Collection, Tamiment Library and Robert F. Wagner Labor Archive, New York University.
15. Forty-one of the fifty-nine women interviewed by researchers at Ellis Island recalled working in domestic service before working in other occupations or

becoming housewives, Irish women's research index, prepared by Danielle Phillips-Cunningham, Ellis Island Immigration Museum's Bob Hope Memorial Library, July 2012.

16. Bertha Devlin, Interview by Dana Gumb, Ellis Island Immigration Museum Oral History Project Interview, 19 Sep 1985.
17. Deborah Gray White, *Too Heavy a Load: Black Women in Defense of Themselves, 1894–1994* (New York: W.W. Norton & Company, 1999), 30
18. See Irma Watkins-Owens, *Blood Relations: Caribbean Immigrants and the Harlem Community, 1900–1930* (Bloomington: Indiana University Press, 1996), 88–89.
19. Peter J. Levin, "Bold Vision: Catholic Sisters and the Creation of American Hospitals." *Journal of Community Health*, 36, no. 1: 2011, 343–47.
20. Maureen Fitzgerald, *Habits of Compassion: Irish Catholic Nuns and the Origins of New York's Welfare System, 1830–1920* (Urbana: University of Illinois Press, 2006), 98.
21. Katherine MaGennis Lamberti, Interview by Paul Sigrist Jr., Ellis Island Oral History Project Interview, 25 Feb 1994.
22. Brenda Clegg Gray, *Black Female Domestics During the Great Depression in New York City, 1930–1940* (New York: Garland Publishing, 1993), 45.
23. Katherine MaGennis Lamberti, Ellis Island Oral History Project Interview, 25 Feb 1994.
24. Country clubs were often racist spaces that hosted minstrel shows, "Crescent Minstrels, One Great Big Hit," *Brooklyn Eagle*, 15 Mar 1914.
25. Brenda Faye Clegg, *Black Female Domestics During the Great Depression in New York City, 1930–1940* (PhD diss., University of Michigan, 1983), 1.
26. Clegg, *Black Female Domestics During the Great Depression*, 18–19.
27. Forrester B. Washington, "A Study of Negro Employees of Apartment Homes in New York City, *Bulletin of the National Urban League Among Negroes* 24.
28. Clegg, *Black Female Domestics During the Great Depression*, 19.
29. Clegg, *Black Female Domestics During the Great Depression*, 25. Also, few Black women were hired for factory jobs partly because white women refused to work with them, see Mary White Ovington, *Half a Man: The Status of the Negro in New York* (New York: Longmans, Green, and Company, 1911) 161–163. For discussion of hiring preference for white women to work in shops, see Vapnek, *Breadwinners*, 78.
30. Hallie Burleson, "Sadie's Servant Room Blues," *History Matters*, http://historymatters.gmu.edu/d/20/.
31. Bessie Smith's "Washwoman's Blues"; See Angela Davis, *Blues Legacies and Black Feminism: Gertrude "Ma" Rainey, Bessie Smith, and Billie Holiday* (New York: Vintage Books, 1999), 98–99.
32. Deborah Gray White, *Too Heavy a Load*, 30.
33. For example, see Hazel Carby's discussion of Jane Edna Hunter and the Phyllis Wheatley Association in "Policing the Black Woman's Body in an Urban Context," *Critical Inquiry* 18 (Summer 1992): 743–745.
34. Charles Lemert and Esme Bhan, *The Voice of Anna Julia Cooper: Including a Voice from the South and Other Important Essays, Papers, and Letters* (New York: Rowman & Littlefield Publishers, 1998), 216, 222.
35. Lemert and Bhan, *The Voice of Anna Julia Cooper*, 219.
36. Lemert and Bhan, *The Voice of Anna Julia Cooper*, 253.
37. Lemert and Bhan, *The Voice of Anna Julia Cooper*, 254.
38. Lemert and Bhan, *The Voice of Anna Julia Cooper*, 254.

39. Lemert and Bhan, *The Voice of Anna Julia Cooper*, 255.
40. Lemert and Bhan, *The Voice of Anna Julia Cooper*, 250.
41. Beverly Guy-Sheftall, *Words of Fire*, 9.
42. Quoted from Beverly Guy-Sheftall, *Words of Fire*, 9.
43. Beverly Guy-Sheftall, *Words of Fire*, 9.
44. "Colored Women to Organize Domestic Workers: National Association of Wage Earners in Big Drive for Ten Thousand Members," *The Pittsburgh Courier*, 22 Mar 1924, 2.
45. Sharon Harley, "When Your Work Is Not Who You Are: The Development of a Working-Class Consciousness among Afro-American Women," *We Specialize in the Wholly Impossible: A Reader in Black Women's History*, eds. Darlene Clark Hine, Wilma King, Linda Reed (New York: Carlson Publishing 1995), 25.
46. Anna Julia Cooper taught Burroughs at the M Street School in Washington, D.C.; see Beverly Guy-Sheftall, *Words of Fire*, 9.
47. Anna Julia Cooper taught Burroughs at the M Street School in Washington D.C.; see Beverly Guy-Sheftall, *Words of Fire*, 9.
48. Irma Watkins-Owens, "Early-Twentieth-Century Caribbean Women: Migration and Social Networks in New York City," *Islands in the City: West Indian Migration to New York* (Los Angeles: University of California Press, 2001), 35.
49. Rosita E. Simmons, "A Brief Study of the Private, Non-Commercial Employment Agencies Operating in Harlem" (master's thesis: Columbia University, 1930), 14–16.
50. Fairclough conducted a study of 334 Black women, a third of whom were Caribbean immigrant women; see Alice Brown Fairclough, "A Study of Occupational Opportunities for Negro Women in New York" (master's thesis: New York University, 1929).
51. Irma Watkins-Owens, "Early-Twentieth-Century Caribbean Women: Migration and Social Networks in New York City," in *Islands in the City: West Indian Migration to New York* (Los Angeles: University of California Press, 2001), 36.
52. "Light colored girls" was the actual term that employers used to describe to employment agencies Black women they preferred to hire; see Simmons, "A Brief Study of the Private, Non-Commercial Employment Agencies Operating in Harlem", 11.
53. Frances Thornton, "Adjustment Problems of certain Negro Women Migrants to Harlem: A Study of 125 Women Seeking Adjustment Aid from the West 137th Street Branch of the Y.W.C.A." (master's thesis. Columbia University, 1936), 3.
54. Irma Watkins-Owens, "Early-Twentieth-Century Caribbean Women, 42.
55. "Domestic Workers Demand 6-Day Week," *New York Amsterdam News*, 10 Oct 1936, 3.
56. Mark Naison, *Communists in Harlem during the Depression* (Champaign: University of Illinois Press, 1983), 140–145.
57. Teresa L. Amot *and* Julie A. Matthaei, eds., Race, Gender, and Work: A Multi-cultural Economic History of Women in the United States (Brooklyn: South End Press, 1996), 171.
58. Vanessa May, *Unprotected Labor: Household Workers, Politics, and Middle-Class Reform in New York, 1870–1940* (Chapel Hill: The University of North Carolina Press, 2011), 155.
59. "The Negro Woman Worker," 1938 Department of Labor-Women's Bureau Bulletin, Cornell University Kheel Center Archive.

60. Vivian Morris, WPA Domestic Workers' Union Interview Unedited Transcript, Library of Congress Digital Collection, 7 Feb 1939.
61. Eileen Boris and Premilla Nadasen, "Domestic Workers Organize!," *Working USA: The Journal of Labor and Society*, 11 (2008): 417.
62. Vivian Morris, WPA Domestic Workers' Union Interview Unedited Transcript, Library of Congress Digital Collection, 7 Feb 1939
63. Suzanne Mettler, *Dividing Citizens: Gender and Federalism in New Deal and Public Policy* (Ithaca: Cornell University Press, 1998), 134.
64. "Servants' Union Urges Old Age Pensions Too: House Sub-Committee is Told of Many Jobless During Depression," *Afro-American*, 23 Feb 1935, 3.
65. Suzanne Mettler, *Dividing Citizens: Gender and Federalism in New Deal and Public Policy* (Ithaca: Cornell University Press, 1998), 135.
66. "Domestics' Medical Test Hearing Sought June 14," *New Rochelle Standard-Star*, 15 May 1937: 1; "Domestics Organize to Fight Ordinance," *New York Times*, 30 Apr 1934, 17; "Domestics Plan to Form Union," *New York Amsterdam News*, 17 Oct 1936, 12; "Domestic Exam Hearing Date Spread Anew by Various Agencies," *New Rochelle Standard-Star*, 9 Jun 1937, 1.
67. "Many to Attend Open Hearing on Domestics' Test," *New Rochelle Standard-Star*, 27 Jun 1937: 1; "Domestic Law Foes Surpass Advocates," *New York Amsterdam News*, 26 Jun 1937, 19; "Opponents Rally against Law for Domestic Tests," *New Rochelle Standard-Star*, 22 Jun 1937, 15. For a full-length study about domestic worker organizations, see Donna L. Van Raaphorst, *Union Maids Not Wanted: Organizing Domestic Workers, 1870–1940* (New York: Praeger, 1988).
68. Vanessa May, *Unprotected Labor*, 149.
69. Belle Taub, "Discovered! A Modern Slave Block," *The Liberator*, 15 Jun 1935, 5.
70. Tom O'Connor, "Negro Domestics Earn Pittance in 'Slave Markets,'" *PM*, 16 Jan 1941, 15.
71. Tom O'Connor, "Negro Domestics Earn Pittance in 'Slave Markets,'" 15.
72. Taub, "Discovered!," 5.
73. Sharon Robinson, Interview by author, Atlanta, GA, 7 Jul 2009.
74. Miss P.G.A., "Jobs, Relief, Opportunity: To the Editor of the Amsterdam News," *Amsterdam News*, 10 Aug 1935.
75. Premilla Nadasen, *Household Workers Unite: The Untold Story of African American Women Who Built a Movement* (Boston: Beacon Press, 2015), 3.
76. After Ella Baker wrote the exposé about the Bronx Slave Markets in *The Crisis*, she was hired by the New York City division of the Workers Education Project where she continued to advocate for domestic workers; see Julie A. Gallagher, *Black Women and Politics in New York City* (Urbana: University of Illinois Press, 2012), 54.
77. Marvel Cooke, "I Was A Part of the Bronx Slave Market," *Sunday Compass Magazine*, section 8, Jan 1950, 14.
78. Ella Baker and Marvel Cooke, "The Bronx Slave Market," *The Crisis*, Nov 1935, 330.
79. Barbara Ransby, *Ella Baker & The Black Freedom Movement: A Radical Democratic Vision* (Chapel Hill: The University of North Carolina Press, 2003), 77.
80. Vivian Morris, WPA Domestic Workers' Union Interview Unedited Transcript, Library of Congress Digital Collection, 2 Feb 1939: 2.
81. Vivian Morris, WPA Domestic Workers' Union Interview, 3.
82. Vivian Morris, WPA Domestic Workers' Union Interview, 4.

83. Vivian Morris, WPA Domestic Workers' Union Interview, 1.
84. For an analysis of sexual exploitation accounts in the interviews conducted by Richard Wright, see Shana Alexssandra Russell's "Domestic Workers, Sex Workers, and the Movement: Reimagining Black Working-Class Resistance in the Work of William Attaway, Richard Wright, and Alice Childress, 1935–1960" (PhD diss., Rutgers, The State University of New Jersey, 2015).
85. Shana Russell, "Domestic Workers, Sex Workers, and the Movement," 22.
86. Mary Frances Gunner, "A Study of Employment Problems of Negro Women in Brooklyn" (master's thesis, Columbia University, 1930), 18.
87. Simmons, "A Brief Study of the Private, Non-Commercial Employment Agencies Operating in Harlem," 13.
88. Untitled, New York Times, 15 Jun 1939.
89. "Charge Woman Brought Maids Here Illegally," The New York Age, 5 June 1937, 1.
90. Vanessa May, Unprotected Labor, 124–125.
91. Bishop W. J. Wells, "Maid of Salem Film Twists History to Disparage Race," Chicago Defender, 13 Mar 1937; Bishop W. J. Wells, "Salem Maid 'Not So Hot, Says Bishop," New York Amsterdam News, 13 Mar 1937.
92. Alfred Duckett, "Virtual Slavery of Negro Women in Brooklyn Reported by Social Worker in Exclusive Interview," The New York Age, 19 Feb 1938.
93. Erik S. McDuffie, Sojourning for Freedom: Black Women, American Communism, and the Making of Black Left Feminism (Durham: Duke University Press, 2011), 4.
94. Claudia May, "Airing Dirty Laundry: Representations of Domestic Laborers in the Works of African American Women Writers," Feminist Formations 27 (Spring 2015): 141.
95. McDuffie, Sojourning for Freedom, 46.
96. Middle-class Black women who ran for political offices in New York City also fought more broadly for domestic workers. Civil rights leader and politician Anna Arnold Hedgeman helped to organize female workers while arguing for the importance of Black women's unions; see Julie A. Gallagher, Black Women and Politics in New York City (Urbana: University of Illinois Press, 2012 51.
97. McDuffie, Sojourning for Freedom, 113–114.
98. Ransby, Ella Baker & The Black Freedom Movement, 72.
99. Ransby, Ella Baker & The Black Freedom Movement, 71.
100. Wesley Curtwright, "Brief History of the Domestic Workers' Association, Brooklyn Local" (Writers' Program, New York City: Negroes of New York Collection, Schomburg Center for Research in Black Culture, Manuscripts, Archives and Rare Books, n.d.), 1.
101. Louise Thompson Patterson, "Toward a Brighter Dawn," Woman Today, April 1936.
102. Curtwright, "Brief History of the Domestic Workers' Association," 1–2.
103. Curtwright, "Brief History of the Domestic Workers' Association," 3.
104. Photograph of Mabel Thompson. Daily Worker and Daily World Collection held at the Tamiment Library, New York University, by permission of the Communist Party USA.
105. Photograph of Mabel Thompson. Daily Worker and Daily World Collection.
106. United Building Service and Domestic Workers Association of Brooklyn, "Facts You Should Know about the Men and Women Who Work in Your Homes and Buildings" (New York University Tamiment Library and Robert F. Wagner Archives' Printed Ephemera Collection on Trade Unions, n.d.).

107. Quoted from Charles Spurgeon Johnson and Elmer Anderson Carter, eds. "Visiting Housekeeper Projects Multiply," *Opportunity: Journal of Negro Life* 13 (1935): 156.
108. Quoted from Johnson and Carter, eds. "Visiting Housekeeper Projects Multiply," 156.
109. Eileen Boris and Premilla Nadasen, "Domestic Workers Organize!," *Working USA: The Journal of Labor and Society* 11 (2008): 420.
110. Esther Victoria Cooper, "The Negro Woman Domestic Worker in Relation to Trade Unionism," (master's thesis: Fisk University, 1940), 6.
111. Marvel Cooke, "I Was a Part of the Bronx Slave Market," *Sunday Compass Magazine*, 8 Jan 1950, 15.
112. Claudia Jones, "An end to the neglect of the problems of the Negro Woman!" (New York: National Women's Commission, Communist Party U.S.A.), 4.
113. Vanessa May, *Unprotected Labor*, 157.
114. Bobbie Patrick, "Women Worth Knowing," *Daily Worker Newspaper*, 1949.
115. Vanessa May, *Unprotected Labor*, 157.
116. Gerald Horne, *Black and Red: W.E.B. DuBois and the Afro-American Response to the Cold War, 1944–1963* (Albany: State University of New York Press, 1986), 141.
117. Photograph of Nina Evans, President of the Domestic Workers' Union, July 7, 1949. *Daily Worker* and *Daily World* Collection, Tamiment Library, New York University, by permission of the Communist Party USA.
118. Ransby, *Ella Baker & The Black Freedom Movement*, 171.
119. Premilla Nadasen, *Household Workers Unite: The Untold Story of African American Women Who Built a Movement* (Boston: Beacon Press, 2015), 9.
120. Trudier Harris, *From Mammies to Militants: Domestics in Black American Literature* (Philadelphia: Temple University Press, 1982), 111.
121. Geraldine Miller, Interview by Debra Bernhardt, 18 Jun 1981 (New Yorkers at Work Oral History Collection, Tamiment Library and Robert F. Wagner Labor Archive, New York University).
122. Nadasen, *Household Workers Unite*, 79.
123. Nadasen, *Household Workers Unite*, 128.
124. For history of Ruby Duncan and Operation Life, see Annelise Orleck's *Storming Caesars Palace: How Black Mothers Fought Their Own War on Poverty* (Boston: Beacon Press, 2006).
125 Eileen Boris and Premilla Nadasen, "Domestic Workers Organize!," 423.
126. Nadasen, *Household Workers Unite*, 142.
127. Nadasen, *Household Workers Unite*, 142.

Conclusion

1. Jared Bernstein and Ben Speilberg, "The Trump administration's ongoing attack on workers, *Washington Post*, 30 Aug 2017, http://wapo.st/2x2iZlJ?tid=ss_mail& utm_term=.f95d55608383; Erica Werner and Kevin Sieff, "How Trump's tariffs on Mexico are taking jobs from U.S. workers," *Washington Post*, 18 Jul 2018; https://wapo.st/2zQOBxF?tid=ss; Ted Genoways,"Farmers voted heavily for Trump. But his trade policies are terrible for them," *Washington Post*, 24 Oct 2017, http://wapo.st/2y1axzW?tid=ss.
2. Katie Reilly, "A Wave of Teacher Activism is Sweeping Red States," *Time* magazine, 5 Apr 2018, http://time.com/5228971/a-wave-of-teacher-activism-is-sweeping-red-states/.

3. A bar in Detroit, Michigan, refused to serve Irish Americans on St. Patrick's Day as part of their experiment to raise awareness among white Americans about racism and its impact on immigrant communities; see *Detroit Free Press*, 17 Mar 2018, https://usat.ly/2GCtHC1.

4. Margaret Lynch-Brennan, *The Irish Bridget: Irish Immigrant Women in Domestic Service in America, 1840–1930* (Syracuse: Syracuse University Press, 2014), xxii.

5. David Roediger's *Wages of Whiteness: Race and Making of the American Working-Class* (New York: Verso, 1991); Noel Ignatiev's *How the Irish Became White* (New York: Routledge, 1995).

6. Beverly Guy-Sheftall, ed., *Words of Fire: An Anthology of African-American Feminist Thought,* (New York: The New Press, 1995), 2.

7. Care in Action, "An Open Letter to Stacey Abrams From Domestic Workers: We'll Keep Fighting With You," *Bustle* magazine, 11 Nov 2018, https://www.bustle.com/p/open-letter-to-stacey-abrams-from-domestic-workers-well-keep-fighting-with-you-13170861.

8. "Black Women Advance Labor's Cause In An Unlikely Setting: 1881 Atlanta," 31 Dec 2009, from the American Postal Workers Union (APWU) website: https://apwu.org/news/black-women-advance-labor%E2%80%99s-cause-unlikely-setting-1881-atlanta

9. Premilla Nadasen, *Household Workers Unite: The Untold Story of African American Women Who Built a Movement* (Boston: Beacon Press, 2015), 154.

10. New York State Department of Labor, *Domestic Workers' Bill of Rights* (n.d.), https://labor.ny.gov/legal/domestic-workers-bill-of-rights.shtm.

11. International Domestic Workers Federation, "USA: Nevada Becomes the 8th State to Pass a Domestic Worker Bill of Rights," 12 Jun 2017, http://idwfed.org/en/updates/usa-nevada-becomes-the-8th-state-to-pass-a-domestic-worker-bill-of-rights; Seattle Office of Labor Standards, "Domestic Workers Ordinance," n.d., https://www.seattle.gov/laborstandards/ordinances/domestic-workers-ordinance.

12. *Living in the Shadows: Latina Domestic Workers in the Texas-Mexico Border Region,* a report published in June 2018 by the National Domestic Workers Alliance. To download the report in English and Spanish, visit https://www.domesticworkers.org/shadows.

13. Bryce Covert, "The New Federal Domestic Workers Bill of Rights Would Remedy Decades of Injustice," *The Nation*, 28 Nov 2018, https://www.thenation.com/article/federal-domestic-workers-bill-of-rights-harris-jayapal-labor/.

Bibliography

Archival Sources

An Gaodhal: A Monthly Journal Devoted To The Preservation and Cultivation of the Irish Language and the Autonomy of the Irish Nation. Brooklyn: Nolan Brothers, Steam Print, 515 and 517 Fulton Street, 1881.

Anonymous. *Our Jemimas: Addressed to the Middle Class by a Victim.* London: Houlston, 1880.

"Appeal for the Children's Aid Society." *New York Times*, 23 Jan 1861.

"A Woman Worker's Plea for her Sex: Leonora O'Reilly, Workingwoman Orator." *The World.* Women's Trade Union League Papers, 30 Mar 1899.

Baker, Ella and Marvel Cooke, "The Bronx Slave Market," *The Crisis*, Nov 1935.

Baldwin, James. "Conversation With James Baldwin: A James Baldwin Interview." By Kenneth Clark. WGBH Media Library & Archives, 24 Jun 1963. http://openvault.wgbh.org/catalog/V_C03ED1927DCF46B5A8C82275DF4239F9.

Barry, Leonora. *General Proceedings of the Knights of Labor*, 1887: 1840–1841.

Barry, Leonora. *General Proceedings of the Knights of Labor*, 1888: 1580–1581.

Barry, Leonora. "Report to the Knights of Labor 1887." In *Tenth Annual Report of the Bureau of Statistics of Labor and Industries of New Jersey*. Somerville, 1888.

Bergheim, Ellen. Ellis Island Oral History Project Interview, 10 Mar 1999.

Besant, Annie. *Annie Besant: An Autobiography*. London: T. Fisher Unwin, 1893.

Borohme, Brian the Younger. *Ireland: A Kingdom and a Colony*. London: C. Dolman, 61 New Bond Street, 1843.

Brady, Ellen. Ellis Island Oral History Project Interview, 7 March 1977.

"Charge Woman Brought Maids Here Illegally." *The New York Age*, 5 June 1937.

"Colored Servants." *The New York Globe*, 29 March 1884.

"Colored Women to Organize Domestic Workers: National Association of Wage Earners in Big Drive for Ten Thousand Members." *The Pittsburgh Courier*, 22 Mar 1924.

Cooke, Marvel Cooke. "I Was A Part of the Bronx Slave Market." *Sunday Compass Magazine*, Section 8, Jan 1950.

Concannon, Catherine. Ellis Island Oral History Project Interview, 15 Oct 1996.

Condon, Mary. New Yorkers at Work Oral History Collection OH.001. New York University Wagner Labor Archives, 2 Nov 1980.

Cooper, Anna Julia. "L'attitude de la France à l'égard de l'esclavage pendant la révolution." PhD diss., University of Paris, 1925.

———. "The Negro Problem in America." *Pan African Conference in London, England,* 1900.

———. "Colored wage-earners." *The Southern Workman,* 1899: 296–297.

———. *A Voice from the South.* New York: Oxford University Press, 1982.

———. "Women's Cause is One and Universal." *The World's Congress of Representative Women.* Chicago: Rand, McNally, 1894.

Cooper, Esther Victoria. "The Negro Woman Domestic Worker in Relation to Trade Unionism." Master's thesis, Fisk University, 1940.

"C.O.P. Justifies Her Position." *Brooklyn Eagle,* 11 Mar 1897.

"Crescent Minstrels, One Great Big Hit." *Brooklyn Eagle,* 15 Mar 1914.

Daily Evening Bulletin. San Francisco. 28 July 1879.

Daniels, Mattie K. "White Rose Mission and Industrial Association, Inc." White Rose Collection, Schomburg Library.

Devlin, Bertha, Interview. By Dana Gumb. Ellis Island Immigration Museum Oral History Project Interview, 19 Sep 1985.

"Domestic Exam Hearing Date Spread Anew by Various Agencies." *New Rochelle Standard-Star,* 9 Jun 1937.

"Domestic Law Foes Surpass Advocates." *New York Amsterdam News,* 26 Jun 1937.

"Domestics' Medical Test Hearing Sought June 14." *New Rochelle Standard-Star,* 15 May 1937.

"Domestics Organize to Fight Ordinance." *New York Times,* 30 Apr 1934.

"Domestics Plan to Form Union." *New York Amsterdam News,* 17 Oct 1936.

"Domestic Servants." *New York Times,* 7 Jul 1872.

"Domestic Service in the South." *New-Orleans Times,* 30 Nov 1889.

"Domestic Workers Demand 6-Day Week." *New York Amsterdam News,* 10 Oct 1936.

Duckett, Alfred. "Virtual Slavery of Negro Women in Brooklyn Reported by Social Worker in Exclusive Interview." *New York Age,* 19 Feb 1938.

Dunbar, Barrington. "Factors in the Cultural Background of the American Southern Negro and the British West Indian Negro That Condition their Adjustment to Harlem." Master's thesis, Columbia University, 1935.

Eaton, Isabel. "Special Report on Negro Domestic Service" in *The Philadelphia Negro: A Social Study.* Philadelphia: University of Pennsylvania, 1899.

"Editor's Drawer." *Harper's New Monthly.* April 1916.

"Effect of the Fifteenth Amendment." *Harper's Bazaar* magazine (New York), 4 Mar 1871.

Ehrhart, S. D. (Samuel D.). "A Look Ahead—But Not So Very Far Ahead, Either." 8 Feb 1899. Repository: Library of Congress Prints and Photographs Division Washington, D.C.

"Ex-Lady." *New York Times,* 17 Feb 1895.

First Annual Report of the Society for the Encouragement of Faithful Domestic Servants in New York. New York: American Tract Society House, 1826.

Good Housekeeping, Jan 1922.

"The Goose that Lays the Golden Egg," *Puck,* 22 Aug 1883.

Grit, Bruce. "A Representative Club Woman." *The Colored American,* 20 Apr 1901.

Gunner, Frances. "A Study of Employment Problems of Negro Women in Brooklyn." Master's thesis, Columbia University, 1930.

Haynes, Elizabeth Ross. "Negroes in Domestic Service in the United States." Master's thesis, Columbia University, 1923.

Henry, Reverend Michael. "A Century of Irish Emigration: Its Causes and Its Results." Mission of Our Lady of the Rosary for the Protection of Irish Immigrant Girls. New York City: Barge Office and 7 State Street, 1900.

Hoffman, Frances Duffy. Ellis Island Immigration Museum Oral History Project Interview, 20 Feb 1997.

Hoarse, Helen. Letter sent from Mobile, Alabama on July 26, 1933. Nannie Helen Burroughs Collection, Library of Congress.

"Hopes 'C.O.P.'s' Girl Did Not Eat the Soap." *Brooklyn Eagle*, 12 March 1897.

"Housekeeping, English and American: By an American. *Every Saturday: A Journal of Choice Reading*, 23 Jan 1869.

Hughes, Mary. *Advice to Female Servants in Letters from Aunt to a Niece.* 4th ed. London: The Christian Tract Society, 1825.

"Incidents in Cottage Place Industrial School." *Twenty Fifth Annual Report of Children's Aid Society.* New York: Wynkoop and Hallenbeck, 1877.

"Irish Housekeeping." *Harper's Weekly*, 1861.

"'Irish Rambler' Suggests a Servant Girl Trust." *Brooklyn Eagle*, 11 Mar 1897.

Jackson, Esther. "The Negro Woman Domestic Worker in Relation to Trade Unionism." Master's thesis, Fisk University, 1940.

Johnson, Charles Spurgeon and Elmer Anderson Carter, eds. "Visiting Housekeeper Projects Multiply." *Opportunity: Journal of Negro Life* 13 (1935).

Jones, Bridget Lacknee. Ellis Island Oral History Project Interview, 16 Nov 1974.

Kendal, Mary. "White Rose Home: Its Work and Need," n.d.

Keyser, Frances R. "Report of the White Rose Home for the Summer of 1906." White Rose Industrial Association Collection, Schomburg Library.

King, Coretta Scott. "Statement of Coretta Scott King on the Nomination of Jefferson Beauregard Sessions, III for the United States District Court Southern District of Alabama, Senate Judiciary Committee." 19 Mar 1986. https://www.documentcloud.org/documents /3259988-Scott-King-1986-Letter-and-Testimony-Signed.html

"Kitchen versus Slop Shop." *New York Times*, 5 Mar 1893.

Lamberti, Katherine MaGennis. Ellis Island Oral History Project Interview, 25 Feb 1994.

Laughlin, Rose Kelley. Ellis Island Immigration Museum's Oral History Collection, April 30, 1995.

Layten, Sarah Willie. "The Servant Problem." *Colored American Magazine*, Jan 1907, 13–15.

Letter to Nannie Helen Burroughs, August 1937. Nannie Helen Burroughs Collection, Library of Congress.

Letter sent from Union Baptist Church on April 21, 1938. Nannie Helen Burroughs Collection, Library of Congress.

Letter sent from Chattanooga, Tennessee, in August 1937. Nannie Helen Burroughs Collection, Library of Congress.

"Letters of the Subject." *New York Times*, 10 Feb 1895.

"Many to Attend Open Hearing on Domestics' Test." *New Rochelle Standard-Star*, 27 Jun 1937.

Materia, Josephine Keenen. Ellis Island Oral History Project Interview, 22 Jun 1994.

Matthews, Victoria Earle, ed. *Black-Belt Diamonds: Gems from the Speeches, Addresses and Talks to Students of Booker T. Washington.* New York: Fortune and Scott, 1898.

———. *Aunt Lindy: A Story Founded on Real Life.* New York: J. J. Little, 1893.

———. "Some of the Dangers Encountered by Southern Girls in Northern Cities." *Hampton Negro Conference Proceedings, no. IL*, July 1898, 62.

———. *Federation.* New York City: Federation of Churches and Christian Organizations in New York City, June 1902, 57–58.

———. "Suggestions of Committee on Domestic Science," *Hampton Negro Conference Number III.* Hampton: Hampton Institute Press, 1899.

McNulty, Bridget Ryan. Ellis Island Oral History Project Interview, 24 Nov 1998.

M.E.P. "Those Servant Girls: Wishes they had one neck so that she could wring it." *Brooklyn Eagle*, 11 Mar 1897.

Miller, Geraldine. Interview by Debra Bernhardt, 18 Jun 1981. New Yorkers at Work Oral History Collection, New York University.

"Miniature Race War at Bay Cliff Villa," *Brooklyn Eagle*, 9 July 1900.

Minutes of the National Association of Colored Women's Meeting, August 1908. Library of Congress NACW Collection, 15–16,

"Miss P.G.A. "Jobs, Relief, Opportunity: To the Editor of the Amsterdam News." *Amsterdam News*, 10 Aug 1935.

"Mistress and Maid." *Harper's New Monthly Magazine*, April 1880.

Money, Louisa Agnes. *History of The Girls' Friendly Society*. London: Wells Gardner & Company. 191, http://anglicanhistory.org/women/money_gfs1911/.

"More Slavery at the South, by a Negro Nurse." *Independent*, 25 Jan 1912.

"Negro House Servants." *The Daily Inter Ocean*, Chicago, 1 Oct 1892.

Nelson, Nell. "City Slave Girls," *Chicago Times*, 30 Jul 1888.

"New Phase of Immigrant Swindling." *New York Times*, 19 Oct 1860.

New York Evening Telegram, 20 September 1897.

New York Globe, 29 Mar 1884.

New York Tribune. Aunt Jemima Pancake Mix Advertisement, 7 Nov 1909.

O' Connor, Tom. "Negro Domestics Earn Pittance in 'Slave Markets.'" *PM*, 16 Jan 1941.

O'Donnell. Lawrence. "Lawrence: 'Stunned' by John Kelly's attack on Rep. Wilson." *The Last Word*, by MSNBC, Aired 9 Oct 2017. https://www.youtube.com/watch?v=Y6_p7hwUl3o.

"Old Colored Servants." *Brooklyn Eagle*, 11 Jul 1897.

O'Neill, Bridget Delia. Ellis Island Oral History Project Interview, 7 Nov 1999.

"Opponents Rally against Law for Domestic Tests." *New Rochelle Standard-Star*, 22 Jun 1937.

O'Reilly, Leonora. "A Few Thoughts Suggested on Reading." Women's Trade Union League Papers, 18 Jun 1907.

———. Sewing a Right to Learned Manual Training?" Master's thesis, Pratt Institute, 1900.

———. "Summer School for Working Girls." The Women's Trade Union League Papers, 1900.

———. "The Sewing Machine as an Opportunity for Self-Expression." Women's Trade Union League Papers, 1911.

"Our Goddess of Liberty." *Frank Leslie's Illustrated Newspaper*, 16 Jul 1870.

Patterson, Louise Thompson. "Toward a Brighter Dawn." *Woman Today*, April 1936.

Pinckney, Edward. "Miss Pinckney's Brother Says a Word." *Brooklyn Eagle*, 20 July 1877.

"Pinckney vs. Halligan." *Brooklyn Eagle*, 12 Dec 1877.

Rogers, Katie. "White Women Helped Elect Donald Trump." *New York Times*, 9 Nov 2016.

Ryan, Mary Ellen. Ellis Island Oral History Project Interview, 6 Nov 1995.

Sandoval, Claudia. "Choosing the Velvet Glove: Women Voters, Ambivalent Sexism, and Vote Choice in 2016." *The Journal of Race, Ethnicity, and Politics* 3, no. 1 (2018): 26–28, doi:10.1017/rep.2018.6.

"Sell the Bloomers and Work, Says One Servant." *Brooklyn Daily Eagle*, 10 Mar 1897.

"Servants' Union Urges Old Age Pensions Too: House Sub-Committee is Told of Many Jobless During Depression." *Afro-American*, 23 Feb 1935.

"Sharp Words for 'J.S.G.'" *Brooklyn Daily Eagle*, 10 Mar 1897.

Simmons, Rosita E. "A Brief Study of the Private, Non-Commercial Employment Agencies Operating in Harlem." Master's thesis, Columbia University, 1930.

"Southern Servant Girls," *Brooklyn Eagle*, 23 Apr 1900.

Stowe, Harriet Beecher. *Uncle Tom's Cabin: A Tale about Life Among the Lowly*. London: George Routledge & Company, 1852.

"Talks on White Slavery: Assistant District Attorney Elder Says Government Should Protect Young Girls." *Brooklyn Daily Eagle*, 21 Apr 1910.

Taub, Belle. "Discovered! A Modern Slave Block," *The Liberator*, 15 Jun 1935.

Terrell, Mary Church. *A Colored Woman in a White World*. Amherst, NY: Ransdell Inc., 1940.

Terrell, Mary Church, "The Progress of Colored Women." *Voice of the Negro* 1, no. 7 (July 1904): 292.

"The ancestral snobbery-microbe," *Puck Magazine*, 16 Mar 1898.

"The Anti-Tuberculosis Movement in Another Small City." *Charities* 13 (Mar 1905): 586–587.

"The Colored Refugees." *New York Times*, 11 Jul 1879.

"The Colored Refugees." *New York Times*, 1 Apr 1880.

"The Goose that Lays the Golden Egg." *Puck Magazine*, 22 Aug 1883.

"The Great 'Scrub' Race." Eureka Advertisement. Library of Congress Prints and Photographs Division, 1870.

"The Irish Declaration of Independence," *Puck Magazine*, 9 May 1883.

"The 'Kitchen-Garden.'" *New York Times*, 24 Mar 1878.

"The Negro Woman Worke." Department of Labor-Women's Bureau Bulletin, 1938.

"The Servant Girl Question." *Brooklyn Eagle*, 18 Mar 1888.

Thornton, Frances. "Adjustment Problems of certain Negro Women Migrants to Harlem: A Study of 125 Women Seeking Adjustment Aid from the West 137th Street Branch of the Y.W.C.A." Master's thesis, Columbia University, 1936.

Tomes, Robert. "Your Humble Servant." *Harper's New Monthly Magazine*, Jul 1864.

"Typhoid Carrier tied to Epidemic: Poor Sanitation on Liner Is Also Blamed for Illness." *New York Times*, 26 Oct 1970.

"Typhoid Mary asks for $50,000 from the City." *New York Times*, 3 Dec 1911.

United Building Service and Domestic Workers Association of Brooklyn. "Facts You Should Know about the Men and Women Who Work in Your Homes and Buildings," n.d., New York University Tamiment Library and Robert F. Wagner Archives' Printed Ephemera Collection on Trade Unions.

Walton, Wilmer. "Colored Servants." *The Daily Register-Call* (Colorado), 4 Aug 1879.

Washington, Forrester B. "A Study of Negro Employees of Apartment Homes in New York City. *Bulletin of the National Urban League Among Negroes*.

Wells, Bishop W. J. "Maid of Salem Film Twists History to Disparage Race." *Chicago Defender*. 13 Mar 1937.

Wells, Bishop W. J. "Salem Maid 'Not So Hot, Says Bishop," *New York Amsterdam News*, 13 Mar 1937.

Wells, Ida B; Frederick Douglass; I. Garland Penn; F. L. Barnett; *The Reasons Why The Colored American Is not in the World's Columbian Exposition: The Afro American's Contribution to Columbian Literature*. Chicago: Clark Street, 1893.

"White Rose Mission Settlement: Girls from Southern Ports Protected, Social Life for Servants, Mothers' Sewing Clubs Help Support Work, Race History Classes, and a Unique Library." *New York Evening Post*, Schomburg Library's White Rose Mission Collection.

"Working Women of Today as Viewed by Miss O'Reilly." Women's Trade Union League Papers, 20 Mar 1899.

"Work to Domestic Service." *New York Times*, 20 Oct 1907.

Yentis, David. "The Negro in Old Brooklyn: An Experiment in Sociological Reconstruction of the Life of a Racial Minority in a Northern City." Master's thesis, Columbia University, 1937.

Zeilen, Cecilia Flanagan. Ellis Island Immigration Museum's Oral History Project Interview, 2 Aug 1994.

Secondary Sources

Amott, Teresa L., and Julie A. Matthaei, eds. *Race, Gender, and Work: A Multi-cultural Economic History of Women in the United States*. Brooklyn: South End Press, 1996.

Anderson, Carol. *White Rage: The Unspoken Truth of Our Racial Divide*. New York: Bloomsbury, 2016.

Anzaldúa, Gloria, and Cherríe Moraga, eds. *This Bridge Called My Back: Writings by Radical Women of Color*. Watertown: Persephone Press, 1981.

Babb, Valerie M. *Whiteness Visible: The Meaning of Whiteness in American Literature and Culture*. New York: New York University Press, 1998.

Baldwin, James. *The Evidence of Things Not Seen*. New York: H. Holt, 1985.

Baptist. Edward E. *The Half Has Never Been Told: Slavery and the Making of American Capitalism*. New York: Basic Books, 2014.

Barkley, Elsa Brown. "Negotiating and Transforming the Public Sphere: African American Political Life in the Transition from Slavery to Freedom." *Public Culture* 7 (Fall 1994): 107–146.

Barrett, James R. *The Irish Way: Becoming American in the Multiethnic City*. New York: The Penguin Press, 2012.

Beckles, Hilary McDonald. A 'riotous and unruly lot': Irish Indentured Servants and Freemen in the English West Indies, 1644–1713." *The William and Mary Quarterly Journal* (1990): 503–522.

Bergquist, James M. *Daily Life in Immigrant America: How the First Great Wave of Immigrants Made Their Way in America, 1820–1870*. Chicago: Ivan R. Dee, 2009.

Bernstein, Jared, and Ben Speilberg, "The Trump administration's ongoing attack on workers, Washinton Post, 30 Aug 2017. https://www.washingtonpost.com/news/posteverything/wp/2017/08/30/the-trump-administrations-ongoing-attack-on-workers/.

Bhan, Esme, and Charles Lemert. *The Voice of Anna Julia Cooper: Including a Voice from the South and Other Important Essays, Papers, and Letters*. New York: Rowman & Littlefield Publishers, 1998.

"Black Women Advance Labor's Cause In An Unlikely Setting: 1881 Atlanta," 31 Dec 2009, from the American Postal Workers Union (APWU) website: https://apwu.org/news/black-women-advance-labor%E2%80%99s-cause-unlikely-setting-1881-atlanta

Blight, David. *Race and Reunion: The Civil War in American History*. Cambridge: Harvard University Press, 2001.

Boris, Eileen, and Premilla Nadasen, "Domestic Workers Organize!" *Working USA: The Journal of Labor and Society* 11 (2008): 413–443.

Brace, Charles Loring. *The Dangerous Classes of New York and Twenty Years' Work among Them*. New York: Wynkoop & Hallenbeck Publishers, 1872.

Brooks, Janet. "The Sad and Tragic Life of Typhoid Mary," *Canadian Medical Association Journal* 6 (March 1996): 915–916

Brooks, Janet. "The Sad and Tragic Life of Typhoid Mary." *Canadian Medical Association Journal*, 15 Mar 1996.

Brown, Leslie, and Annie Valk. *Living with Jim Crow: African American Women and Memories of the Segregated South.* New York: Palgrave Macmillan, 2010.

Bularzik, Mary J. "The Bonds of Belonging: Leonora O'Reilly and Social Reform." *Labor History* 24 (1983): 60–83.

Burleson, Hallie. "Sadie's Servant Room Blues," http://historymatters.gmu.edu/d/20/.

Burrell, William Patrick, and D.E. Johnson. *Twenty-Five Years History of the Grand Fountain of the United Order of True Reformers.* Richmond, VA: Grand Fountain, United Order of True Reformers, 1909.

Canny, Nicholas P. "The Ideology of English Colonization: From Ireland to America." *William and Mary Quarterly Journal* (1973): 575–598.

Capehart, Jonathan. "'Trump's Benghazi': Frederica Wilson wants the truth about what happened to La David Johnson in Niger." *Washington Post*, 19 Dec 2017

Carby, Hazel. "Policing a Black Woman's Body in an Urban Context." *Critical Inquiry* 18 (1992): 738–755.

Care in Action. "An Open Letter to Stacey Abrams From Domestic Workers: We'll Keep Fighting With You." 11 Nov 2018. https://www.bustle.com/p/open-letter-to-stacey-abrams-from-domestic-workers-well-keep-fighting-with-you-13170861

Carle, Susan D. *Defining the Struggle: National Organizing for Racial Justice, 1880–1915.* New York: Oxford University Press, 2013.

Cavanah, Frances, ed. *We Came to America.* Philadelphia: Macrae Smith Company, 1954.

Clark-Lewis, Elizabeth. *Living In, Living Out: African American Domestics in Washington D.C., 1910–1940.* Washington: Smithsonian Institute Press, 1996.

Cleek, Ashley. "The Route of Division." http://projects.aljazeera.com/2015/05/birmingham-bus/.

Clegg, Brenda Faye. "Black Female Domestics during the Great Depression in New York City, 1930–1940." PhD diss. University of Michigan, 1983.

Coffey, Michael, ed. *The Irish in America.* New York: Hyperion, 1997.

Coldrey, Barry M. "Child Migration and the Catholic Church." Journal of the Royal Australian Historical Society 79 (1993): 199–213.

Colen, Shellee. "With Respect and Feelings: Voices of West Indian Workers in New York City." In J. B. Cole, ed. *All American Women: Lines That Divide and Ties That Bind.* New York: Free Press, 1986.

Coles, Robert. *The South Goes North: Volume III of Children of Crisis.* Boston: Little, Brown, and Company, 1967.

Collins, Patricia Hill. *Black Feminist Thought: Knowledge, Consciousness, and the Politics of Empowerment.* Boston: Unwin Hyman, 1990.

Cooper, Brittany C. *Beyond Respectability: The Intellectual Thought of Race Women.* Urbana: University of Illinois Press, 2017.

Cooper Owens, Deirdre Benia. *Medical Bondage: Race, Gender, and the Origins of American Gynecology.* Athens: University of Georgia Press, 2018.

———. "'Courageous Negro Servitors' and Laboring Irish Bodies: An examination of Antebellum-Era Modern American Gynecology." PhD diss., University of California-Los Angeles, 2008.

———. Perfecting the Degraded Body: Slavery, Irish-Immigration, and American Gynecology." *Power in History: From Medieval Ireland to the Post-Modern World,* eds. Anthony McElligott, Liam Chambers, Ciara Breathnach, Catherine Lawless. Dublin: Irish Academic Press, 2011.

Crenshaw, Kimberlé. "Demarginalizing the Intersection of Race and Sex: A Black Feminist Critique of Antidiscrimination Doctrine, Feminist Theory, and Antiracist Politics." *The University of Chicago Legal Forum* 1 (1989): 139–166.

Crenshaw, Kimberlé, Leslie McCall, Sumi Cho, eds. "Toward a Field of Intersectionality Studies: Theory, Applications and Praxis." *Signs: Journal of Women and Culture in Society* 38, no.4 (2013): 785–810.

Cowan, Ruth Schwartz. *The 'Industrial Revolution' in the Home: Household Technology and Social Change in the 20th Century.* Baltimore: Johns Hopkins University Press, 2003.

———. *More Work for Mother: The Ironies of Household Technology from the Open Hearth to the Microwave.* New York: Basic Books, 1983.

Cox, Karen L. *Dixie's Daughters: The United Daughters of the Confederacy and the Preservation of Confederate Culture.* Gainesville: University Press of Florida, 2003.

Curtis, L.P. Jr., *Anglo Saxons and Celts: A Study of Anti-Irish Prejudice in Victorian England* Bridgeport: University of Bridgeport, Connecticut, 1968.

Curtwright, Wesley. "Brief History of the Domestic Workers' Association, Brooklyn Local." Writers' Program, New York City: Negroes of New York Collection, Schomburg Center for Research in Black Culture, Manuscripts, Archives and Rare Books.

Cusumano, Katherine. "The Women of the Women's March: Meet the Activists Who Are Planning One of the Largest Demonstrations in American History." *W* magazine, 19 Jan 2017. https://www.wmagazine.com/story/womens-march-on-washington-activists-organizers.

Daugherty, Alex, Anita Kumar, and Douglas Hanks, "Video of Frederica Wilson's 2015 speech shows John Kelly Was Wrong." *Miami Herald*, 20 Oct 2017. http://www .miamiherald.com/news/politics-government/article179952536.html,

Davis, Angela. *Blues Legacies and Black Feminism: Gertrude "Ma" Rainey, Bessie Smith, and Billie Holiday.* New York: Vintage Books, 1999.

Diffee, Christopher. "Sex and the City: The White Slavery Scare and Social Governance in the Progressive Era." *American Quarterly* 57(June 2005): 416.

Dill, Bonnie Thornton. *Across The Boundaries of Race and Class: An Exploration of Work and Family Among Black Female Domestic Servants.* New York: Garland Publishing, 1994.

———. "'Making Your Job Good Yourself': Domestic Service and the Construction of Personal Dignity." In Ann Bookman and Sandra Morgen, eds., *Women and the Politics of Empowerment* (Philadelphia: Temple University Press, 1998).

———. "The Dialectics of Black Womanhood," *Signs: Journal of Women and Culture in Society* 4, no. 3 (Spring 1979): 543–555.

Diner, Hasia. *Erin's Daughters in America: Irish Immigrant Women in the Nineteenth Century.* Baltimore: The John Hopkins University Press, 1983.

Diner, Hasia, and Michael W. Grunberger. *From Haven to Home: 350 Years of Jewish Life in America.* New York: George Braziller Press, 2004.

Douglass, Frederick. *My Bondage and My Freedom.* New York and Auburn: Miller, Orton, and Mulligan, 1855.

Du Bois, W.E.B. *The Philadelphia Negro: A Social Study.* Philadelphia: University of Pennsylvania, 1899.

———. *Black Reconstruction in America: An Essay Toward a History of the Part Which Black Folk Played in the Attempt to Reconstruct Democracy in America, 1860–1880.* New York: Athenaeum, 1935.

Dudden, Faye. *Serving Women: household service in nineteenth-century America.* Middletown: Wesleyan University Press, 1983.

Duffy, Jennifer Nugent. *Who's Your Paddy? Racial Expectations and the Struggle for Irish American Identity.* New York: New York University Press, 2014.

Dunn, Richard S. *A Tale of Two Plantations: Slave Life and Labor in Jamaica and Virginia.* Cambridge: Harvard University Press, 2014.

England, Kim and Bernadette Steill. "'They think you're as stupid as your English is': constructing foreign domestic workers in Toronto." *Environment and Planning* 27 (1999) 195–215.

———. "Jamaican Domestics, Filipina Housekeepers and English Nannies: Representations of Toronto's Foreign Domestic Workers." In Janet Henshall Momsen, ed. *Gender, Migration, and Domestic Service* (London: Routledge, 1999) 43–61.

Enstad, Nan. *Ladies of Labor, Girls of Adventure: Working Women, Popular Culture, and Labor Politics at the Turn of the Twentieth Century.* New York: Columbia University Press, 1999.

Firth, Violet M. *The Psychology of the Servant Problem: A Study in Social Relationships.* London: C.W. Daniel Company, 1925.

Fitzgerald, Maureen. *Habits of Compassion: Irish Catholic Nuns and the Origins of New York's Welfare System, 1830–1920.* Urbana: University of Illinois Press, 2006.

Flynn, Peter. "How Bridget Was Framed: The Irish Domestic in Early American Cinema, 1895–1917." *Cinema Journal* 50 (Winter 2011) 1–20.

Foner, Nancy, ed. *Islands in the City: West Indian Migration to New York.* Berkley: University of California Press, 2001.

Foner, Eric. *Reconstruction: America's Unfinished Revolution, 1863–1877.* New York: Harper Perennial Modern Classic, 2014.

Eric Foner. *Gateway to Freedom: The Hidden History of the Underground Railroad.* New York: W.W. Norton &Company, 2015.

Foner, Eric, Walter Johnson, and Richard Follett. *Slavery's Ghost: The Problem of Freedom in the Age of Emancipation.* Baltimore: The Johns Hopkins University Press, 2011.

Frank, Dana. "White Working-Class Women and the Race Question," *International Labor and Working-Class History* 54 (Fall 1998): 80–102.

Gallagher, Julie. *Black Women and Politics in New York City.* Urbana: University of Illinois Press, 2012.

Garner, Steve. *Racism in the Irish Experience.* London: Pluto Press, 2004.

Giddings, Paula. *When and Where I Enter: The Impact of Black Women on Race and Sex in America.* New York: W. Morrow, 1984.

Gayles, Gloria Wade. "Black Women Journalists in the South, 1880–1905: A Study of Black Woman's History," *Caliloo* 11/13 (Feb-Oct 1981).

Gellerman, Bruce. "'It Was Like a War Zone': Busing in Boston," http://www.wbur.org/2014 /09/05/boston-busing-anniversary, 5 Sep 2014.

Genoways, Ted. "Farmers voted heavily for Trump. But his trade policies are terrible for them,." *Washinton Post,* 24 Oct 2017, https://www.washingtonpost.com/news /posteverything/wp/2017/10/24/farmers-voted-heavily-for-trump-but-his-trade-policies -are-terrible-for-them/?utm_term=.bd72feafo432

Glasco, Lawrence. "Ethnicity and Social Structure: Irish, Germans and Native-Born of Buffalo, New York, 1850–1860. PhD diss., State University of New York at Buffalo, 1973.

Glenn, Evelyn Nakano. *Unequal Freedom: How Race and Gender Shaped American Citizenship and Labor.* Cambridge: Harvard University Press, 2002.

———. "Racial Ethnic Women's Labor: The Intersection of Race, Gender, and Class Oppression." In *Women, Culture, and Society, A Reader (Second Edition),* Barbara Balliet and Patricia, eds. McDaniel. Dubuque: Kendall/Hunt Publishing Company, 1992.

Golway, Terry and Michael Coffey. "The Work: Where The Irish Did Apply." In *The Irish in America.* Hyperion: New York, 1997.

Gordon, Linda. *The Great Arizona Orphan Abduction.* Boston: Harvard University Press, 2001.

Gossett, Thomas F. *Race: The History of an Idea in America* (Dallas: Southern Methodist University Press, 1963.

Gourevitch, Alex. *From Slavery to the Cooperative Commonwealth: Labor and Republican Liberty in the Nineteenth Century.* New York: Cambridge University Press, 2015.

Gray, Brenda Clegg. *Black Female Domestics during the Depression in New York City, 1930– 1940.* New York: Garland Publishing, 1993.

Greenberg, Cheryl. *Or Does it Explode? Black Harlem in the Great Depression.* New York: Oxford University Press, 1991.

Guglielmo, Jennifer, and Salvatore Salerno. *Are Italians White: How Race Is Made in America.* New York: Routledge Press, 2003.

Guy-Sheftall, Beverly. *Daughters of Sorrow: Attitudes toward Black Women, 1880–1920.* Brooklyn: Carlson, 1990.

———. (ed.) *Words of Fire: An Anthology of African-American Feminist Thought.* New York: The New Press, 1995.

Hale, Grace Elizabeth. *Making Whiteness: The Culture of Segregation in the South.* New York: Vintage Books, 1998.

Haley, Sarah. *No Mercy Here: Gender, Punishment, and the Making of Jim Crow Modernity.* Chapel Hill: University of North Carolina Press, 2016.

Harley, Sharon. "When Your Work Is Not Who You Are: The Development of a Working-Class Consciousness among Afro-American Women." In *Gender, Class, Race and Reform in the Progressive Era,* edited by Noralee Frankel and Nancy S. Dye. Lexington: University of Kentucky Press, 1991.

Harris, Leslie M. *In the Shadow of Slavery: African Americans in New York City, 1626–1863.* Chicago: University of Chicago Press, 2004.

Harris, Leslie, and Daina Ramey Berry, eds. *Slavery and Freedom in Savannah.* Athens: University of Georgia Press, 2014.

Hart, Tonya. *Race, Poverty, and the Negotiation of Women's Health in New York City.* New York University Press, 2015.

Harris, Trudier. *From Mammies To Militants: Domestics in Black American Literature.* Temple University Press, 1982.

Haskell, Rob. "Serena Williams on Pregnancy, Power, and Coming Back to Center Court." *Vogue* magazine, 15 Aug 2017. https://www.vogue.com/article/serena-williams-pregnancy -vogue-september-issue-2017.

Hearn, Mona. *Below Stairs: Domestic Service Remembered in Dublin and Beyond, 1880–1922.* Dublin: The Lilliput Press, 1993.

Hendricks, Wanda A. *Fannie Barrier Williams: Crossing the Borders of Region and Race.* Urbana: University of Illinois Press, 2013.

Hicks, Cheryl. *Talk with You Like a Woman: African American Women, Justice, and Reform in New York, 1890–1935.* Chapel Hill: North Carolina University Press, 2010.

Higginbotham, Evelyn Brooks. "African-American Women's History and the Metalanguage of Race." *Signs: Journal of Women and Culture in Society* 17 (Winter 1992): 251–274.

Hogarth, Rana A. *Medicalizing Blackness: Making Racial Difference in the Atlantic World, 1780–1840.* Chapel Hill: The University of North Carolina Press, 2017.

Hooper and Litvack, eds. *Ireland in the Nineteenth Century: Regional Identity.* Portland: Four Courts Press, 2000.

Howes, Marjorie. "How Irish Maids Are Made: Domestic Servants, Atlantic Culture, and Modernist Aesthetics," in *The Black and Green Atlantic: Crosscurrents of the African and Irish Diaspora,* eds. Peter D. O'Neill and David Lloyd. New York: Palgrave McMillan, 2009.

Hounmenou, Charles. "Black Settlement Houses and Oppositional Consciousness." *Journal of Black Studies* 43 (September 2012): 646–666.

Horne, Gerald. *W.E.B. DuBois and the Afro-American Response to the Cold War, 1944–1963* Albany: State University of New York, 1986.

Hull, Gloria T. ed. *The Works of Alice Dunbar-Nelson.* Vol 1. New York: Oxford University Press, 1988.

Hull, Gloria T. (Akasha), Patricia Bell Scott, and Barbara Smith. *All the Women are White, All the Blacks are Men, But Some of Us Are Brave: Black Women's Studies.* New York: The Feminist Press, 1982.

Hunter, Tera. *To Joy My Freedom: Southern Black Women's Lives and Labors after the Civil War.* Cambridge: Harvard University Press, 1997.

Hutchinson, Louise Daniel. *Anna J. Cooper: A Voice from the South* (Washington D.C.: Smithsonian Institution Press, 1981.

Ignatiev, Noel. *How the Irish Became White.* New York: Routledge, 1996.

Jacobson, Matthew Frye. *Whiteness of a different color: European immigrants and the Alchemy of race.* Cambridge: Harvard University Press, 1999.

Johnson, Stanley Currie. *Emigration from the United Kingdom to North America, 1763–1912.* New York: Routledge, 2013.

Johnson, Walter. *Soul by Soul: Life Inside the Antebellum Slave Market.* Cambridge: Harvard University Press, 1999.

Jones, Claudia. "An End to the Neglect of the Problems of the Negro Woman!" In *Words of Fire: An Anthology of African-American Feminist Thought,* edited by Beverly Guy-Sheftall. New York: The New Press, 1995.

Jones, Jacqueline. *Labor of Love, Labor of Sorrow: Black Women, Work, and the Family, from Slavery to the Present.* New York: Vintage Books, 1986.

Jones, Mary. *These Obstreperous Lassies: A History of the IWWU.* Dublin: Gill and MacMillan, 1988.

Jordan, Don, and Michael Walsh, eds. *White Cargo: The Forgotten History of Britain's Whites Slaves in America.* New York: New York University Press, 2008.

Kaplan, Carla. *Miss Anne in Harlem: The White Woman of the Black Renaissance.* New York: Harper Perennial, 2013.

Kandaswamy, Priya. "Gendering Racial Formation Theory." In *Racial Formation in the Twenty-First Century,* edited by Daniel Martinez HoSang, Oneka LaBennett, and Laura Polido. Berkeley: University of California Press, 2012.

Katzman, David. *Seven Days a Week: Women and Domestic Service in Industrializing America.* Champaign: University of Illinois Press, 1981.

Kautt, William H. *The Anglo-Irish War, 1916–1921.* Westport, Connecticut: Praeger, 1999.

Kelley, Robin D. G. *Race Rebels: Culture, Politics, and the Black Working Class.* New York: Maxwell Macmillan International, 1994.

Kellor, Frances A. "Southern Colored Girls in the North: The Problem of Their Protection." *Charities* 13 (18 Mar 1905): 584–585.

Kelly, John. *The Graves Are Walking: The Great Famine and the Saga of the Irish People.* New York: Henry Holt and Company, 2012.

Kinealy, Christine. "Was Ireland a Colony? The Evidence of the Great Famine." In *Was Ireland a Colony?: Economy, Politics, Ideology and Culture in Nineteenth Century Ireland,* edited by Terence McDonough. Dublin: Irish Academic Press, 2005.

King, Deborah. "Multiple Jeopardy, Multiple Consciousness: The Context of a Black Feminist Ideology." *Signs: Journal of Women and Culture in Society* 14 (Autumn 1988): 42–72.

Kenny, Kevin. *The American Irish: A History.* New York: Routledge, 2014.

Kessler-Harris, Alice. *Out to Work: A History of Wage-Earning Women in the United States.* New York: Oxford University Press, 1982.

Kleinberg, Susan J. "Technology's Stepdaughter: The Impact of Industrialization Upon Working Women, Pittsburgh, 1865–1890." PhD diss., University of Pittsburgh, 1973.

Kramer, Steve. "Uplifting our 'Downtrodden Sisterhood': Victoria Earle Matthews and the New York City's White Rose Mission, 1897–1907. *The Journal of African American History* 91 (2006): 243–266.

Leavitt, Judith Walzer. *Typhoid Mary: Captive to the Public's Health.* Boston: Beacon Press, 1996.

Lee, J. J. *Ireland 1912–1985: Politics and Society.* Cambridge: Cambridge University Press, 1989.

Lerner, Gerda Lerner. *Black Women in White America: A Documentary History.* New York: Vintage Books, 1972.

Lerner, Gerda, ed. *Black Women in White America: A Documentary.* New York: Vintage Books, 1972.

Levin, Peter J. "Bold Vision: Catholic Sisters and the Creation of American Hospitals." *Journal of Community Health* 36, no. 1 (2011): 343–47.

Levine, Susan. "Labor's True Woman: Domesticity and Equal Rights in the Knights of Labor." *The Journal of American History* 70 (1983): 323–339.

———. *Labor's True Woman: Carpet Weavers, Industrialization, and Labor Reform in the Gilded Age.* Philadelphia: Temple University Press, 1984.

Lewis, David Levering. *W.E.B. Du Bois: Biography of a Race, 1868–1919.* New York: H. Holt, 2000.

Lloyd, David; O'Neill, eds. *The Black and Green Atlantic: Cross-Currents of the African and Irish Diasporas.* Palgrave McMillan: New York, 2009.

Logan, Shirley Wilson, ed. *With Pen and Voice: A Critical Anthology of Nineteenth-Century African-American Women.* Carbondale: Southern Illinois University Press, 1995.

Lopez, Ian Haney. *White By Law 10th Anniversary Edition: The Legal Construction of Race.* New York: New York University Press, 2006.

Lowe, Lisa. *Immigrant Acts: On Asian American Cultural Politics.* Durham: Duke University Press, 1996.

Lowery, Wesley. "Read the Letter Coretta Scott King wrote opposing Sessions's 1986 federal nomination," 10 Jan 2017. https://www.washingtonpost.com/news/powerpost/wp/2017/01/10/read-the-letter-coretta-scott-king-wrote-opposing-sessionss-1986-federal-nomination

Luddy, Maria. *Women in Ireland: A Documentary History* 1800–1918. Cork: Cork University Press, 1995.

Ludlow, Helen W. "Industrial Classes for Colored Women and Children." *The Southern Workman* 31 (1902).

Lynch-Brennan, Margaret. "Ubiquitous Bridget: Irish Immigrant Women in Domestic Service in America, 1840–1930." In *Making the Irish American: History and Heritage of the Irish in the United States,* edited by J. J. Lee and Marion Casey. New York: New York University Press, 2006.

———. *The Irish Bridget: Irish Immigrant Women in Domestic Service in America, 1840–1930.* New York: Syracuse University Press, 2009.

"Many to Attend Open Hearing on Domestics' Test." *New Rochelle Standard-Star,* 27 Jun 1937.

Marshall, D. "The history of Caribbean migration: The case of the West Indies." *Caribbean Review* 11 (1982): 6–11.

Matthews, Glenda. *Just a Housewife: The Rise and Fall of Domesticity in America*. New York: Oxford University Press, 1987.

May, Claudia. "Airing Dirty Laundry: Representations of Domestic Laborers in the Works of African American Women Writers." *Feminist Formations* 27 (Spring 2015): 141.

May, Vanessa H. *Unprotected Labor: Household Workers, Politics, and Middle-Class Reform in New York, 1870–1940*. Chapel Hill: North Carolina Press, 2011.

May, Vivian. *Anna Julia Cooper, A Visionary Black Feminist: A Critical Introduction*. New York: Routledge, 2007.

McBride, Theresa. *The Domestic Revolution: The Modernisation of Household Service in England and France, 1820–1920*. New York: Homes and Meier Publishing, 1976.

McCurdy, Jesselyn. "The Justice Department Continues to Roll Back Civil Rights Protections," 20 Nov 2017. https://www.aclu.org/blog/criminal-law-reform/justice-department-continues-to-roll-back -civil-rights-protections

McClaughlin, Trevor. "Lost Children? Irish Famine Orphans in Australia." *History Ireland* 8 (2000): 30–34.

McClintock, Anne. *Imperial Leather: Race, Gender, and Sexuality in the Colonial Contest*. New York: Routledge,1995.

McCoole, Sinéad. *No Ordinary Women: Irish Female Activists in the Revolutionary Years, 1900–1923*. Dublin: The O'Brien Press, 2004.

McDonough, Terrence, ed. *Was Ireland a Colony? Economics, Politics, and Culture in Nineteenth Century Ireland*. Dublin: Irish Academic Press, 2005.

McDuffie, Erik S. *Sojourning for Freedom: Black Women, American Communism, and the Making of Black Left Feminism*. Durham: Duke University Press, 2011.

McManus, Edgar J. *Black Bondage in the North*. Syracuse: Syracuse University Press, 1973.

Mettler, Suzanne. *Dividing Citizens: Gender and Federalism in New Deal and Public Policy*. Ithaca: Cornell University Press, 1998.

Miller, Kerby. *Emigrants and Exiles: Ireland and the Irish Exodus to North America*. New York: Oxford University Press, 1985.

Miller, Kerby, and Patricia Mulholland Miller, "From 'Bridget' to 'Mother Machree,'" In *Journey of Hope: The Story of Irish Immigration to America*. San Francisco: Chronicle Books, 2001.

Morgan, Jennifer. "Some Could Suckle Over their Shoulder': Male Travelers, Female Bodies, and the Gendering of Racial Ideology, 1500–1770." *The William and Mary Quarterly Journal* 54 (Jan 1997) 167–192.

Moriarty, Theresa. "'Who Will Look After the Kiddies?' Households and Collective Action during the Dublin Lockout, 1913. In *Rebellious Families: Household Strategies and Collective Action in the Nineteenth and Twentieth Centuries*, edited by Jan Kok. (New York: Berghan Books, 2002).

Morris, Vivian. WPA Domestic Workers Interview Unedited Transcript, Library of Congress Digital Collection, 2 Feb 1939.

Morton, Samuel. *Crania Americana: or a Comparative View of the Skulls of Various Aboriginal Nations of North and South America*. Philadelphia: J. Dobson Press, 1839.

Murphy, Angela. *American Slavery, Irish Freedom: Abolition, Immigrant Citizenship and the Transatlantic Movement for Irish Repeal*. Baton Rouge: Louisiana State University, 2010.

Murphy, Maureen. "Birdie, We Hardly Knew Ye: The Irish Domestics." In *The Irish in America*, edited by Michael Coffey and Terry Golway. Hyperion, New York, 1997.

Nadasen, Premilla. *Household Workers Unite: The Untold Story of African American Women Who Built a Movement.* Boston: Beacon Press, 2015.

Naison, Mark. *Communists in Harlem during the Depression.* Champaign: University of Illinois Press, 1983.

Newkirk, Vann R. II. "How Voter ID Laws Discriminate: A New Comprehensive Study Finds Evidence That Strict Voting Laws Do Suppress Along Racial Lines." *Atlantic,* 18 Feb 2017. https://www.theatlantic.com/politics/archive/2017/02/how-voter-id-laws -discriminate-study/517218/

New York State Department of Labor, "Domestic Workers' Bill of Rights, https://labor.ny .gov/legal/domestic-workers-bill-of-rights.shtm

Nolan, Janet A. *Ourselves Alone: Women's Emigration from Ireland, 1885–1920.* Kentucky: University Press of Kentucky, 1989.

O'Ferrall, Charles T. Speech at the dedication of the White House of the Confederacy in Richmond, *Memoriam Sempiternam.* Richmond: Confederate Museum, 1896.

Omi, Michael and Winant, Howard. *Racial Formation in the United States: From the 1960s to the 1990s.* 2nd ed. New York: Routledge, 1994.

O'Donnell, Ed. "United Front: The Irish and Organized Labor." In *Irish in America,* edited by Michael Coffey and Terry Golway. New York: Hyperion, 1997.

O'Hearn, Denis. "Ireland in the Atlantic Economy." In *Was Ireland A Colony?: Economics, Politics and Culture in Nineteenth Century Ireland,* edited by Terrence McDonough. Dublin: Irish Academic Press, 2005.

Olson, James and Robert Shadle, eds. *Historical Dictionary of the British Empire, A–J* Westport: Greenwood Press, 1996.

Orleck, Annelise. *Storming Caesar's Palace: How Black Mothers Fought Their Own War on Poverty.* Boston: Beacon Press, 2005.

———. *Common Sense and a Little Fire: Women and Working-Class Politics in the United States, 1900–1965.* Chapel Hill: University of North Carolina Press, 1995.

"Our New Congested Districts—the City Hospitals." *Charities* 13 (Mar 1905): 581–584.

Ovington, Mary White. *Walls Came Tumbling Down.* New York: Harcourt, Brace and Company, 1947.

———. *Half a Man: The Status of the Negro in New York.* New York: Longmans, Green, and Company, 1911.

Owens, Eleanore. Interview conducted by author, 28 Nov 2007.

Painter, Nell Irvin. *The History of White People.* New York: W.W. Norton and Company, 2010.

———. *Standing at Armageddon: The United States 1877–1919.* New York: W.W. Norton & Company, 2008.

Palmer, Phyllis. *Domesticity and Dirt: Housewives and Domestic Servants in the United States, 1920–1945.* Philadelphia: Temple University Press, 1991.

Patrick, Bobbie. "Women Worth Knowing." *Daily Worker Newspaper,* 1949.

Perry, Jeffrey B. *Hubert Harrison: The Voice of Harlem Radicalism, 1882–1913.* New York: Columbia University Press, 2008.

Phillips-Cunningham, Danielle. "Moving with the Women: Tracing Racialization, Migration, and Domestic Workers in the Archive." *Signs: Journal of Women and Culture in Society* 38 (Winter 2013): 379–404.

Phillips, Kimberly. *AlabamaNorth: African-American migrants, community, and working class activism in Cleveland, 1915–1945.* Urbana: University of Illinois Press, 1999.

Pleck, Elizabeth. "A Mother's Wages: Income Earning Among Married Italian and Black Women, 1896–1911." In *A Heritage of Her Own: Toward a New Social History of American*

Woman, edited by Nancy Cott and Elizabeth Pleck. New York: Simon and Schuster Press, 1979.

———. *Black Migration and Poverty: Boston 1865–1900.* New York: Academic Press, 1979.

Quigley, Joan. *Just Another Southern Town: Mary Church Terrell and the Struggle for Racial Justice in the Nation's Capital.* New York: Oxford University Press, 2016.

Raaphorst, Donna L. *Union Maids Not Wanted: Organizing Domestic Workers, 1870–1940.* New York: Praeger, 1988.

Ransby, Barbara. *Ella Baker and the Black Freedom Movement: A Radical Democratic Vision.* Chapel Hill: The University of North Carolina Press, 2003.

Reilly, Katie "A Wave of Teacher Activism is Sweeping Red States," *Time* magazine, 5 Apr 2018. http://time.com/5228971/a-wave-of-teacher-activism-is-sweeping-red-states/

Roberts, Diane. *The Myth of Aunt Jemima: White Women Representing Black Women.* New York: Routledge, 1994.

Roberts, Dorothy. *Killing the Black Body: Race, Reproduction, and the Meaning of Liberty.* New York: Pantheon Books, 1997.

Robinson, Sharon. Interview by author, Atlanta, GA, 7 Jul 2009.

Roe, Clifford G. and Samuel B. Steadwell. *The Great War on White Slavery, or, Fighting for the Protection of Our Girls,* 1911.

Roediger, David. *The Wages of Whiteness: Race and the Making of the American Working Class.* New York: Verso, 1999.

Rollins, Judith. *Between Women: Domestics and Their Employers.* Philadelphia: Temple University Press, 1986.

Rosenberg, Chaim. *America at the Fair: Chicago's 1893 World's Columbian Exposition.* Charleston: Arcadia Publishing, 2008.

Runstedtler, Theresa. *Jack Johnson, Rebel Sojourner: Boxing in the Shadow of the Global Color Line.* Berkley: University of California Press, 2012.

Russell, Shana Alexssandra. "Domestic Workers, Sex Workers, and the Movement: Reimagining Black Working-Class Resistance in the Work of William Attaway, Richard Wright, and Alice Childress, 1935–1960. PhD diss., Rutgers, The State University of New Jersey, 2015.

Sacks, Marcy. *Before Harlem: The Black Experience in New York City Before World War I.* Philadelphia: University of Pennsylvania Press, 2006.

Salmon, Lucy Manard. *Domestic Service.* New York: The MacMillan Company, 1901.

Sanders, Kimberly Wallace. *Mammy: A Century of Race, Gender, and Southern Memory.* Ann Arbor: University of Michigan Press, 2008.

Saturday Evening Post. Aunt Jemima Pancake Advertisement, 3 Aug 1918.

Saturday Evening Post. Aunt Jemima Pancake Advertisement, 12 Mar 1921.

Scanlon, Jennifer. *Inarticulate Longings: The Ladies' Home Journal, Gender, and the Promises of Consumer Culture.* New York: Routledge, 1995.

Schiebinger, Londa. *Nature's Body: Gender in the Making of Modern Science.* Boston: Beacon Press, 1993.

Schrom, Nancy Dye. *As Equals and as Sisters: Feminism, Unionism, and the Women's Trade Union League of New York.* Columbia: University of Missouri Press, 1980.

Schultz, April. "The Black Mammy and the Irish Bridget: Domestic Service and the Representation of Race, 1830–1930." *Éire-Ireland Journal* 48, nos. 3, 4 (Fall/Winter 2013): 176–212.

Schwartz, Laura. "'What we think is needed is a union of domestics such as the miners have': The Domestic Workers' Union of Great Britain and Ireland 1908–1914." *Twentieth Century British History* 25 (June 2014): 173–198.

Scupin, Raymond. *Race and Ethnicity: An Anthropological Focus on the United States and the World.* Prentice Hall: New Jersey, 2002.

Shapiro, Laura. *Perfection Salad: Women and Cooking at the Turn of the Century.* Los Angeles: University of California Press, 2009.

Sharpless, Rebecca. *Cooking in Other Women's Kitchens: Domestic Workers in the South, 1865–1960.* Chapel Hill: The University of North Carolina Press, 2012.

Simonsen, Jane E. *Making Home Work: Domesticity and Native American Assimilation in the American West, 1860–1919.* Chapel Hill: The University of North Carolina Press, 2006.

Smith, Hudsy. "Partial History of White Rose Mission Industrial Association," 1899.

Smith, Warren B. *White Servitude in Colonial South Carolina.* University of South Carolina Press, 1961.

Solari, Mary M. *Confederate Veteran* 13 (Mar 1905): 123–124.

Stein, Melissa N. *Measuring Manhood: Race and the Science of Masculinity, 1830–1934.*

Steinberg, Stephen. *The Ethnic Myth: Race, Ethnicity, and Class in America.* Boston: Beacon, Press, 1989.

Stoddard, Eve Walsh. *Positioning Gender and Race in (Post)Colonial Plantation Space: Connecting Ireland and the Caribbean.* New York: Palgrave MacMillan, 2012.

Sutherland, Daniel. *Americans and Their Servants: Domestic Service in the United States from 1800 to 1920.* Baton Rouge: Louisiana State University Press, 1981.

Swift, Roger, ed. *Irish Migrants in Britain, 1815–1914: A Documentary History.* Ireland, Cork University Press, 2002.

Terrell, Mary Church. *A Colored Woman in a White World.* Amherst, NY: Ransdell Inc., 1940.

Testimony of Alfred Richardson, *United States Congress Report: Testimony Taken by the Joint Select Committee to Inquire into the Conditions of Affairs in the Late Insurrectionary States, Volume 1: Georgia.* Washington, D.C.: Government Printing Office, July 1871.

Tompkins, Kyla Wazana. *Racial Indigestion: Eating Bodies in the 19th Century.* New York: New York University Press, 2012.

Trotter, Joe, ed. *The Great Migration in Historical Perspective: New Dimensions of Race, Class, and Gender.* Bloomington: Indiana University Press, 1991.

Turbin, Carole. *Working Women of Collar City: Gender, Class, and Community in Troy, New York, 1864–1886.* Urbana: University of Illinois Press, 1992.

Urban, Andrew T. *Brokering Servitude: Migration and the Politics of Domestic Labor During the Long Nineteenth Century.* New York: New York University Press, 2018.

———. "Irish Domestic Servants, 'Biddy' and Rebellion in the American Home, 1850–1900" *Gender and History* 21(August 2009): 263–286.

Valenze, Deborah. *The First Industrial Woman.* New York: Oxford University Press, 1995.

Vapnek, Lara. *Breadwinners: Working Women and Economic Independence, 1865–1920.* Urbana: University of Illinois Press, 2009.

Vickerman, Milton. *Crosscurrents: West Indian Immigrants and Race.* New York: Oxford University Press, 1999.

Walden, Sarah. "Marketing the Mammy: Revisions of Labor and Middle-Class Identity in Southern Cookbooks, 1880–1930." In *Writing in the Kitchen: Essays on Southern Literature and Foodways*, edited by David A. Davis and Tara Powell. Jackson: University of Mississippi, 2014.

Walsh, Ann. Ellis Island Immigration Museum Oral History Project Interview, 26 Jun 1986.

Walter, Bronwen. *Outsiders Inside: Whiteness, Place and Irish Women: Gender, Racism, Ethnicity.* New York: Routledge, 2001.

———. "Irish Domestic Servants and English National Identity." In *Domestic Service and the Formation of European Identity*, edited by A. Fauve-Chamoux. London: Oxford, 2004.

———. "Strangers on the Inside: Irish Women Servants in England, 1881." *Immigrants & Minorities* 27 (July/November, 2009) 279–299.

Watkins-Owens, Irma, *Blood Relations: Caribbean Immigrants and the Harlem Community, 1900–1930*. Bloomington: Indiana University Press, 1996.

———. "Early-Twentieth-Century Caribbean Women: Migration and Social Networks in New York City," In *Islands in the City: West Indian Migration to New York*. Los Angeles: University of California Press, 2001.

Weisenfeld, Judith. *African American Women and Christian Activism: New York's Black YWCA, 1905–1945*. Cambridge: Harvard University Press, 1997.

Wells, Ida B., Frederick Douglass, I. Garland Penn, F.L. Barnett. *The Reasons Why The Colored American Is not in the World's Columbian Exposition: The Afro American's Contribution to Columbian Literature*. Chicago: Clark Street, 1893.

Weir, Robert E. *Knights Unhorsed: Internal Conflict in a Gilded Age Social Movement*. Detroit: Wayne State University Press, 2000.

Werner, Erica and Ed O'Keefe. "White House Chief of Staff: Trump not expected to extend DACA Deadline," 6 Feb 2018. https://www.washingtonpost.com/powerpost /white-house-chief-of-staff-trump-not-expected-to-extend-daca-deadline/2018/02/06 /7e459e4a-0b54–11e8–95a5-c396801049ef_story.html?utm_term=.1badf8b7abdf

Werner, Erica, and Kevin Sieff. "How Trump's tariffs on Mexico are taking jobs from U.S. workers." *Washington Post*, 18 Jul 2018. https://www.washingtonpost.com/business /economy/trumps-tariffs-on-mexico-are-causing-layoffs-in-the-united-states/2018/07/18 /03ec1e74-8473–11e8–9e80–403a221946a7_story.html?utm_term=.7749877c6ea6,.

White, Deborah Gray. *Arn't I a Woman: Female Slaves in the Plantation South*. New York: W.W. Norton & Company, 1999.

———. *Too Heavy a Load: Black Women in Defense of Themselves, 1894–1994*. New York: W. W. Norton, 1999.

Wilkerson, Isabel. *The Warmth of Other Suns: The Epic Story of America's Great Migration*. New York: Vintage Books, 2010.

Williams, Fannie Barrier. "The Intellectual Progress of Colored Women since the Emancipation Proclamation." In *The World's Congress of Representative Women*, edited by May Wright Sewell. Chicago: Rand, McNally, 1894.

Williams, Katt. "Great America" Comedy Tour, Jacksonville, Florida, Netflix Original, 2018.

Winant, Howard. *The World is a Ghetto: Race and Democracy since World War II*. New York: Basic Books, 2001.

Witt, Doris. *Black Hunger: Food and the Politics of U.S. Identity*. New York: Oxford University Press, 1999.

Woodward, C Vann. *The Burden of Southern History*. Baton Rouge: Louisiana State University Press, 1960.

Zaniewski, Ann. "Detroit pub refused to serve Irish people at St. Patrick's Day Parade—to make a point." *Detroit Free Press* (USA Today Network), 18 Mar 2018. https://www.freep .com/story/news/nation-now/2018/03/17/detroit-pub-refused-serve- irish-people-detroit-st-paddys-pub-refused-serve-irish-people-make-point-m/435650002/

Index

Page numbers in *italics* indicate a photograph or illustration.

About the Author

DANIELLE T. PHILLIPS-CUNNINGHAM is an associate professor of multicultural women's and gender studies at Texas Woman's University.